REDISCOVERING GANDHI

VOLUME 3
Satyagraha: Gandhi's Approach to Conflict Resolution

Series Editor: ***Prof. R.P. Misra***

Vol. 1. Hind Swaraj: *Gandhi's Challenge to Modern Civilization*
—R.P. Misra

Vol. 2. Ahimsa: *The Way to Peace*
—Jonathan K. Crane & Jordi Agusti-Panareda

Vol. 3. Satyagraha: *Gandhian Approach to Conflict Resolution*
—Jai Narain Sharma

Forthcoming Volumes

Vol. 4. Consensual Democracy: *Gandhi on State, Power, and Politics*
—Ashu Pasricha

Vol. 5. Humanizing Science and Technology: *Some Case Studies*
—Vinnie Jauhari and Parul Goyal

Vol. 6. Truth is God: *Gandhi's Search for Religion of Religions*
—R.P. Misra

About the Author

Dr. Jai Narain Sharma (b. 1951) Currently a professor in the department of Gandhian Studies, University of Punjab, Chandigarh, Dr. Jainarain Sharma (born 1951) obtained his MA and Ph.D. degrees from Punjab University, Chandigarh; and M. Phil degree from Himachal University, Shimla. Among his especial interests are: Gandhian Economics, Human Resource Management, Political Power, Modern Political Thought, and Research Methodology.

Dr. Sharma is associated with a number of academic institutions in different capacities. He is a member of the Board of Studies of Nagpur Vidyapeeth (University), Nagpur; Mahatma Gandhi Kashi Vidyapeeth, Varanasi; and Jain Vishwabharati Institute (Deemed to be University), Ladunu, Rajasthan. He is also a member of the Research Degree Committee of the Department of Political Studies, Himachal University, Shimla.

Dr. Sharma has been the Secretary General of the Indian Association of Gandhian Studies (IAGS) during 2002-04. He is the Editor of 'Gandhian Studies', the bi-annual Journal of the IAGS. Among the books he has published are: Economic Thoughts of Mahatma Gandhi; Economics of Defense: A Study of the SAARC Countries; Human Resource Management; Alternative Economics; Economics of Mahatma Gandhi and Globalization, Defense Economics; and Power, Politics and Corruption: A Gandhian Solution. Currently, he is engaged in writing a series of books on Modern Indian Political Thought.

REDISCOVERING GANDHI

Series Editor
Prof. R.P. Misra

Volume 3

Satyagraha
Gandhi's Approach to Conflict Resolution

By
Professor Jai Narain Sharma
Department of Gandhian Studies
Panjab University, Chandigarh

In Collaboration with
GANDHI SMRITI & DARSHAN SAMITI, NEW DELHI

Published by
CONCEPT PUBLISHING COMPANY,
NEW DELHI-110059

Cataloging in Publication Data—DK
Courtesy: D.K. Agencies (P) Ltd. <docinfo@dkagencies.com>

Sharma, Jai Narain, 1951-
Satyagraha : Gandhi's approach to conflict resolution / by Jai Narain Sharma.
p. cm. — (Rediscovering Gandhi ; v. 3)
Includes bibliographical references (p.).
Includes index.
ISBN 13: 9788180694806
ISBN 10: 8180694801

1. Gandhi, Mahatma, 1869-1948.—Philosophy. 2. Passive resistance. 3. Nonviolence. 4. Conflict management. 5. India—Politics and government—1919-1947. I. Title. II. Series: Rediscovering Gandhi ; v. 3.

DDC 954.035 092 22

ISBN-13: 978-81-8069-374-8 (Series)
ISBN-10: 81-8069-374-0 (Series)
ISBN-13: 978-81-8069-480-6 (Vol. 3)
ISBN-10: 81-8069-480-1 (Vol. 3)

First Published 2008

Published and Printed by
Ashok Kumar Mittal
Concept Publishing Company
A/15-16, Commercial Block, Mohan Garden
New Delhi-110 059 (INDIA)
Phones : 25351460, 25351794 *Fax* : 091-11-25357103
Email : publishing@conceptpub.com

Preface

In times such as ours violence is the order of the day and the unprecedented economic and technological changes in offing engender more fear than hope. It appears we have gone back to the times when war considered indispensable and the only means to settle disputes, interpersonal or international. People knew more about how to wage war than how to wage peace, intermittent voices of sanity notwithstanding. Virtues like bravery, valour, patriotism, and sacrifice came to be associated with violence. As if it were not enough to inflict physical harm and vandalize humanity, we have now invented the weapons of mass destruction – the weapons, which can kill millions within minutes and seconds. Each conflict or war is followed by another, more devastating than the previous one.

History is witness to the fact that conflict is built in the very social system man has created since he descended on this earth as the *Homo sapiens*. There is recurrent feeling of injury and injustice, either because the individuals, groups, and nations feel, rightly or otherwise, their interests injured, or because some individuals, groups and nations consider it their right to rule over others. Thus was born economic exploitation of other peoples, and rise and fall of many kingdoms and empires. Great souls like Ram, Krishna, Buddha, Jesus, Zoroaster, and Mohammad tried hard to dissuade man from the path of violence, and showed him the way to peace and harmony. But man preferred to ritualize their teachings than following them in his day-to-day life. And thus the wars not only continue unabated but have also become more devastating.

Man is not only waging war against his fellow humans but also against nature. He is cutting the very branch on which he is perching. The danger inherent to global warming and consequent climatic change has the potentials of eliminating all life from planet earth. There is therefore a search for new paradigm of development – a paradigm that drowses the fire of violence that has gripped human mind. No two humans are alike, think alike, and perceive the world around them alike. In fact that is the beauty of being human being with body, mind and soul. Differences of opinion are, therefore, built in human psyche and society. The question is: should these differences be resolved by fighting as animals do or by understanding each other, convincing each other and converting each other by love and compassion so that both sides feel being winners leaving no ill feelings behind.

Unfortunately, man has tried to resolve conflicts by brute force with honourable exceptions here and there. Evil cannot be cured by evil; fire cannot be extinguished by fire; and hatred cannot be subdued by hatred. To extinguish the fire, we need water; to win over the evil, we need goodwill; and to remove hatred we need love.

This is what Gandhi said and demonstrated in real life situations. What he said was not new, but the way he said and demonstrated the efficacy and effectiveness of his praxis were definitely new. His uniqueness lay in practicing the wisdom he gained through meditation and research before asking other to follow him. Further, his method of combating violence was not limited to solving the interpersonal problems; it extended to inter-group, inter-religious, and even international problems. For him the salvation of individual human beings was possible only if they can act individually as well as collectively as nonviolent warriors to pour love on the tormentors until their hearts melt and they become one with them. Gandhi succeeded in making the British realize their folly and leave the India as a friend. Had he fought the British they way they enslaved India, he would have not added even an iota to the existing theory and practice of resolving disputes.

Somehow the academia has not responded to the human desire for peace. It has contributed little, if at all, to theory of and practice of conflict resolution. How else can we explain the causes and consequences of the last two World Wars, leave aside the thousands of small and big wars man engaged himself through time? How else can we explain all the preparations we have made for atomic war and outer space wars which would no doubt end in the end of human civilization? How else can we explain the cruelty man imposed on nature and now he is beginning for peace for the global warming is threatening his very existence?

Is violence a part of human nature? Scientist of the world say emphatic NO. Then, how is it that social theories have failed so far to construct theories and models, which are in tune with human nature while at the same time are conducive to peace and harmony in the world. It was left to Mahatma Gandhi, by no means a social scientist fit to be a professor in a University, to advance a theory which he called *Satyagraha*. Gandhi rejected outright the Darwinian formulation that man is essentially violent because he, like other animals, has to survive in not always hospitable environment, and hence has to fight to protect himself and his progenies. The very fact that man has survived points to the Darwin's theory of the survival of the fittest. He rejected Hobbes's formulation that human life as 'struggle of all against all'.

Gandhi propounded the theory of interdependence, mutual aid, cooperation, and sacrifice as the foundation of human survival and development. He went along with the Vedantic Theory that 'all life is one and the same', which the Christians proclaimed that 'we are member one of another'. Human life is organic (it is not an inanimate machine), and so is human society. One cannot injure the neighbour without injuring himself. In Gandhi's own words man should earnestly desire the well-being of all God's creation and pray that he might have the strength to do so. In desiring the well-being of all lies his own welfare; he who desires only his own or his community's welfare is selfish and it can never be well with him.

This means that human life, individual and group, social, economic and political cannot be divided into air-tight compartments. What is good and moral conduct in one department of life must be so in others. The confusion and chaos that exists today in the collective life of humanity has recognized a dual standard of morality, one for regulating individual and family life and another, a contrary one, for regulating conduct in corporate life – the field of political, social, and international relations each contaminating the other.

This volume has been written with this perspective in mind. Lot of has already been written on *Satyagraha* and its various nuances. I claim no originality except that I have added one more supportive volume to the need for India going back to the Gandhian ways. My aim is to interpret and trace the working of the Mahatma's mind through time to rediscover to myself what Gandhi stood for. His thoughts are so deep and stimulating and his life so absorbing to his students like me that the more I read and write about him the less I appear to know him. What we lack most is the will to translate his ideas into action.

Personal acknowledgements are no easy matters where so many have been kind. My special thanks are due to Professor R.P. Misra and Professor K.D. Gangrade, who were kind enough to go through the manuscript and include the volume in the series 'Rediscovering Gandhi', and Professors S.L. Malhotra, R.N. Pal, N. Radhakrishnan, Dr. Savita Singh, Dr. K.S. Bharathi, Dr. R.P. Dwvedi, Dr. A. D. Mishra, Professor B.R. Duggar, Professor Raj Bir Singh Yadav, Professor M.L. Sharma, Dr. Meena Dutta, Dr. Ashu Pasricha and Dr. Rashmi Sharma. Beyond that, I can make only an all embracing salute to the galaxy of the scholars whose works I have consulted.

Chandigarh **Jai Narain Sharma**

Contents

Editor's Foreword

During the year 2006-07, India reminded itself of the epochal contribution Mahatma Gandhi made a century ago in 1906 to give in the hands of the weak, whether individuals, or groups or nations, a new weapon to fight oppression and injustice. The weapon was Passive Resistance later renamed as Satyagraha. In recognition of this gift of Gandhi to humanity, the United Nations declared October 2, the birth anniversary of Mahatma Gandhi, as the International Day of Nonviolence.

Gandhi's mission was not without obstacles. It was difficult to convince people that soul force could subdue brute force not by defeating it but by transforming it into a love force. That apart, a number of men and women in public life including some of Gandhi's own colleagues argued against it. Some of the points they raised were fundamental, while others tactical. Even today there are people who think that Satyagraha might have been good to fight a colonial government but it has no relevance in a democratic set up irrespective of the cause. Those who consider Satyagraha as a weapon of the weak and meek are not few. This editorial reviews these and other arguments for and against Satyagraha advanced from time to time, and tries to bring to the fore not only its contextual relevance but also its spiritual content and civilizational import.

When Gandhi pitched his soul force against the brute force of British emperialism, he had no bitterness towards the British people; he rather loved them as he loved his own countrymen. But he was against the British Raj for it was imposed on India against its will and it brought untold miseries to its people. His offensive, even if nonviolent, began in South Africa in 1906 and ceased in India in 1948 not because his goal was achieved but because he was assassinated by the very people he loved so enormously and for whose transformation into a spiritually more advanced human beings, he worked incessantly.

HOW IT ALL BEGAN?

Over a century back, in a distant land in Africa, a young Indian lawyer was thrown out of a train unjustly and illegally. His fault: he dared to travel in an upper class compartment reserved for 'whites'. He was a Coolie (Indian) Barrister, and hence he had no right to sit besides a white man. He spent that cold night awake and musing over the fate of millions of people who were treated worst for the only fault that their skin was 'coloured'. By the time the sun was up on the eastern horizon, someone from within told Gandhi: 'Well, what you have gone through has been the fate of many others. Look, what is happening in your own country. It can change only if persons like you come forward and oppose it.' Gandhi sat down, shuddered for a while as his inner-self was aroused; he decided to fight it out to secure equality before law and justice, for all.

It was 1893; to be exact, June 7, 1893. And the place was: Pietermaritzburg in South Africa, a small non-descript railway station on the way to Johanesburgh from Durban. Barrister Mohan Das Karamchand Gandhi experienced a deep spiritual awakening within him and decided not to rest content until the discriminatory treatment against Indian settlers by the then South African government was ended. Like Buddha, he appears to have got a ray of enlightenment. He decided not to renounce the world but to live in it and reform it by reforming himself and finally reforming others around him.

Gandhi decided to fight against injustice done to him for it was not only a question of dignity of one individual being defiled; it was the injustice done to masses and that too in the name of 'higher civilization'. He went round, talked to the fellow sufferers and launched a movement designed to oppose the wrongdoings of the whites of South Africa against the Asians and Africans. He called for a joint action without the use of violence. Since violence breeds violence; the fight must be cooperative and nonviolent. And the fight must be against the injustice, not against those who perpetrated injustice. The soul force should be able to melt the hardened hearts of the whites. And once it happened, they would be on the side of the oppressed.

A number of meetings were held; and it was decided to oppose all discriminatory laws and rules. But the movement must remain nonviolent. By suffering jointly and collectively, he decided to win over even the most hardened oppressors by love. After all, the oppressors too were human beings. 'If we can change them by love, they will become part of us once again; and if we are members of one human family, we can always settle our disputes without recourse to violence' said Gandhji to himself. The movement came to be known as passive resistance. By 1911 it was renamed as Satyagraha and made more compressive and philosophically sound.

Satyagraha demanded complete dedication to truth and non-violence and this was possible only if the life of the person practicing it was pure and simple. In order that he is not afraid of losing anything, he should not be attached to anything but truth and non-violence. Gandhi took the vow of celibacy and stepped out of the narrow confines of the biological family to embrace the entire humankind as his own. He lost the sense of enemy; all became his family members, even those who considered him their enemy number one.

It was also in the year 1906, 11th September to be precise, when he put his concept of Satyagraha in practice on a scale he had not done before and opened the path for nonviolent mass movement against even the mightiest empire of the world. A century later in 2006-07, we are celebrating the centenary of Satyagraha. This volume is a contribution to this epochal search for peace and is dedicated to the Mahatma.

I prefer to call Satyagraha 'as a weapon of war' because Gandhi unleashed love towards his opponents with such a great fury that they, being human beings, had no choice but to give in. As he walked on foot on the roads of South Africa and India millions followed, prepared to suffer and die, but never to give in. He stopped the march only when the rules of the game he laid down were broken or the opponents came forward to debate, dialogue, and settle the issues he had raised peacefully even if step by step. Gandhi fought his battled not using swords, guns and atom bombs; he used what he called 'soul force' pitched against 'brute force'. Following Tolstoy, he called his offensives 'passive resistance'; later he fine tuned it and termed it 'Satyagraha'.

Satyagraha is often misunderstood as a means to eliminate conflicts in human relations. It is not so. Conflict is a part of human nature; but violence is not. Even the most saintly persons would have differences of opinion, for the perception of right and wrong differ depending upon the cultural and intellectual background of individuals. If the differences are settled peacefully without the opinion holders using violence and becoming each other's enemy, there is no problem. Unfortunately, most people use violence to settle disputes. The violence takes several forms. It may take form of hatred towards the opponent, or abusive language to hurt his dignity, or brute force to subdue him. Satyagraha is a means to resolve conflicts peacefully without resorting to violence or leaving behind bitter memories of the past.

Man has never been in peace; he has always been struggling against nature, then against the institutions he built to manage his affairs. Each struggle, he hopes, would be a precursor of peace, but alas it leads to more and far more serious conflicts. So man is ever engaged in perpetual wars, big or small, to secure peace but it has, so far, remained illusive. The world he lives in is thus conflict ridden and war torn. The very built of man with a brain that directs his body to act in a particular way on particular occasions, is so unique that conflicts arising out of differences in perceptions are but to arise. It is these differences, which have led to even global wars in the past; and may lead to more devastating inter-planetary wars in future.

Gandhi is one of the latest men of wisdom to show the way to resolve the conflicts, as and when they arise, peacefully without resorting to violence. There must be a human way to solve our problems; we need not return to our animal past and use brute force to settle our disputes, said he. And the method he prescribed was nonviolence, which, when converted into an strategy, was called Satyagraha. Satyagraha was not only a model of peaceful resolution of conflicts; it was a practical exercise he laid bare through live demonstrations in the field.

Satyagraha, therefore, has engaged the attention of all those who love peace. Literature on this is so copious that no aspect of it has remained untouched. It has been criticized as an impractical exercise. It has also been hailed as the only way to establish a peaceful social order. Questions were raised, and are being raised about the relevance of Satyagraha in a fast changing world. It could not stop the partition of India in 1947. Some say that the traditional revolutionary method of securing the independence of the country, as advocated by Subhas Chandra Bose, for example, would have brought Hindus and Muslims closer and India would have gained independence even earlier than 1947 without partition. There is some truth in it. No force could have stopped India from gaining its independence sooner or later by resorting to violence as has been the case with countries like China. But if what is happening in our neighbouring countries which gained independence either as a fall out of India's Independence or as fighting a violent war, one doubts if India would have remained united and democratic too at the same time, had it not got its freedom the Gandhian way.

There is another point to take note of. India could have gained Independence as the USA did in 1776 from Britain or Russia did in 1917 when it threw the Tzar Nicholas II out; or as China went through a bloody revolutionary war of several decades. The French Revolution; the Vietnam's fight against a degenerate government; and Indonesia's rise in South-East Asia as an independent nation, are the other examples. There aren't many countries in the world, which did not go through bloody wars to gain independence. India too could have followed suit but that would have amounted to rejecting the uniqueness of Indian civilization and succumbing to the culture of war that had dominated the world since millenniums. By introducing Satyagraha it introduced a new philosophy and methodology of war, a war without violence in thought, words or action. And thus it opened a new way of getting freedom from repression, exploitation and injustice whether at the personal or global level.

Interestingly, while this unique war of independence was on, it was stirring the minds and hearts of many others all over the world. There was sympathy for India and Indians and great admiration for Gandhi, the progenitor of Satyagraha. Many people suffered and even died on both sides when the rules of Satyagraha were violated. Gandhi had to stop it mid-way when violence took control of the situation. The British administration had to concede the right of India to govern itself on August 15, 1947. And soon, in 1953 Martin Luther King Jr. in the USA followed suit and launched a Civil Rights Movement to secure basic human rights for coloured Americans. The beginning of the end of the oppressive USSR regime emerged in the form of Solidarity Movement in Poland in 1980. It was a nonviolent movement quite akin to Satyagraha. It had its innings in many other countries – in Europe, Latin America, and Asia. Today, Satyagraha stands recognized as the ultimate weapon of peaceful resolution of conflicts. But the world has yet to learn how to use this weapon creatively.

SATYAGRAHA AFTER GANDHI

After Mahatma's death in 1948 many of his followers tried to use satyagraha to solve the emergent problems of democratic India. Vinoba

Bhave, Gandhi's spiritual heir, and Jai Prakash Narain whose Sampoorna Kranti (Total Revolution) led to the imposition of Emergency in India by Smt. Indira Gandhi, deserve special attention.

Vinoba Bhave laid down four principles of satyagraha in 1958 to make it consistent with democratic India:

1. It must be positive;
2. It should proceed from gentle, to gentler and finally gentlest;
3. The very word Satyagraha should arouse happiness; and
4. There should be no insistence on the part of the satyagrahi; insistence should come from truth itself.

Placing high premium on swaraj or self-rule, he defined it as ruling over oneself and that was not possible if one was under some other person's captive, physically or mentally. The second requirement of Swaraj was that no one should exercise control over any other person, institution or nation. This ruled out coercion in any form, and recognized and respected the dignity of the opponent. It was possible only if satyagraha was spiritualized and was used in a 'more subtle and finer forms'. Gandhi's science of satyagraha had to be converted into science and art of satyagraha; it had to be pure and unadulterated. Emphasis had to be on constructive work more than on coercive nonviolence.

The Bhoodan Movement he launched was a great success. Had it received the backing of the Indian government, the rural landscape of India would have changed drastically. Unfortunately, the government looked the other way round as Viboba trudged from village to village to receive land gifts. Jai Prakash Narain (JP) was one of his main pillars of support. May be, it was because of this that the government became lukewarm about the Movement and the land donated was never distributed to the poor the way Vinoba had envisaged. .

Jayaprakash Narayan had spent most of his life as a major actor on the political stage. In the 1920s, JP undertook seven years of higher education in the United States where he studied Marx and completed a highly praised M.A. dissertation analyzing societal changes from a Marxist perspective. On his return to India he worked closely with Nehru and became a spokesman for the socialist members of the Indian National Congress. During the Second World War, JP was imprisoned.

He escaped and spent a year 'underground' and emerged a revolutionary.

Disenchanted with power politics as the means to correct the deteriorating socio-political situation in India, JP returned to Gandhi to work for a social revolution, which Gandhi initiated but could not, give full attention to. He joined Vinoba, distanced himself from active politics, and dedicated the rest of his life to Bhoodan and Sarvodaya. After some time, he launched a satyagraha called Sampoorna Kranti but he removed from it the otherworldly underpinnings. He tried to become Gandhi the politician minus Gandhi the saint.

These two persons apart, there were and are many others who took one or the other cause ranging from Chipko Movement of launched by Chandi Prasad Bhat and expanded and popularized by Sundarlal Bahuguna to protect the forests and other natural gifts in the Himalaya to Medha Patkar's movement for the rehabilitation of Sardar Sarovar Dam oustees in Gujarat, and then on to Mamta Banerjee's movement against SEZ in Nandigram in West Bengal. All of these constitute a form of Satyagraha chiseled to specific social, political and economic contexts. Innovation is the hallmark of Gandhian praxis.

Not only India, the civil society all over the world on many occasions, organized peaceful sit-ins and demonstrations to impress on various international agencies, and national governments to save the earth from getting barren and change their ways in favour of the poor and deprived masses no matter where they were. The Velvet Revolution in East European countries to throw away the Soviet iron chain was in no small measure influenced by Gandhi's theory and practice of Satyagraha.

A form of non-cooperation and civil disobedience was used to oust the military dictatorships in El Salvadore and Guatemala in 1944; Civil Rights Movement in the USA during 1950-60; Hungarian Revolution in 1956-57; the Czech and Slovak Resistance in 1968-69; Solidarity Movement in Poland in 1980-90; South African Struggle for Freedom in 1950-90; Nonviolent Uprisings in Philippines in 1986 and 2001; Stalling of the Soviet Hard-line Coup d'etat in 1991; nonviolent struggles to end communist dictatorships in East Germany, Estonia, Latvia and Lithuania in 1991; recent changes of governments in Ukraine, Georgia, Chile and Argentina, Ghana and Liberia; and ousting of Kaunda of Zambia. Among the ongoing movements are: struggle against military rule in Mynamar (Burma) since 1988; Tibetan Struggle for Autonomy since 1958; and movement for People's Power in Latin America.

People all over the world see a ray of hope in peaceful demonstrations against war, against ecological destruction, against trade in arms and armaments, and against gender bias. Gandhi inspires them all even if indirectly.

CRITIQUES OF SATYAGRAHA

Despite global recognition of satyagraha as the ultimate way of conflict resolution, its critics have not been scarce. There are people who reject it in toto on the ground that violence has a cleansing effect when the oppressed rise against their oppressors. Some limit their criticism to its aftereffects on the civil society in the form of indiscipline. Even Gene Sharp, who has done so much to spread the message of Gandhi, has some critical notes on the way Gandhi applied nonviolence. He considers Gandhi's approach too fundamentalist, and therefore less productive in terms of results. It would be more pragmatic and within the reach of all if emphasis was laid on defeating the opponent without the use of any physical force than on converting him.

Marxists have never been sympathetic to Gandhi and the way he fought the British. They reject the idea that self-suffering would soften the hearts of the oppressors. They cite the example of women, who suffered for centuries under the patriarchal system but the hearts of the males never softened. And those who feel that Gandhi's methods could work only because the British were liberal are in plenty. It would have not worked, they think, in Nazi Germany or Stalin's USSR. Some feel that Gandhi thought of ahimsa and satyagraha only when he realized that a disarmed India could not fight a hot war.

It appears that much of the criticism of Satyagraha was ideological more than realistic. Gandhi had a point of departure, which was outside the main currents of thinking of his time. That was the strength as well as the weakness of Gandhi: strength because it emanated from the basic values of Indian culture, and weakness because it stood apart from how man had handled his problems in the past. Given below is a commentary on the criticism of satyagraha.

Satyagraha Is Not an Effective Force

Many critics of Mahatma Gandhi contend that those who enjoyed power and privilege would not give these up unless forced to do so.

Attachment to power is so alluring that rarely do people abjure it willingly. To such people Love has only one meaning i.e. lust. History is witness to the fact that no one has ever secured his rights by suffering or begging, and Gandhi's nonviolence was just a bit better than begging. The only force the tormenters understand is superior brute force.

Among those who wanted to free India from colonial rule, there were those who preferred to launch a revolutionary war, something like the 1857 War of Independence or the American War of Independence (1776) to free India. Some of them wanted India to be a strong Hindu Rashtra (nation). Veer Savarkar can be considered as the representative leader of this group. Then there were the nationalists like Subhas Chandra Bose who were highly secular but in matters of strategy they were with Savarkar and the likes. Veer Savarkar (1883-1966) was wedded to the violent revolutionary ways. He was a disciple of Shiva Ji, and advocated the use all possible tactics of war – Sam, Dam, Danda, Bheda – to throw the British out. When he was incarcerated in Port Blair Jail (Andaman & Nicobar Isls) for life, he appealed for mercy and promised never to use violence again. After his release he broke the undertaking and was back on his revolutionary path. Gandhi, as we know, would have neither asked for mercy nor broken his pledge. Some people think that Savarkar should not be judged by Gandhian principles? He should rather be judged by Leninist standards, even if he were not a Leninist.

Subhas Chandra Bose (1897-1945) had a great regard for the Mahatma but begged to differ from him on the means to fight the British. He had no faith in Satyagraha. But he had a deep faith in the Mahatma. It was Subhas who called Gandhi, the Father of the Nation. He organized the Indian National Army (INA) with the help of Axis powers during the Second World War to occupy India as Japan advanced westward from South East Asia. Japanese defeat in the War, forced him to abandon the plan. He died in a plane crash, so it is said. His mission failed but it stirred the soul of young India. It would not be an exaggeration to say that Gandhi's success in no small measure lay in the sacrifices Subhas and other revolutionaries made.

Saul Alinsky (1909-1970), a master political agitator, tactical planner and social activist and mobilizer organized the Back of the Yard neighbourhood in Chicago. He believed that nonviolence should be used in human relations only as a last resort, when nothing else worked. "If Gandhi had had the weapons and the people to use them, this means would not have been so unreservedly rejected as the world would like to think'. Gandhi's campaigns 'were a striking example of the selection of means'. Given the passivity of the Indian masses, his choice of passive resistance was the only intelligent, realistic, expedient programme at his disposal. 'Gandhi organized the inertia.' The spirituality and morality that he weaved around his movement was designed to give his programme a rationale to do or die. 'If he had had guns he might well have used them in an armed revolution against the British, which would have been in keeping with the traditions of revolutions for freedom through force."

Alinsky thinks that Gandhi faulted on the issue of ends and means too for the important question is not whether the end justifies the means; it has always been "Does this particular end justify this particular means?" Nonviolence has never worked against violent opponents. Had violence been available to Gandhi in South Africa he would have used it and the idea of Satyagraha would have not come to his mind. Nonviolence is the weapon of the weak and Gandhi began his epic journey with weakness. And hence 'ends and means' debate is theoretical. To be practical, each case has to be seen on its own merit irrespective of what passive non-doers, as Alinsky seems to label Gandhi, may say. If violence can win, it should be used. The Gandhian response to this debate is best formulated by Aldous Huxley when he says "Good ends ... can only be achieved by the employment of appropriate means", and that "The end cannot justify the means, for the simple reason that the means employed determine the nature of the ends produced."[1]

Charles Dobson who teaches creative problem solving at the Emily Carr Insitute of Art and Design in Vancouver has compared the techniques of Alinky and Gandhi in terms of some rules. It is reproduced below for the benefit of the reader.

Alinsky's Rules:

Rule 1: Power is not only what you have, but what an opponent thinks you have. Hence pose yourself to be more powerful than you may be.

Rule 2: Never go outside the experience of your people. The result is confusion, fear, and retreat.

Rule 3: Whenever possible, go outside the experience of an opponent. Here you want to cause confusion, fear, and retreat.

Rule 4: Make opponents live up to their own book of rules. "You can kill them with this, for they can no more obey their own rules than the Christian church can live up to Christianity."

Rule 5: Ridicule is man's most potent weapon. It's hard to counterattack ridicule, and it infuriates the opposition, which then reacts to your advantage.

Rule 6: A good tactic is one your people enjoy. "If your people aren't having a ball doing it, there is something very wrong with the tactic."

Rule 7: A tactic that drags on for too long becomes a drag. Commitment may become ritualistic as people turn to other issues.

Rule 8: Keep the pressure on. Use different tactics and actions and use all events of the period for your purpose. "The major premise for tactics is the development of operations that will maintain a constant pressure upon the opposition. It is this that will cause the opposition to react to your advantage."

Rule 9: The threat is more terrifying than the thing itself. When Alinsky leaked word that large numbers of poor people were going to tie up the washrooms of O'Hare Airport, Chicago city authorities quickly agreed to act on a longstanding commitment to a ghetto organization. They imagined the mayhem as thousands of passengers poured off airplanes to discover every washroom occupied. Then they imagined the international embarrassment and the damage to the city's reputation.

Rule 10: The price of a successful attack is a constructive alternative. Avoid being trapped by an opponent or an interviewer who says, "Okay, what would you do?"

Rule 11: Pick the target, freeze it, personalize it, polarize it. Don't try to attack abstract corporations or bureaucracies. Identify a responsible individual. Ignore attempts to shift or spread the blame. According to Alinsky, the main job of the organizer is to bait an opponent into reacting. "The enemy properly goaded and guided in his reaction will be your major strength."

To sum up, we can say that Alinsky asks the social activists to "Agitate + Aggravate + Educate + Organize". Use any means to achieve a given objective.

Gandhi on the other hands puts forward a different set of rules. These are:

Mahatma Gandhi's Rules for Social Activism:

Rule 1. Refrain from violence and hostility.

Rule 2. Attempt to obtain your opponent's trust by being truthful, being open about your intentions, using chivalry (for example, being kind if the other side experiences an unrelated difficulty), and making behavior inoffensive without compromising the issue at hand.

Rule 3. Refrain from humiliating an opponent.

Rule 4. Make visible sacrifices for one's cause. Here it is best if the suffering of the aggrieved is made visible.

Rule 5. Carry on constructive work. Address parts of the problem you can address. Make improvements where you can. Participate in activities that all people see as contributing to everyone's common welfare.

Rule 6. Maintain contact with an opponent. This is absolutely necessary if conversion is to succeed.

Rule 7. Demonstrate trust in an opponent.

Rule 8. Develop empathy, goodwill, and patience toward an opponent. This is the best you can do from your end. If you fail to convert an opponent it may be due to external factors beyond your control.[2]

Gandhi's ends were far more ambitious and intrinsic than what Alinsky credits him with. Gandhi's vision went beyond throwing the oppressors out by hook or by crook. He considered the oppressors part of the society and so long as they are not transformed into a new human beings, the oppression would continue in some other garb. In the context of India, he wanted the British to go away but with a feeling they were wrong in occupying India and they should go because Indians had in their armory a weapon (satyagraha), which was more powerful than the guns. It so melted their hearts that they were unable to use the conventional weapons against them.

For Gandhi the fight against the British was a radical experiment, which would give rise to a new India, an India unique, and in its true colours. He wanted to use the new India to create a peaceful and just global society. His time frame was much longer than that of Alinsky. Moreover, his understanding of the finer nuances of satyagraha was inadequate, if not faulted. Who could be more courageous than Gandhi? Satyagraha was never conceived as a weapon of the weak.

Thoroughly opposed to Gandhi and his approach to British

imperialism, Marxists were no admirers of satyagraha. Being Marxists, and inseparably aligned to the USSR, they were not in favour of even Quit India Movement of 1942 not because of strategic differences but because Britain and USSR were parts of the Allied Powers. Even earlier, they considered Gandhi's nonviolent strategy as a stumbling block in proletarian revolution, which alone could reorder the society in favour of the working class, and throw the capitalists and feudalists out from the position of power they occupied. They alleged that capitalists supported Gandhi and he in turn rewarded them in various ways. Gandhi's dream of one big family in India and his philosophy of satyagraha, said the Marxists, suited the Indian capitalists. For Marxists, Gandhi was a lackey of the bourgeoisie.

Taking the Marxist line, George Orwell claimed that the British saw in Gandhi their best ally for he helped them rule India peacefully with some pinpricks here and there. Gandhi was well treated in the prisons so that he lived longer. His death could herald the advent of another hero who believed less in 'soul force' and more in bombs. Marxist, while comparing the nonviolent movement of Gandhi with their model of revolution suggested that the latter aimed at 'defending life' violently while the former at 'sacrificing life' nonviolently. The nonviolent activists were only offered "an opportunity to be beaten, arrested, or tortured". The reluctance to finish off an oppressor when he was down was characterized as naive, self-defeating, or against the very nature of man. It amounted to accepting the dictum of capitalism and fascism that the weak must be ruled by the strong. Orwell also raises the question: "It is difficult to see how Gandhi's methods could be applied in a country where opponents of the regime disappear in the middle of the night and are never heard of again. Without a free press and the right of assembly, it is impossible not merely to appeal to outside opinion, but to bring a mass movement into being, or even to make your intentions known to your adversary."

"One feels of him (Gandhi) that there was much he did not understand, but not that there was anything that he was frightened of saying or thinking. I have never been able to feel much liking for Gandhi, but I do not feel sure that as a political thinker he was wrong in the main, nor do I believe that his life was a failure. It is curious that when he was assassinated, many of his warmest admirers exclaimed sorrowfully that he had lived just long enough to see his life work in ruins, because India was engaged in a civil war, which had always been foreseen as one of the byproducts of the transfer of power. But it was not in trying to smooth down Hindu-Moslem rivalry that Gandhi had spent his life. His main political objective, the peaceful ending of British rule, had after all been attained. As usual the relevant facts cut across one another. On the other hand, the British did get out of India without fighting, and event which very few observers indeed would have predicted until about a year before it happened. On the other hand, this was done by a Labour government, and it is certain that a Conservative government, especially a government headed by Churchill, would have acted differently. But if, by 1945, there had grown up in Britain a large body of opinion sympathetic to Indian independence, how far was this due to Gandhi's personal influence? And if, as may happen, India and Britain finally settle down into a decent and friendly relationship, will this be partly because Gandhi, by keeping up his struggle obstinately and without hatred, disinfected the political air? That one even thinks of asking such questions indicates his stature. One may feel, as I do, a sort of aesthetic distaste for Gandhi, one may reject the claims of sainthood made on his behalf (he never made any such claim himself, by the way), one may also reject sainthood as an ideal and therefore feel that Gandhi's basic aims were anti-human and reactionary: but regarded simply as a politician, and compared with the other leading political figures of our time, how clean a smell he has managed to leave behind!"[3]

The Marxist saw Gandhi within the confines of a narrow vision of materialism and power politics. The larger spiritual vision of Gandhi was irrelevant or should we say incomprehensible to them. The problem thus lies in the bankruptcy of Marxist vision and the thinking derived from it rather than in Gandhian praxis. Interestingly, the very bastions of Marxism, USSR and People's Republic of China, have abandoned Marxism. The USSR along with its former colonies of Eastern Europe has adopted western democracy and China has kept the one party system intact but integrated itself with world capitalism. As Gandhi returns slowly and surely to the world political scene while Marxian bastions collapse, the Marxists have kept silent on Gandhi and his nonviolent ways because it is no longer popular. Interestingly, it is India, the largest democracy of the world where Marxists rule over two states: West Bengal and Kerala; in West Bengal because they have identified themselves with Bengali sub-nationalism and in Kerala because the other parties are too disparate to come together.

It is not only Orwell and the Marxists who considered nonviolence a weapon of the helpless. Many literary figures too expressed doubts about the efficacy of nonviolence in certain extreme political situations. V.S. Naipaul, the Trinidad fiction writer of Indian origin sees India as a wounded civilization, trapped in an uncritical and dysfunctional glorification of the past, noting that "The past must be seen to be dead; or the past will kill." He seems to blame Gandhi for retaining class relations in India by stifling a modern outlook with his quaint village-centred model of spatial society.

Naipaul wrote about 30 years back. He accused Gandhi of glorifying poverty (simplicity). He dismissed Gandhi's insistence on simple living and high thinking as primitivism. Naipaul wanted India to catch up with the west in economic development and technological achievements.[4] As we enter the 21st century, Nailpal appears to be losing and Gandhi, even after his death sixty years back, gaining ground. Today more people than ever before feel convinced that we must "live simply so that others may simply live". It is quite another thing that the people who practice in what they believe, is not yet large. Naipal's understanding of Gandhi does not appear to be deep. Gandhi never glorified poverty nor did he equate it with simplicity.

Constitutionalists' Criticism of Satyagraha

Prominent among persons who considered satyagraha extra-constitutional in a democratic set up was Bhimrao Ramji Ambedkar, Chairman of the Drafting Committee of the Constitution of India. Ambedkar and Gandhi had a common goal: to free India from the British rule and the depressed classes of Indian society from the tyranny of untouchability. They appreciated and respected each other but differed on the way to achieve the goals they set before them. While Gandhi admired Indian civilization, and considered it fountain head of a truly humane civilization. The defects like untouchability were deviations from its original course. They have to be removed to purify it. For Ambedkar "The Hindu Civilisation.... is a diabolical contrivance to suppress and enslave humanity. Its proper name would be infamy. What else can be said of a civilisation which has produced a mass of people... who are treated as an entity beyond human intercourse and whose mere touch is enough to cause pollution?" But he proved wrong in asking for separate electorate for the depressed classes (dalits). Had it been introduced, Mayawati, a dalit woman, would have never become the Chief Minister of UP, the largest state of India and strived for the prime ministership of the country.

At the same time Ambedkar was critical of Islam and its practices in South Asia. He condemned practices of Child-Marriage in Muslim society, as well as the mistreatment of women. He also condemned the prevalence of caste practices and slavery among Muslims in South Asia. He considered Muslim society "even more full of social evils than Hindu Society is" and criticized Muslims for sugarcoating their sectarian Caste System with euphemisms like brotherhood. Ambedkar had warned that the division of India into India and Pakistan would be extremely problematic with massive population transfers and border disputes. He proved right.

While presenting his report to the Constituent Assembly on the new constitution of Republican India, he said: "If you want to maintain democracy not merely in form but also in fact, what must we do? The first thing in my judgment is to hold fast to constitutional methods of achieving social and economic objectives. It means that we must abandon the method of civil disobedience, non-cooperation and satyagraha. When there was no way left for constitutional methods for achieving economic and social objectives, there was a great deal of justification for unconstitutional methods. But when constitutional methods are open, there can be no justification for these unconstitutional methods. These methods are nothing but Grammer of Anarchy, and the sooner are they abandoned better for us."

Ambedkar admired Gandhi for his sacrifices and efforts to get India rid of colonialism, but his admiration was limited to the political mobilization and awareness it generated. He was totally against the spiritualization of the freedom movement as he was against using extra-constitutional methods to paralyze the government. The later he objected because once people get used to breaking the law, they would continue such practices even when India became free. Let it be clear to the reader that Ambedkar and Gandhi never saw eye to eye on many issues. They had respect and affection for each other but they never tried to hide their differences.

Annie Besant was very close to Gandhi. They derived strength from each other. But at the Lahore Congress of 1920, she along with five others stood against the overwhelming flood of support in favour of Gandhiji's plan to launch Satyagraha movement. Being a constitutionalist, she had a deep distrust in massive lawbreaking irrespective of the cause and the method. While addressing the All

India Women's Conference in 1927, she (the leader of the Home Rule Movement) warned Gandhi, that satyagraha could be misused by the politicians, trade unions or even unscrupulous people in free India. But the Mahatma did not agree with her. Given the circumstances of the time, he had no other alternative to compel the British to leave India. Where the choice was between violence and nonviolence, he not only preferred the later but also refused to do anything with the first. Gandhi was a firm believer in the dignity of man and in the need to abjure violence in thought, words and deed no matter who the opponent was. He was trying to be just to the British; he would never hurt their dignity; but he would never submit to their dictates.

Rabindranath Tagore too did not like Gandhian ways of throwing the British colonialism out. He counseled: "Try to build up your country by your own strength because realization becomes complete through creation." Tagore asked his people, to win back the country, not from the British, but from apathy and indifference. His method for liberation was an internal, intellectual movement: "Unreasoning faith, blind habits of mind, adherence to customs that had no merit save their age, the repression of intellect and heart in the unproductive channel of inaction - all of this is the antithesis of the forces that reveal people in all their full glory and dignity. This is the root cause of degeneration."[5]

Tagore did not support the non-cooperation movement as he felt the end result of disassociation from the British would be futile, since the future would only lead back to assimilation. Mahatma Gandhi and Rabindranath Tagore differed in this way in their thinking on how to free India but they had fond love and respect for each another. Gandhi termed Tagore as his 'Gurudev' and Rabindranath termed Gandhi as 'Mahatma'. Gandhi consulted Gurudev quite often and considered him a spiritual ally. Yet they differed on the issue of Satyagraha.

Tagore equated Satyagraha to a thunderbolt; it required the rain god Indra to wield it, he wrote in an essay entitled 'Voices of Humanity'. He felt that "Passive Resistance is a force, which is not necessarily moral in itself; it can be used against truth as well as for it. The danger inherent in all force grows stronger when it is likely to gain success, for then it becomes temptation." Tagore acknowledged the moral right of a Mahatma '*frail in body and devoid of all resources*' to lead the country but he was deeply troubled by the negative impulses non-cooperation could generate. He was particularly disturbed by

Gandhi's call to the students to boycott schools and colleges. Gandhi, however, remained unconvinced of Tagore's pleadings for his message of non-cooperation, non-violence and Swadeshi was not for India alone; it was for the whole world. All he was doing was to experiment it in India first and foremost because India provided a fertile ground for it.

Being a lawyer by profession, Mohammad Ali Jinnah was averse to Gandhi's non-cooperation movement ever since his Congress days in 1920s. But he was well aware that there was a reason why Gandhi launched the movement. Addressing the Calcutta Session of Muslim league in 1920, Jinnah said 'I cannot ask the people to submit to wrong after wrong. Yet, I will still ask the government not to drive the people of India to desperation or else there is no other course open except to inaugurate the policy of non-cooperation, though not necessarily the programme of Mr. Gandhi.' Apparently, Jinnah was not so much against non-cooperation movement as against the spiritual underpinnings of it. Moreover, he wanted to be sure that the movement succeeded. This is clear from what he said the next day in his address at the Special Session of the Indian National Congress at Calcutta presided over by Lala Lajpat Rai. "I am fully convinced of non-cooperation. I see no other way. But before I put this policy into practice, I want to take stock of the situation to find what are the materials and forces. We are all one. We have got our opponent and we want to make him feel that if he does not behave, we will make government impossible. When you have understood the whole situation you could begin to practice." This session was specially called to discuss and approve the programme of Non-Cooperation. The programme was read out by Gandhi, and after a thorough discussion the draft was approved for formal adoption at the Nagpur Session of the Congress held later, the same year. Among the members who unsuccessfully sought some changes in it were Chittaranjan Das, Vipin Chandra Pal, Madan Mohan Malaviya, Md. Ali Jinnah and Mrs. Annie Besant.

Gandhi's programme of non-cooperation was formally adopted in the Nagpur Session of the Congress (1920). Jinnah expressed dissatisfaction over the whole issue and said: "You are making a declaration, which you do not have the means to carry out. ...Our president who is sitting here said, at the moment destiny of the country is in the hands of two men (one of them being Gandhi). Therefore, standing on this platform, knowing as I do know that he commands the majority in this Assembly, I appeal to him to pause, to cry halt before it is too late." Soon, Jinnah resigned from the Congress and returned to Bombay. He was not bitter. He respected Gandhi and his followers because he knew 'of what noble stuff they were made'. He was proud of them all. He objected to the movement because what ought to have been a political movement was converted into a socio-cultural movement.

"The first essential thing for any country to resist the government was to mobilize the forces. If they were going to regulate everything in their country by the doctrine of nonviolent non-cooperation, he was afraid they were forgetting human nature. They were forgetting that they were human beings, not saints. If they really wanted to serve their country at the present moment they must let the political movement go on. The programme was based on the doctrine of soul-force and it was an essentially spiritual movement....Nonviolent non-cooperation will be a miracle if accomplished." Md. Ali Jinnah.

Three years later in 1924, Jinnah, appears to have changed his views and came very close to Gandhi. While addressing the teachers and students of Hindu College, Delhi University on March 14, 1924 on 'Parties and Politics in India', he said: "If the government persistently continues a policy of indifference and injustice, and the constitutional party fails, then those who believe in direct action must come into prominence."

Gene Sharp[7] on Satyagraha

No other thinker has done more to bring to focus the theory of pragmatic nonviolence than Gene Sharp, but he too considers its moral underpinnings unrealistic and at times confusing. Rarely have people used nonviolence against repressive opponents for moral reasons. And when they used it they could not organize required physical force to defeat the opponent. And least they were guided by a desire to make peace, to convert opponents or to self-suffer.

The religious symbolism and language, which Gandhi used "more often confuses than clarifies." That is the reason the western mind is unable to adequately evaluate Mahatma's political importance. To help the westerners understand Gandhi, Sharp tried to secularize Gandhi and his message. By doing so he abandoned Gandhi and made nonviolence a tactics. Having done that, Gandhi for Sharp became a liability because instead of using nonviolence as a technique, Gandhi "tried to convince people who did not believe in *ahimsa* (nonviolence) on ethical grounds to adopt nonviolent methods as a practical expedient, a technique that works." Once it is placed in the hands of imperfect people in an imperfect world, it can become highly dangerous. This he makes clearer in his foreword to a later edition of Krishnalal Shridharani's 1939 classic study of War Without Violence. Sharp was not interested in the religious and moral arguments in favour of nonviolence as advanced by Gandhi; he was interested in its use as a strategy. Sharp was right when he emphasized that many people use nonviolence only because it can help them achieve their objectives with least cost. He does not consider it wrong to be a 'moral pacifist,' but given the world as it is, the use of nonviolence without its moral underpinnings would be more productive of peace, than one soaked in moral and spiritual decoction.

'The Politics of Nonviolent Action', a three-volume magnum opus by Sharp explains the notion of power, and how nonviolence had been used in the past, and could be used in future. According to him the nonviolent action "consists of acts of protest and persuasion, non-cooperation and nonviolent intervention designed to undermine the sources of power of the opponent in order to bring about change." He refers to Gandhi time and again but only as Gandhi the strategist, not Gandhi the moral philosopher set upon to create a new world order based on morality and ethics. Sharp takes out nonviolence from Gandhi's armory and converts it into an instrument of waging struggles against oppression and injustice as a soldier in modern warfare uses his guns and bombs. It produces good results without bloodshed. He treats nonviolence as an "alternative weapons system", as a "means of combat, as is war. It involves the matching of forces and the waging of 'battles', it requires wise strategy and tactics, employs numerous 'weapons' and demands of it's 'soldiers' courage, discipline, and sacrifice." It is "political jiu-jitsu" rather than the "moral jiu-jitsu" of Gandhi that constitutes the central dynamics of the struggle. Conflict is seen as a relationship between antagonists with incompatible interests and the goal is to defeat the opponent.[8]

The Gandhian analysts and scholars like Richard Gregg[9] do not go along with Gene Sharp who reduces Satyagraha to a mere strategy or tactics. To them the reestablishment of communication to convince the opponents of the error of their ways, and to converting rather than coercing them, must be the goal. In the words of Robert Burrowes, true Gandhians "choose (nonviolent action) for ethical reasons and believe in the unity of means and ends. They view the opponent as a partner in the struggle to satisfy the needs of all; if anyone suffers, it is the practitioner of nonviolence. More fundamentally, this practitioner may view nonviolence as a way of life." Sharp would be happy if the Gandhian approach brings results. But as long as there is violence in the human relations, the use of violence to counter violence has to exist. First, people should use Satyagraha as a strategy. Once it is widely accepted as a viable means to counter wrong, people can "consider and deal with the finer ethical problems, which arise in the application of nonviolent sanctions."

When writing about the meaning of "success" in nonviolent action Sharp takes a far more "objective" view than many other nonviolent activists. The important questions for him are: were the opponent's objectives frustrated, what factors in the social or political situation allowed the opponent to be defeated? Or whether the stated goals of the nonviolent group were achieved because of the struggle. The subjective, and we could say existential, payoffs that are so important to Gandhi are not important to Sharp. While Sharp is concerned with social and political freedom, Gandhi's focus is on a search for Truth. And, according to Hayes, this means that in "a theoretical-practical sense, Gandhi's ideals can be seen to be directly aimed at addressing many of the existential effects of being dominated, and of being a dominator," and "what nonviolent actors might be or become as a result of their struggle."[10]

Nevertheless, a friend of Sharp has pointed out that this debate must be seen in its proper context. Ralph Summy notes that Sharp is trying to promote nonviolence in a highly acquisitive capitalist society. He thinks that Gandhi would be the first to proclaim that "a satyagraha that discounted the views and passions rife in its society and proceeded blindly on its own purist path was tantamount to pursuing merely personal redemption and not societal change." In short, the reasons for a Gandhian or more pragmatic approach to nonviolence, and hence the way that it is conducted, need to be determined by each individual practitioner of nonviolence.

Is Satyagraha Relevant in a Democratic Set Up?

A debate has been on ever since Gandhi's days on the relevance of satyagraha in a democratic set up. The very origin of satyagraha was firmed up in South Africa where Gandhi had to fight discrimination against Indians, and was perfected in India where British imperialism had taken away the human rights of Indians. India is now a democratic country; it has a government of the people, by the people and for the people. People can change the government as and when they like through the ballot. There are law courts and several other constitutional means to correct the government if it goes wrong. This is what the textbooks say. Why should the people then use Satyagraha or any other coersive method against their own government? This raises the larger question of the role of individuals, groups, and the civil society in general in the governance of the country. Democracy is the best form of government but not necessarily the ideal one. Should man not try to move towards the ideal? And if he should, then what that ideal is and what means should he adopt to achieve it? Isn't the Gandhian way a right way, if not the only way?

To find an answer to this question, let us look at satyagraha as conceived and practiced by Gandhi. Satyagraha is a relentless search for truth; and is an effective substitute for violence. Truth is the destination; nonviolence is the way, and Satyagraha the vehicle to move forward. Fearlessness, and willingness to suffer constitute the powers that drives the vehicle. Only those who are strong willed can tread on this path. It teaches us the art of living as well as of dying for a cause gracefully yet without adding to the violence that already fills this world. A true satyagrahi should not harbour contempt for the opponent even if he deserves no respect. Satyagraha thrives on injustice, oppression and repression.

Satyagraha needs no outside help; it derives all its strength from within. The method of Satyagraha requires that the Satyagrahi should never lose hope. Nor should he harbour ill will and enmity towards the opponent. Satyagraha being a method of conversion and conviction, it prohibits the use of coercion. But its use as a coercive method is certainly less evil than the use of brute force. Much depends on where and in what situation it is used. If it is used in societies where the ethical and moral principles underlying it are not easily understood, it can be used as a coercive method even if in its unadulterated form it should never be used so. In any case violence in any form is barred, no matter what the social context.

Satyagraha not only involves direct action but also the education of the people involved in it as participants or recipients. People include those for whom the action is taken as also those against whom it is taken. Only those are eligible to join a Satyagraha brigade who believe in nonviolence and Truth; who have infinite patience, abundant faith in others, and ample hope. A true Satyagrahi would not take recourse of law courts for a personal wrong, nor would he ever surrender or use brute force.

Many thinkers, however, believe that, to be more realistic, satyagraha should be stripped of its moral content. There is no harm in using violence in thoughts and words to coerce the opponent to change his ways or to concede the rights due to the protesters. This is the western model of satyagraha widely used in different parts of the world both before and after Gandhi. Thus two models of Satyagraha appear to have emerged: the first is the unadulterated original model as perfected by Gandhi; and the other as a simplified method devoid of Satya and limited to Non-Cooperation and Civil Disobedience. In the later case, there is no love or sympathy for the opponent; nor is there any blanket prohibition on the use of coercion. In both cases physical force is prohibited.

Should satyagraha be used against the doings and un-doings of a democratic government? To answer this question, we have to first see the nature of the government including a democratically elected government. According to Eric Hoffner, "When watching men of (coercive political) power in action it must be always kept in mind that, whether they know it or not, their main purpose is the elimination or neutralization of the independent individual — the independent voter, consumer, worker, owner, thinker — and that every device they employ aims at turning men into a manipulable 'animated instrument' which is Aristotle's definition of a slave."[11]

In his book 'Why Government Doesn't Work,' Harry Browne a Libertarian Party president candidate in USA (1996), writes: "The distinctive feature of government is coercion — the use of force and the threat of force to win obedience. This is how government differs from every other agency in society. The others persuade; government compels. So what is government? Very simply, it is an agency of coercion. Of course, there are other agencies of coercion — such as the Mafia. So to be more precise, government is the agency of coercion that has flags in front of its offices. Or, to put it another way, government is society's dominant producer of coercion. The Mafia and independent bandits are merely fringe competitors — seeking to take advantage of the niches and nooks neglected by government."[12]

Similar is John Hospers caricature of Government when he says: "By far the most numerous and most flagrant violations of personal liberty and individual rights are performed by governments... The major crimes throughout history, the ones executed on the largest scale, have been committed not by individuals or bands of individuals but by governments, as a deliberate policy of those governments... that is, by the official representatives of governments, acting in their official capacity."[13]

"All government, in its essence, is organized exploitation, and in virtually all of its existing forms it is the implacable enemy of every industrious and well-disposed man." Says H. L. Mencken.[14] And to add punch to the comments, George Washington has said: "How soon we forget history...Government is not reason, it is not eloquence, it is force; like fire, a dangerous servant and fearful master." Concurring with these thinkers, Gandhi said: "The state represents violence in a concentrated and organized form. The individual has a soul, but as the state is a soulless machine, it can never be weaned from violence to which it owes its very existence."[15]

Two more comments before we close this discussion. Two hundred years ago, the French philosopher Rousseau said: "The less government, the better off its citizenry." This simple but axiomatic statement points to the duties enjoined on people to strive for individual freedom for they are free only to the extent that governments are inefficient. People do need government but they also need least government. In his seminal work, 'The Wealth of Nations', Adam Smith set forth three, and only three, legitimate functions of any government: The judiciary; protection of the country against foreign enemies; and the infrastructure, such as highways, power etc. To these functions can be added the 'safety net'.

This being the nature of the government, there is always a scope and need for movements to contain it and bring it on right course. But who would contain it and bring it on the right course? It will be people as individuals and groups who would be far less power hungry and corrupt than the government. What satyagraha of Gandhi aimed at was to bring the government on the righteous path and at the same time training the people to be more righteous. He wanted to change the course of the government at the same time he wanted to change the people too in the hope that a day will come sometimes in the future when good people and good government would coincide. Good people would emerge only if individuals feel them selves bound in common bond of life; in the unity of the existence in the long run and that of humanity in the immediate run. "People are related to each other in a way that is transcendental in nature and conflict should be seen as a gift providing a rich opportunity, potentially to the benefit of all, to realize a higher self. A desired outcome of conflict, in this line of argument, is nothing short of the creation of a new social structure and a "higher level of self-purification in both actors." But unlike Sharp, Gandhi considered satyagraha not merely a useful technique for the resolving conflicts, and satyagrahi not merely a practitioner of certain skills. He considered satyagraha as a means to change the nature of the government, and the satyagrahi an embodiment of an ideal.

In an article published in New York Times on January 21, 1968, under the caption 'Rebels without a Program', George F. Kennan, (1904-2005), a distinguished US diplomat and historian, and one of the primary architects of US strategy during the Truman Administration remarked that the acceptance of the democratic system by a people implied that they were prepared to put up with its workings good or bad. In his own words, "This willingness to accept in principle, the working of a system based on the will of the majority even if your self are in minority is simply the essence of democracy. Without it there could be no system of representative self-government at all. When you attempt to alter the system by means of violence or nonviolence, this, it seems to me, have only one of the two implications: either you do not believe in democracy at all, and consider that society ought to be governed by enlightened minorities such as the one to which you of course belong, or you consider the present system to be so imperfect that it is not truly representative, that it no longer serves adequately as a vehicle for the will of the majority, and this leaves to the unsatisfied no adequate means of self-expression other than the primitive one of calling attention to themselves and their emotions by mass demonstration and mass defiance of established authority."[16]

Pointing to Gandhi's Civil Disobedience wherein the participants in the movement were prepared to willingly accept the penalty for breaking the law, he said: "The violation of the law is not, in the moral and philosophical sense, a privilege that lies offered for sale with a given price tag." When poet W. H. Auden reminded him that: "A law is positively unjust if it commands an action, which is unjust or immoral. It is only in such circumstances that a man can be said to 'accept' the penalty for defiance." History owes a lot to martyrs! Kennan retorted: "for a Gandhi or a Tolstoy civil disobedience was one thing, for a Thoreau another. It seems to me that the citizen who lives under a system that assures him not only voting right but extensive guarantees for inviolability of his person and property, and who accepts the protection of this state in the enjoyment of these rights owes to the state, at least in high measure, of respect and forbearance in those instances where he may not find himself not in agreement with its policies."[17]

Concluding Remarks

As time flows, generations of men and women come and go to merge in infinity leaving behind a legacy of memories and traditions that shape the future. Each generation has contributed to making of the world we live in today. Whether the currents forming the ebbs and flows of the ocean of life are clear or muddy depends on how the outgoing generations handled their problems in response to the challenges of their own time and place. The twists and turns in human history determine the content and shape of the world in making.

Thus the present is what we made of yesterday and what we are doing today would shape the tomorrow. Two contrasting forces have ever been active: man's eternal cravings for peace; and his abiding faith in the instrument of war to secure it. The wars he wages are both within and without. The whole message of Bhagvat Gita – The Song Eternal – centers on the war that rages within each of human being – the war between good and evil; hate and love; greed and sacrifice. There is Kurukshetra, the battleground of Mahabharata, in each of us. It needs the intervention of super-conscious among us (Lord Krishna who personified Truth), to end the war. Christ sacrificed his life so that others may live in peace. But they did not. Buddha showed the path of peace through nonviolence. Mohammad taught his followers to launch Jehad against the enemy within. Many others came and left behind sobering messages in words and deeds. But wars did not die; they have continued and become more ferocious than ever before.

They all came when faith reigned supreme. Man invested them with the power of divinity and distanced himself from them. They were no longer super-conscious human beings. They became God, the Son of God, or the Messenger of God. And the business of war continued, one after the other, both within the individual and the society he built. No wonder then that much of the written history of humankind is the story of wars and warmongers. We are more familiar with the wars that man has been waging against nature and his own fellow human beings for millennia than with peace, the eternal craving of human species. The sacrifices that the common people as individuals and communities have made and continue to make in order that those who are near and dear live in peace is great indeed but it never gets the attention of the historians for it never leaves a lasting imprint on the wider world to get attention. And thus the wars and conflicts continue in various garbs: religious wars, ethnic wars, wars among neighbouring countries, and international wars. As time goes, it becomes more devastating and all embracing.

Until 1600 AD or so, wars were fought with the help of horses, elephants, sticks, arrows and spears. Those who won had their way. In these wars the human sufferings were limited even if large scale from the reckonings of the time. There were limits to even killing, for the reach of the tormenters and armies were limited in space and time. The technological advances have now enabled us to engage in wars without the involvement of soldiers and weapons operated manually. Rockets, missiles and laser beams can now kill all that is live on planet earth within minutes.

The war against nature that man started thousands of years ago has brought us on the threshold of climatic change – a change that would make human survival on planet earth impossible. We have used nature not as a nest to live but as a resource for exploitation. We are cutting the very branch on which we are sitting. And we think it is progress; it is development. The number of people who would be homeless and who would die because of global warming and consequent flooding of the coastal areas the world over is indeed imminent unless man launches satyagraha against his own thinking and doings.

Not content with these two devastating onslaughts, a new culture of war has been unleashed: it is terrorism. Symptoms of a form of localized terrorism were already there even earlier. Nomadic peoples attacked the civilized societies and spread terror. Innocents were trampled and butchered by invading horsemen not because they had done any wrong to them but because they were 'lesser human beings' in the eyes of the invaders. More they killed, larger the wealth they laid their hands on. That ancient method of mass extermination has now taken the form of Terrorism. Hundreds and thousands of innocent people – children and women included – are being exterminated not because they have done any harm to anyone, but because their deaths would help them achieve their ulterior ends.

The world we live today is the world of violence: violence against nature; violence against fellow human beings; and violence against oneself.

To bring peace in the conflict-torn world we have to work on two fronts. First, we have to educate ourselves to be at peace within. We must move forward from our animal ancestry, which Gandhi called brute force. We must become more human and learn to respect the dignity of man and nature; and we must find social and political solution to the conflicts so that they do not reach flash points of violence. These solutions have first to be found within. The germs of conflicts and wars lie in the minds of the people and so long as the human mind is ready to harbour the germs, there can be no peace.

Man has fought innumerable wars since times immemorial and each war has been fiercer than the earlier ones. Interestingly, each war was fought to bring peace. During the twentieth century we fought two World Wars; as if not satisfied with the enormous loss of life and property, we are preparing to engage ourselves in the Third, and perhaps the last, World War. In fact, if we sum up all the deaths and destructions that man has caused since the end of the Second World War in 1944, it has been far more than those perpetrated during the First and Second World Wars taken together. Wars have thus not ceased; they have only taken forms, which appear less spectacular than world wars. To quote Lao Tzu:

> "A country may be governed with justice,
> And a war may be won with cunning,
> But people can only be mastered by following them.
> How can this be known?
> By looking!
> The more people are controlled, the poorer they become;
> The poorer they become, the more restless they get;
> The more restless they get, the more forcefully they are restrained.
> When people are forcefully restrained, their defiance becomes ingenious.
> And the more ingenious their defiance, the stranger are the things that happen.
> Now when strange things begin to happen, laws and regulations become stricter;
> Then stricter laws and regulations mean more criminals and fugitives.
> Soon everyone is either a criminal or a fugitive,

And no one can untangle the mess.
Therefore,
The sage does nothing and people govern themselves,
Provokes no one and people are peaceful,
Does not interfere and people prosper,
Is without desire and people fulfill themselves.
The more people are controlled, the less contented they become.
But when will leaders understand the significance of this?"

—*Lao Tzu, tr. Ray Grigg*; stanza 57-58
(trad.), 20-21 (MaWangTui

The time has come to pause and think. Should we continue to advance materially at the cost of our survival; should we continue to use science and technology for our own annihilation; and should we lead a style of life that makes us sick? Should we not consider material advancement as a means, rather than an end to become more advanced human beings? Should we not use the growing pool of knowledge that we have accumulated to make this world a better place to live? And should we not develop ourselves individually and collectively into personalities that are physiologically, well functioning, mentally alert and emotionally loving? These and many others are the questions that confront us all; they aroused response in Gandhi, which he called Truth and Nonviolence. When translated into action, they together, gave rise to Satyagraha.

While violence and non-violence do sound, and are contradictory, they are marked with commonalities in many ways. Both are conflict resolution vehicles; both need bravery, courage and will power. Only the goals are different. Violence aims at subduing or finishing the opponent by brute force; nonviolence aims at winning over the opponent without hurting him and by soul force. In the words of Gandhi "I have said time and again that Satyagraha (non-violent struggle) is not same as making peace. It is still a fight that has to be fought as bravely as a soldier in a war — just the weapon is different."[18]

REFERENCES

1. Saul David Alinsky, *Rules for the Radicals: A Pragmatic Primer for Realistic Radicals,* (out of print), 1971.

2. Charles Dobson, *The Troublemaker's Teaparty: A Manual for Effective Citizen Action*, New Society Publishers, 2003.
3. George Orwell: *Reflections on Gandhi,* London, *Partisan Review*. January 1949.
4. V.S. Naipaul, *India: A Wounded Civilization*, London: Knoff Publishing Group, 1975.
5. Dutta, K. & A. Robinson, *Rabindranath Tagore: An Anthology,* St. Martin's Press, 1997.
6. Jalal, Ayesha. *The Sole Spokesman: Jinnah, the Muslim League and the Demand for Pakistan.* Cambridge: CUP, 1994. See also, French, Patrick, Liberty or Death: India's Journey to Independence and Partition, NT: Harperr Collins, 1997.
7. Gene Sharp, *Gandhi as a Political Strategist, with Essays on Ethics and Politics*, Introduction by Coretta Scott King, Boston: Porter Sargent, 1979.
8. ——— *The Politics of Nonviolent Action*, Introduction by Thomas C. Schelling, Harvard University Center for International Affairs, Boston: Porter Sargent. 1974; paperback edition in 3 vols.: I. *Power and Struggle*. p. 114; II. *The Methods of Nonviolent Action*, p. 348; and III. *Dynamics of Nonviolent Action*, p. 466.
9. Joseph Kip Kosak, "Richad Gregg, Mohandas Gandhi, and the Strategy of Nonviolence", *Journal of American History,* No. 4(2005), pp. 1318-48.
10. Gene Sharp, *Ibid.*
11. Eric Hoffner, *Reflections on Human Conditions,* ISBN 1-933435-14.
12. Harry Browne, *Why Government Doesn't Work: How Reducing Government will Bring us Safer Cities, Better Schools, Lower Taxes, More Freedom, and Prosperity for All, 1995. Amazon.Com.*
13. John Hospers. *www.liberty-news.com/quotes.php.*
14. H.L. Menken. *www.lewrockwell.com/orig2/bradley1.html.*
15. George Washington, *humanscaleblog.blogspot.com/.../george-washington-on-government.html-57k.*
16. George F. Kennan, "Rebels without a Program", *The New York Times Magazine,* January 21, 1968.
17. *Ibid.*

R.P. Misra
Series Editor

1
Introduction

A path breaking method of conflict resolution was born almost a century ago, far away from India in South Africa. The father of the method was Mohandas Karamchand Gandhi, a lawyer by profession. Following Tolstoy, he called it passive resistance. But the action that followed was not passive, it was proactive. So he renamed it *Satyagraha.*

Satyagraha, as practised by Gandhi, was a technique of action designed to set in motion a process to achieve lasting peace. It emerged from the realisation that violence breeded violence; war fought to end wars and bring peace brought greater and more devastating wars. *Satyagraha* replaced brute force by soul force, also known as love force through self-suffering with the sole objective of drowsing hatred in the opponent and arousing in him the inherent capacity, even if muted, to love the 'enemy'.

The doctrine of *Satyagraha* was an extension of the rule of family life into the political arena. Gandhi held that family disputes and differences were generally settled according to the 'Law of Love'. The injured member had so much regard for the others that he suffered injury for the sake of his principles without retaliating and without anger against those who differed with him. As repressing of anger and self-suffering were difficult processes, he did not dignify trifles into principles, but in all non-essentials readily agreed with the rest of family and thus continued to gain the maximum of peace for himself without disturbing that of others. Thus, his action whether he resisted or resigned was always calculated to promote the common welfare of his family.

The doctrine of *Satyagraha* was meant to show how the man of conscience could engage in heroic action in the vindication of truth and freedom from all tyranny, in his appeal to justice against every social abuse and sectional interest. Gandhi challenged the conventional notions of authority, law and obligation by appealing to his conception of natural law or *dharma* and self-suffering or *tapas*. *Satya* and *ahimsa* alone could secure an unending basis for social consensus and political loyalty.

In times such as ours when conflict is the order of the day and the potentials of technology offer more to fear than to hope, social and political theories face their gravest challenge. Theoretical and political systems have grown increasingly suspect and intellectual formulations tend less to challenge than to repel. But there is rapidly developing demand hitherto neglected by social and political theory: this is the demand for solutions to the problem of conflict not for theoretical systems of end-structure aimed at ultimately eliminating conflict, but for ways of confronting conflict when it arises: ways, which are constructive and not destructive. Such a demand must be met by a theory of process and of means and not of further concern for structure, for pattern and for ends; basic to such a theory is a philosophy of action.

In the arena of power politics, power experts meet power experts and the struggle continues to be cast in power-play manoeuvers if not in terms of outright or subtle coercion. The framework of assumptions, which underlies the strategy of power conflicts may make it impossible for rivals or antagonists to choose the mutually advantageous course because there is nothing in their experience, which allows them to make the assumption of similarity in regard to their relative positions. If they could do this, they might solve the dilemma to the benefit of both. Indulgence in *himsa* is the result of short-sightedness, lack of vision, arising out of the inability to put oneself in the position of the antagonist and to disarm or convert him so that he ceases to regard himself as an irreconciable enemy.

Far from denying the existence or reality of conflicts of interest in human mind and society, Gandhi admitted their existence in every walk of life and sought to make *ahimsa* the basis of a method of action, which could cope with such conflicts by limiting, if not wholly removing, the *himsa* involved. It is part of liberal and democratic doctrine that the method of persuasion is morally and even practically superior to that of pressure; that free discussion and rational argument are better than coercion or brute force. We commonly distinguish between force, which usually means physical constraint; power, which implies the use of reason or of other skills, and authority, which presupposes the recognition by those who accept it of the moral and political legitimacy of its exercise by its holder. T.H. Green's dictum "will, not force, is the basis of the State"; the earlier attempt to invoke the notion of a social contract; Locke's 'tacit consent'; Hume's 'appeal to political prudence and the artificial virtues; and Rousseaus' "general will", are all traditional examples of the present-day sociologists' concern with the social consensus, which provides the framework for peaceful conflict resolution under recognised rules of the game. The notion of non-coercion is essential to the respect that we accord to the human personality, and the concern with justifying minimum coercion as a necessary evil to secure a larger good is itself a recognition of the superiority of *ahimsa* over *himsa.* There was an anarchistic and utopian element in Gandhi's doctrine of *ahimsa* in that he proclaimed the ultimate need for the State and for all institutions totally to abjure all *himsa.* This was because he recognised that, in the broader meaning of *ahimsa*, even a liberal who abstained from physical force or shrinked from slaughter could indulge in subtler forms of *himsa* or pressure. The main thing for Gandhi is that more and more people must be prepared to accept the absolute moral value of *ahimsa,* not as an elusive ideal or a pious hope, but as a widely relevant principle of social and political action. Force thrives on fear but if more and more individuals and groups become fearless, force increasingly fails to serve its intended purpose and its exercise may be effectively opposed and even consistently frustrated. Today, we are prepared to question the retributive theory of punishment and to condemn forms of *himsa* like capital punishment, dueling, slavery, torture, collective retaliation or revenge, acts of aggression by states, preventive wars, cruelty to animals, flogging and corporal punishment, which were all quite respectable at one time or the other. We are now stricter about the notion of minimal coercion or the use of force as a last resort and we also increasingly recognize that a progressive reduction of the content of minimal coercion is the mark of civilization, progress and enlightenment. But we still base our degrees of repugnance or condemnation of force upon our valuation of the rightness of the cause in which it is employed and upon our assessment of the amount of suffering caused in relation to existing suffering or the future suffering avoided.

Gandhi insisted that force did not change its immoral character according to the circumstances of its use, and denied that the use of force to prevent a greater evil could ever acquire any inherent moral or political legitimacy. His attitude towards *ahimsa* was never literalist, but it was nonetheless absolutist rather than utilitarian. He declared that a votary of *ahimsa* could not subscribe to the utilitarian formula. He would strive for the greatest good of all and die in an attempt to realise the ideal.

He was, therefore willing to die so that others might live. The absolutist's sphere of destruction will always be the narrowest possible. The utilitarians had no limit. Judged by the standard of non-violence, every war was wholly wrong. Judged by the utilitarian standard, each party was justified according to its idea of utility. Precisely on the same ground, the anarchist justified his assassinations. But none of these acts could possibly be justified on the principle of greatest-good-of-all.

Although Gandhi's conception of *ahimsa* was absolutist on the ethical plane, it was anything but an abstract moral attitude for he was convinced beyond doubt that individuals and groups and even the masses could be trained in "the white art of non-violence" just as they could be in "the black art of violence".[1] The individual votary of *ahimsa* must learn that he needed far greater physical and mental courage than the one needed for delivering of physical blows. He had to pass many a sleepless nights and go through many a mental torture before he could even be within measurable distance of the goal of utter humility and goodwill even towards his most bitter opponent. In any conflict between two parties, he was bound, when the occasion arose, to say, which side was just but he could not grade different species of violence according to whether it was defensive or offensive. Strength did not come from physical capacity but from indomitable will.

The votary of *ahimsa* must cultivate the habit of unremitting toil, sleepless vigilance, ceaseless self-control. Such a man would not meekly submit to the will of an evil-doer but put his whole soul against the will of a tyrant. "Working under this law of our being, it is possible for a single individual to defy the whole might of an unjust empire." Gandhi recognised that it would be difficult to get large masses of men to be nonviolent in this exalted sense, but he was convinced that if even a band of intelligent and honest men with an abiding faith in *ahimsa* could be formed and trained, it could ensure the nonviolent atmosphere required for the working of civil disobedience in accord with *ahimsa*. It should be possible to train small communities in the difficult art of nonviolence and use their influence for peaceful mass action and to get large numbers of people to learn to do without the protection of both the military and the police during communal troubles. Gandhi thought it was gross self-deception to believe that man could risk death only if they had learned and practiced the art of killing but not otherwise. There was no *prima facie* reason why the masses, if trained in non-violent action, be incapable of showing the discipline displayed usually by a fighting force. The example of a few men and women if they fully imbibed the spirit of non-violence was bound to infect the whole mass in the end.

From *Ahimsa* in politics flowed the individual freedom. Gandhi was against any kind of impositions even if it was imposed for the benefit of the person concerned. He upheld the dignity and authority of the individual throughout his life. In Champaran where he conducted his first *Satyagraha* in India, he was served with a notice to leave the district. But he refused to comply with the directive. A summon was served on Gandhi to appear before the court. He pleaded guilty and read a brief statement before the court wherein he said, "I have disregarded the order served upon me, not for want for respect for lawful authority, but in obedience to the higher law of our being, the voice of conscience."[2]

Writing in 1939 in connection with the People's movement, he observed, "Civil liberty consistent with the observance of non-violence is the first step towards Swaraj. It is breath of political and social life. It is foundation of freedom. There is no room there for dilution or compromise. It is the water of life. I have never heard of water being diluted."[3] With the outbreak of Second World War, India was made a party to the War. Rigorous curbs were put on civil liberties of the people. He strongly pleaded for freedom of speech as an inviolable fundamental right of the citizens even during the war. Explaining his mind at a greater-length he observed, "But if they (the British) fight unto death for their freedom, and if they are at all reasonable, they must recognise our right.... It is our duty to fight for that right...This liberty is a concrete issue, which needs no defining. It is the foundation of freedom, especially when it has to be taken nonviolently. To surrender it, is to surrender the only means for attaining freedom."[4] He asked, "If the individual ceases to count, what is left of society? Individual freedom alone can make a man voluntarily surrender himself completely to the service of society. If it is wrested from him, he becomes an automation and the society is ruined."[5] He regarded the individual as the centre of the power. He was categorical in his estimate of relation between individual and the state. He held that the state derived its existence and power from the individual.

The concept of the ultimate authority of the individual logically paved the way for the enunciation of the theory of nonviolent non-cooperation with the state and the exploitative system that stood in the way of the all round evolution of the individual. The emphasis on the moral power of the individual was the keynote of his philosophy. His anguish and indignation expressed in the pages of 'Hind Swaraj' against modern civilization was based on this fundamental belief.

Gandhi did, however, try to reconcile individual freedom with social obligation. He considered society like a family, and the relation between the individual and the society as interdependent. He rejected unrestricted individualism that ignored social obligations as well as the individual freedom as a mere cog in the social machine. He wrote, "I value individual freedom, but you must not forget that man is essentially a social being. He has risen to this present status by learning to adjust his individualism to requirements of social progress. Unrestricted individualism is the law of the beasts of the jungle. We have learnt to strike the mean between individual freedom and social restraint. Willing submission to social restraint for the sake of the well-being of the whole society, enriches both the individual and the society of which one is a member."[6] But between the individual and society, the individual came first, though society was, by no means neglected. The individual was the unit and in any scheme of social progress the first step always began with him. Society must provide opportunities for the maximum growth of individual and individual in his turn must discharge his duties faithfully. In case, either of the two went wrong, the other must resist nonviolently. Thus nonviolence reconciled individual freedom with social restraints. Nonviolence implied that the mechanics of control, which maintained social cohesion consisted of internal and non-coercive external sanctions. The individual used his opportunities to advance the greatest good of all while society gave to the individual maximum opportunity to be good.

Gandhi suggested a moral alternative to violence. The international community, so far, has adopted the method of violence, physical power, as the means for resolving conflicts, which accrue due to the clash of national interests as well as for other reasons. The achievements of science and technology have proved the futility of war, as in modem times, it means total annihilation of the world. This inadequacy of violence has raised the question of resolving conflicts without inviting disaster and use of physical power? We are in search of a functional alternative to violence.

Gandhi's contribution lies in the fact that he dispelled the common place notion that leads to a belief in the unavoidability of war. He applied his theory of unity and purity of means and ends in dealing with the problem of international relation also. War, as a method of struggle is the means and the object for which it is waged is the end. Even if the end of war is to get justice, it cannot be realised through the impure means of war. To get justice through war is unjust for if one cannot give life, how can one take it? Thus he rejects even the concept of just war as a method of resolving conflict.

In modern age concept of "just war" is not tenable even if the peaceful methods prove ineffective. The destructive nature of war does not permit us to resort to war. The contention that war is in the interest of peace, is fallacious. For it overlooks the fact that the suppression of force can only prevent the expression of the evil in acts, but cannot remove the source of the evil itself. Gandhi held: "There is a law of Nature that a thing can be retained by the same means by which it has been acquired. A thing acquired by violence can be retained by violence alone while one acquired by truth can be retained only by truth".[7] Further, "It is an inevitable law that the weapon which is responsible for victory is the only one which can preserve the fruits of victory and win more."

Even the nuclear armament cannot prevent war. In his view, "The atomic weapons might have created a temporary revulsion against war, but the world would return to violence as soon as the feeling of revulsion was over." Thus, Gandhi rejects war as a method of conflict resolution and suggests a novel technique of *Satyagraha* based on the principle of non-violence which may legitimately be regarded as moral alternative to war for the resolution of conflicts. He holds: "I do justify entire nonviolence and consider it possible in relations between man and man and nation and nation, but it is not 'a resignation from all real fighting against wickedness. On the contrary the nonviolence of my conception is more active and real fighting against wickedness than retaliation whose very nature is to increase wickedness. I contemplate a mental and, therefore, a moral opposition to immoralities."[8] The Gandhian technique of international conflict resolution consists in the principle of struggle without arms and, positively speaking, a fight with the help of truth, self-suffering, love, character and moral powers, which is known as the 'principle of nonviolent resistance.

This technique of *Satyagraha,* however, requires greater courage and training than is required for military personnel. "To seek to win in a clash of arms would be pure bravado. Not so if in defying the might of one who would deprive me of my independence, I refuse to obey his will and perish unarmed in the attempt." Further, "To kill and be killed in fighting an enemy is comparatively speaking an act of bravery but to stand the blows of your adversaries and not to retaliate is a greater form of bravery." The technique of nonviolent resistance not only holds good for resolving the interpersonal conflicts but for the international conflicts also. To Gandhi, 'It is blasphemy to say that nonviolence can only be practiced by individuals and never by nations which are composed of individuals.'

Aggression by any nation on others takes place due to certain motive behind it. The motive may be certain natural greed or lebensraum. In the former case Gandhi suggests the proper study of the motives of the possible aggressor and removing that motive by providing suitable alternative. Speaking about the frequent tribal raids in the North West Frontier Provinces Gandhi said in 1938 that the raider's motive was chiefly economic, *i.e.* the satisfaction of primary needs. Therefore, he suggested to teach them industries and thereby remove their principal motive that forced them into the raiding habit.

If the possibility of invasion is due to certain differences, Gandhi forbids to take it into law court. In his view, 'We should use a variety of possible approaches dictated to us by our hearts and minds, including negotiation, conciliation, mediation, sharing of differences, co-responsibility and the co-creation of a valid and creative compromise, which is a recognition of the element of truth within 'the other' out there."[9] He realised that "for two disagreeing parties to go to law court there could often be "another form of exhibition of brute force". "Having recourse to judiciary as a form of the Law of Aggression rules out the chance for one to practice the Law of Love". If we resolve the differences with the help of judiciary, it will amount to taking recourse to fear, constraint and force, which will never give us justice and the conflict finally will remain unsolved". Therefore, "A theory of nonviolence must lay the greatest stress on negotiations as the chief peaceful means of international disputes".

Gandhi prescribed another approach for a nation when it is faced with an armed attack. Here, the technique consists in fighting nonviolently to the last consequences without any bitterness and hatred against the invader. In 1940 Gandhi wrote in the *Harijan* "If the Czechs, the Poles, the Norwegians, the French and the English had all said to Hitler, 'You need not make your scientific preparation for destruction. We will meet your violence with nonviolence. You will, therefore, be able to destroy our nonviolent army without tanks, battleships and airships.' the history of Europe would have been written differently," the same year in July, he appealed to every Briton "to accept the method of nonviolence instead of that of war for the adjustment of relation between nations and other matters".[10] In this context his advice to Britain is also worth noting. He said, "I want you to fight Nazism without arms. I would like you to lay down the arms you have as being useless for saving you or humanity. You will invite Hitler and Signor Mussolini to take that they want of the countries, you call your possessions. Let them take possession of your beautiful island, with your many beautiful buildings; you will give all these, but neither your souls nor your minds. If these gentlemen choose to occupy your houses, you will vacate them, if they do not give free passage out, you will allow yourself: man, woman and child to be slaughtered, but you will refuse to owe allegiance to them."[11] The same type of advice is given to Abyssinia, Czechoslovakia, China and India during Italian, German and Japanese invasions. In 1935 he said: "If Abyssinia were nonviolent, she would have no arms, would want none, she would make no appeal to the League of Nations or any other power for armed intervention. She would never give any cause for complaint. And Italy would find nothing to conquer. If Abyssinians would not offer armed resistance, nor would they give co-operation willing or forced. Italian occupation in that case would mean that of the land without its people. That, however, is not Italy's object. She seeks submission of the people of that beautiful land.[12] Against Japanese aggression to China, he advised. "The Chinese would say to Japan, "bring all your machinery we present half of our population to you. But the remaining two hundred millions won't bend their knee to you". If the Chinese did that Japan would become China's slave. He argued: "If it is brave, as it is, to die to a man fighting against odds, it is braver still to refuse to fight and yet to refuse to yield to the usurper. If death is a certainty, in either case, is it not nobler to die with the breast bared to the enemy without malice against him within.[13] During Second World War at the time of Japanese aggression, he advised people of India to opt for nonviolent resistance. "The underlying belief in such nonviolent resistance is that, the aggressor will, in time, be mentally, even physically, tired of killing nonviolent resisters. He will begin to search what this new force is, which refuses co-operation without seeking to hurt, and will probably desist from further slaughter". But one can doubt it's efficacy during aerial warfare and blast of atom bomb. Gandhi's reply was, 'Behind the death dealing bomb there is the human hand that releases it, and behind that still is the human heart that gets the hand in motion.' The remorse that gripped those who talked of atom bomb as also of those who dropped it on Hiroshima and Nagasaki is a sufficient proof of Gandhi's thesis.

Gandhi denounced not only the use of arms in war, but also the help of armed forces from other nations to one side or the other. He wrote in the *Harijan* 'It is clear that small nations must either come or be ready to come under the protection of the dictators or be a constant menance to the peace of Europe. In spite of all the goodwill in the world, England and France cannot save them. Their intervention can only mean bloodshed and destruction such as has never been seen before."[14] "If I were Czech, therefore, I would free these two nations from the obligation to defend my country. And yet I must live, I would not be a vassal to any nation or body. I must, have absolute independence or perish".[15] He always advised the nations small and big to fight with their soul-force, the force lying within, and not to take help from the outward circumstances.

In spite of the best of the efforts, if a nation loses its territory and becomes the slave of the aggressor, Gandhi prescribes a third type of behaviour called non-cooperation. A voluntary non-cooperation with the victor will make him realize his fault and arouse his moral consciousness. At least, it will not strengthen his evil designs and pride and will cause ultimate defeat to him. According to Gandhi "Non-cooperation is not merely an ideal but also a safe and quick way to freedom for India. I do suggest that the doctrine holds good also as between states and states". This is why, he suggested Abyssinia to non-cooperate with Italy. In 1942 during the anticipated Japanese attack on India, Gandhi wrote to Meerabehn: "Remember that our attitude is that of complete non-cooperation with the Japanese army. Therefore, we may not help them in any way, nor may we profit by any dealings with them. Therefore, we cannot sell any thing to them.

The question of having any dealings with the Japanese does not and should not arise. They will handle nothing from Japanese hands".

To sum up, Gandhian technique of international conflict resolution consists in resolving differences with the help of nonviolence and truth in the form of *Satyagraha* and non-cooperation. In normal cases, it suggests the method of conciliation, negotiation, arbitration, and direct dialogue with the opponents for resolving conflicts.

According to the doctrine of *Satyagraha,* social and political conflicts can best be resolved in an atmosphere in which the contestants respect each other's moral worth, distinguish between measures and persons, conduct their battles in a spirit of self-criticism and abstain from the cruder forms of coercion. When the coercive element is strong in conducting a conflict, it demoralizes the winner and humiliates the loser and leaves behind it a trail of continuing bitterness or suppressed resentment. Fear is always a bad counsellor, and solutions that rest on the appeal to fear are less lasting or satisfying than agreement achieved in the context of a consensus of goodwill. Further, when a conflict takes place between unequal parties, it is tempting for the stronger to regard itself as invulnerable, to identify its interests with the general good or to think it can ignore with impunity the just claims of others. In such situations, the appeal to force is useless for the weaker party and merely increases the complacency of the stronger. The weaker can compel the attention of the materially stronger by showing their reserves of moral and spiritual strength and by casting doubt on the self-assurance and moral conceit of their opponents. Even if those who resort to *Satyagraha* fail to secure their ends, they retain their self-respect and are morally enhanced, although they have sometimes to pay the price of political or physical martyrdom.

NOTES

1. D.G. Tendulkar, *Mahatma*, New Delhi, Publications Division, Ministry of Information and Broadcasting, Government of India, 1952, pp. 209-10.
2. *Collected Works of Mahatma Gandhi*, New Delhi, Publications Division, Ministry of Information and Broadcasting, Government of India, 1965. Vol. XIII, p. 375, Hereinafter as *CWMG*.
3. *Ibid.*, Vol. LXIX, p. 356.
4. *Harijan*, 22-9-1940, p. 292.

5. *Ibid.*, 1-2-1942, p. 521.
6. *Ibid.*, 25-7-1939, p. 139.
7. M.K. Gandhi, *Satyagraha in South Africa*, Ahmedabad, Navajivan, Publishing House, 1975, pp. 338-39.
8. *Harijan*, 12-11-1938, p. 328.
9. Guyde Mallac, *Seven Steps to Global Changes: Gandhi's Message for Today*, Santa Fe, New Mexico, Ocean Tree Book 1987, p. 33.
10. *Ibid.*, 6-7-1990, p. 185.
11. *Ibid.*
12. *Ibid.*, 12-10-1935, p. 276.
13. *Ibid.*, 8-10-1938, p. 282.
14. *Ibid.*, 15-10-1938, pp. 290-91.
15. *Ibid.*

2

Satyagraha: Essence, Percepts and Techniques

The word *Satyagraha* is Sanskrit in origin. It is a compound word formed of *Satya* and *Agraha*. *Satya* means truth and *Agraha* means holding fast, adherence, insistence. Thus *Satyagraha* means clinging to truth, holding fast to truth, insistence on truth, or firm adherence to truth come what may.

The term *Satya* itself is derived from *sat*, which means being, that which exists. *Satya* is that which is in accordance with *sat* or being, that is, truth. Thus, that which is in accordance with correct knowledge of things as they are, is truth. Action according to truth, or right action, has a special word for it in the Vedas. It is *rta.* From *rta* is derived *anrta,* what is not right, a lie. *Satya* is knowledge of truth and *rta* is action according to truth. The Vedic Rishis insisted that *satya* and *rta* must go together; sometimes the words are used alternately.

The term *Satyagraha* was coined by Gandhi when he felt that the English term "passive resistance", which is largely derived from the Christian concept of non-resistance to evil and which he borrowed from Tolstoy, failed to express adequately the nature of nonviolent resistance in the active form developed by him. For about a decade he ran passive resistance against the racist policies of South African government. It was in 1906 that the need for a new name for his movement was felt by him for the first time.

In his 'Autobiography' Gandhi has narrated the circumstances in which, the term was coined: "The principle called *Satyagraha* came into being before that name was invented. Indeed when it was born, I myself could not say what it was. In Gujarati also we used the English phrase 'passive resistance' to describe it. When in a meeting with Europeans I found that the term "passive resistance" was too narrowly construed, it was supposed to be a weapon of the weak, that it could be characterized by hatred, and that it could finally manifest itself as violence, I had to demur to all these statements and explain the real; a new word must be coined by the Indians to designate their struggle."[1]

In 1906 Gandhi organized the Indians in South Africa and led a new kind, of resistance movement against the unjust laws under which they were then suffering. This movement was called in the beginning 'Passive Resistance'. Gandhi himself used this term in the early stages, but later he 'felt ashamed' of using an English word which could not be easily understood and used as current coin by the Indian people. What was more important, he felt, that the movement he had started was essentially from what was ordinarily known as 'passive resistance'. This term was not rejected but the new movement launched by Indians in South Africa had only outword resemblance to passive resistance, which was distinguishable from active or violent armed resistance. But there the resemblance ended. The approach, the underlying philosophy, and the technique of the new movement were all different from those of simple passive resistance. Gandhi felt the need for an appropriate word for the new kind of resistance and as nothing suggested itself to him, he announced a prize in his weekly, *Indian Opinion,* to any reader suggesting one. Perhaps the best among the many entries that were submitted was the word '*sadagraha*' suggested by Maganlal Gandhi, meaning 'firmness in a good cause' or 'adherence to a good cause'. Bearing in mind the difference between '*sat*' and '*satya*' mentioned above, Gandhi modified Maganlal's suggested word to '*Satyagraha*', to connote the full meaning, which he wished to express, namely, 'truth-force' or the power of truth, force born of truth and love or nonviolence.[2] For Gandhi, truth and nonviolence or love have always clung together.

Discussing the origins of *Satyagraha* with Joseph J. Doke, one of Gandhi's earliest biographers, Gandhi appears to have stated:

> "I remember, how one verse of a Gujarati poem, which, as a child, I learned at school, clung to me.' In substance it was this:
>
> 'If a man gives you a drink of water and you give him a drink in return, that is nothing. Real beauty consists in doing good against evil.'

As a child, this verse had a powerful influence over me, and I tried to carry it into practice. Then came the 'Sermon on the Mount".

" 'But,' said I, 'surely the *Bhagavad Gita* came first?' 'No,' he replied, 'of course I knew the *Bhagavad Gita* in Sanskrit tolerably well, but I had not made its teaching in that particular a study.' It was the New Testament which really awakened me to the rightness and value of Passive Resistance. When I read in the 'Sermon on the Mount' such passages as 'Resist not him that is evil but whosoever smiteth thee on thy right cheek turn to him the other also', and 'Love your enemies and pray for them that persecute you, that ye may be sons of your Father, which is in heaven,' I was simply overjoyed, and found my own opinion confirmed where I least expected it. The *Bhagavad Gita* deepened the impression, and Tolstoy's *The Kingdom of God Is Within You* gave it permanent form."[3]

But *Satyagraha*, according to Gandhi, is not a method limited merely to a conflict-situation that subsisted between an alien rule and a subject community. The scope of *Satyagraha* is wider than that. For Gandhi, "the law of *Satyagraha,* the law of love, is an eternal principle."[4] It is this 'eternal principle' of love in which, it is presumed, lies the global significance of Gandhi. But this message of love to the world preached as an abstract norm shorn of the dynamic method of *Satyagraha* does not carry any social relevance; it becomes a platitude or, at its best, a pious wish of a group of 'good' but ineffective men.

As discussed in chapter one, the doctrine of *Satyagraha* was for Gandhi an extension of the rule of domestic life into the public life. Normally, the family disputes and differences were settled according to the "Law of Love."

It is this Law which, silently but surely, governs the family for the most part throughout the civilized world. I feel that nations cannot be one in reality, nor can their activities be conducive to the common good of the whole humanity, unless there is this definition and acceptance of the law of the family in national and international affairs, in other words, on the political platform. Nations can be called civilized only to the extent that they obey this law.[5]

This rule of domestic life or the Law of Love may require self-suffering or some form of non-cooperation. If the father does an injustice, it is the duty of his children to leave the parental roof.

Similarly, argued Gandhi, if the headmaster of a school conducts his institution on an immoral basis, the pupils must leave the school. If the chairman of a corporation is corrupt, the members must wash their hands clean of his corruption by withdrawing from it. Even so, if a government does grave injustice, the subjects must withdraw cooperation wholly or partially, but sufficiently to wean the ruler from his wickedness.

A *Satyagrahi* who wants to vindicate his inherent, sacred right, should be prepared to bear all kinds of suffering. Self-suffering, thus, replaces retaliation, which has been traditionally recognised as the technique of the redemption of right. If Hampden and Wat Taylor would not have been able to bear suffering, they could not have raised the standard of revolt.[6] The aspirant after the vindication of truth has necessarily to undergo all types of suffering for its sake. Real, organic nonviolence based on suffering can become a mighty force and can be used against the most powerful government. Gandhi wrote in an article:

"Suffering is the mark of the human tribe. It is an eternal law. The mother suffers so that her child may live. Life comes out of death. No country has ever risen without being purified through the fire of suffering.... It is impossible to do away with the law of suffering which is the one indispensable condition of our being. Progress is to be measured by the amount of suffering undergone...the purer the suffering the greater is the progress."[7]

Ahimsa, which is the life blood of *Satyagraha*, meant for Gandhi, infinite love and this in its turn meant infinite capacity for infinite suffering.

"Non-violence in its dynamic condition means conscious suffering.... I have ventured to place before India the ancient law of self-sacrifice, the law of suffering. The Rishis who discovered the law of non-violence in the midst of violence were greater geniuses than Newton, greater warriors than Wellington. Having themselves known the use of arms, they realized their uselessness and taught a weary world that salvation lay not through violence but through non-violence.... The religion of non-violence is not meant merely for the Rishis and Saints. It is meant for the common people as well. Non-violence is the law of our species, as violence is the law of the brute. This dignity of the man requires obedience to a higher law – to the strength of the spirit....I want India to practise nonviolence, being conscious of her strength and power. I want India to recognise that she has a soul that cannot perish and that can rise triumphant above every physical weakness and defy the physical combination of a whole world."[8]

The Gandhian theory of *Satyagraha* or dynamic soul-force, thus, is based on the acceptance of the concept of suffering for the vindication of truth and justice. *Satyagraha* is, in its innermost essence, an attempt at self-purification through suffering. It signifies a genuine, intense and sincere quest for the vindication of Truth, which is God, through suffering. It is, hence, based on an invincible belief in the ultimate triumph of divine justice.

The deliberate acceptance of suffering for a great cause not only purifies and ennobles the sufferer, but it creates a powerful social situation of invincible potency whose dynamic effect almost physically compels the oppressor to yield to the demands of truth and justice, for the voluntary acceptance of suffering does make an appeal to the implicit moral sense of the oppressor. Its intensity would show the hollowness of the moral foundations of the antagonist's position. Furthermore, it would also solicit the sympathy of the vast number of people who may not be immediately involved in the situation.

Thus, suffering serves three purposes. First, it purifies the sufferers. Secondly, it makes a direct appeal to the soul of the oppressor. Thirdly, it intensifies favourable public opinion. The potency of suffering is revealed also in the history of early Christianity. Jesus Christ is a symbol of victorious suffering. Against the imperialism of Rome, early Christianity offers several examples of ennobling martyrdom.

It is true that the sacrifice of one evokes sympathetic feelings in others and thus big movements are produced. But the success of *Satyagraha* depends on individual purification and discipline. In armed struggles, the stress is on collective attack and defence. But in *Satyagrahi* struggle, the individual effort at self-suffering and the conversion of the heart of the oppressor is the vital element, because *Satyagraha* as soul-force is the force of love. It is based on the conception that triumph against injustice can be the achievement of only the moral will, because the active nonviolent resistance of the "heroic meek" makes an immediate appeal to the heart of the oppressor.

As early as 1919 Gandhi regarded "the Law of *Satyagraha*"—the Law of Love—as an eternal principle,[9] although the principles of

Satyagraha constitute gradual evolution. Once its simple basic principles—adherence to truth and insistence upon it by self-suffering—are understood, anybody can practice it. "It is as difficult or as easy to practice as any other virtue"[10] and it is not necessary for its practice that everyone should understand the entire philosophy of *Satyagraha*. In 1914, he described it as a "force" that may be used by individuals as well as by communities, in political as in domestic affairs. "Its universal applicability is a demonstration of its permanence and invincibility. It can be used alike by men, women and children".[11] The reason why it is universally applicable is that it is independent of pecuniary or other material assistance. Gandhi stressed the universal scope of *Satyagraha* until he died. In 1946 he still described it as a law of universal application. "Beginning with the family, its use can be extended to every other circle."[12]

When Gandhi spoke about the universality of the scope of *Satyagraha* he combined two completely separate notions. He believed that *Satyagraha* being a law all men must accept—acceptance involving no more than a moral preference for nonviolence – and also that it being a force, it must be universally present in nature and society.[13] It would bc difficult to challenge the latter as he claimed assumption of this force to be non-physical and "works silently and apparently slowly."[14] A similar confusion or combination of two quite different senses of "law", as a moral precept and as an opperative force or process in nature, may be detected in some thinkers in the West who employed the concept of Natural Law. What Gandhi meant by calling this divine force in nature (expressed in man as soul-force) universal is merely that it "necessarily makes no distinction between kinsmen and strangers, young and old, man and woman, friend and foe."[15] There is also a third sense closely connected with the second, in which Gandhi regarded *Satyagraha* as universal and this is the easiest to grasp as well as the most useful way of recording it. In this sense, he meant simply that it is an effective method of action, an instrument, which he regarded as universally applicable in society. When he called *Satyagraha* a universal law, he meant that "it is a universal principle of universal application." The former two senses were important to him insofar as he wanted to show that this instrument was based upon an ethical principle or precept, which all men must accept and that it is invariably bound to be effective if soul-force was properly employed. It is easier to make the notion of the universal scope of *Satyagraha* in society intelligible when we remember Gandhi's stress on the educative role of *Satyagraha*. "*Satyagraha* is a process of educating public opinion, such that it covers all the elements of society and, in the end, makes itself irresistible. Violence interrupts the process and prolongs the real revolution of the whole structure."[16]

BASIC PRECEPTS

On January 9, 1920, Gandhi appeared before the Disorders Inquiry Committee at Ahmedabad presided over by Lord Hunter. A brief extract from his oral evidence will explain the basic precepts of *Satyagraha*.

"Q. I take it, Mr. Gandhi, that you are the author of the *Satyagraha* movement.

A. Yes, Sir.

Q. Will you explain it briefly?

A. It is a movement intended to replace methods of violence and a movement based entirely upon Truth. It is, as I have conceived it, an extension of the domestic law on the political field and my experience has led me to the conclusion that that movement and that alone can rid India of the possibility of violence spreading throughout the length and breadth of the land, for the redress of grievances.

Q. People differ as to the justice or injustice of particular laws?

A. That is the main reason why violence is eliminated and a *Satyagrahi* gives his opponent the same right of independence and feelings of liberty that be reserves to himself and he will fight by inflicting injuries on his person...."[17]

Gandhi's enunciation of the doctrine shows that a few tenets are basic to *Satyagraha*. Truth, non-violence and self-suffering are the principles on which this technique is based. Understanding of these fundamentals combined with the skill in application determines the effective functioning of *Satyagraha*. The failure to comprehend these underlying assumptions and the methods based on them may lend the impression that any unarmed mass action wearing outwardly a nonviolent appearance could be termed a *Satyagraha*. *Satyagraha* is to be sharply distinguished from *Duragraha*. Appearance is not enough, he would emphasise; the strength of this technique lies in soul-force. So in order to comprehend the technique one must try to have a precise grasp of the concepts of truth, non-violence and self-suffering as understood by Gandhi and as employed by him in *Satyagraha*.

TRUTH

'*Satyagraha* is literally holding on to Truth, and it means therefore Truth-force.' What is this 'truth' which Gandhi incorporated as an essential element of his premier technique? How does it become a 'force', and how does it relate to man's action on the field of conflict? 'It excludes the use of violence,' Gandhi asserted, 'because man is not capable of knowing the absolute truth and therefore not competent to punish.'

Gandhi made his life into 'numerous experiments with truth'. In 'holding on to the truth' he did not suggest that such truth need be or could be a universally valid object of acknowledgement. He said, simply,

"...I am but a seeker after Truth. I claim to have found the way to it. I claim to be making a ceaseless effort to find it. But I admit that I have not yet found it. To find Truth completely is to realise oneself and one's destiny, that is, to become perfect. I am painfully conscious of my imperfections, and therein lies all the strength I possess, because it is a rare thing for a man to know his own limitation."[18]

And, so, Gandhi, in search of an absolute truth, concerned himself more intensively with the means whereby the realisation of such truth might be advanced. The 'truth' concept which enters into the technique of *Satyagraha* is clearly not that of the absolute. As he pursued his experiments with *Satyagraha*, the relative character of truth as an operative principle became the stronger. *Satyagraha*, the technique, developed at once as the tool whereby Gandhi dealt with practical social or political problems and the statement of his philosophical beliefs. Commenting on the derivation of the word *Satyagraha*, Gandhi wrote:

> 'The word "*Satya*" (Truth) is derived from "*Sat*", which means being. And nothing is or exists in reality except Truth. That is why "*Sat*" or Truth is perhaps the most important name of God. In fact it is more correct to say that Truth is God, than to say that God is Truth.... it will be realised that "*Sat*" or "*Satya*" is the only correct and fully significant name for God.'[19]

Early in his public comments on the concept of truth, Gandhi had identified God with Truth. In 1925, in a talk with Christian missionaries in Darjeeling, Gandhi had said that for him 'God and Truth are convertible terms'.[20] The following year in an address at Wardha he had declared: '... to me Truth is God and there is no way to find Truth except the way of non-violence.'[21] When he was later (in 1931) asked by a group of conscientious objectors in Switzerland why he regarded God as Truth, Gandhi explained how he had come to believe that the phrase 'God is Love' was inadequate and how he had further concluded that God is Truth. He then added that he had found it necessary to go a step further and to say that Truth is God.

"You will see the fine distinction between the two statements, "God is Truth" and "Truth is God". I came to that conclusion after a continuous and relentless search after truth which began fifty years ago. I then found that the nearest approach to truth was through love."[22]

Gandhi, in search of an absolute truth, concerned himself more intensively with the means whereby the realization of such truth might be advanced. As noted by Bondurant, "the 'truth' concept, which enters into the technique of *Satyagraha*, is clearly not that of the absolute. As he pursued his experiments with *Satyagraha* the relative character of truth as an operative principle became stronger."[23] The correctness of this interpretation would be evident from the extract given below:

Sir Chimanlal: "With regard to your *Satyagraha* doctrine, so far as I understand it, it involves the pursuit of Truth and in that pursuit you invite suffering on yourself and do not cause violence to anybody else.

Mr. Gandhi: Yes, Sir.

Q. However honestly a man may strive in his search for Truth, his notions of Truth may be different from the notions of others. Who then is to determine the truth?

A. The individual himself would determine that.

Q. Different individuals would have different views as to Truth. Would that not lead to confusion?

A. I do not think so.

Q. Honestly striving after Truth is different in every case.

A. That is why the non-violence part was a necessary corollary. Without that there would be confusion and worse."[24]

Every mode of social action directed at the determination of the truth of any matter, then, requires 'necessary corollary' of non-violence. What is the criterion of judging the truth as it functions in *Satyagraha*? "The quest for Truth", said Gandhi, "cannot be prosecuted in a cave. One may live in a cave in certain circumstances, but the common man can be tested only in society."[25]

Gandhi frequently emphasised the partial manifestations of truth like honesty and integrity. These were derived from an implied social epistemology which led him, necessarily, back to the realm of ethics.

NON-VIOLENCE

Explaining the connexion between truth and non-violence, he wrote in a letter to Jamnalal Bajaj:

"As I proceed in my search for trust, it grows upon me that Truth comprehends everything. It is not *ahimsa*, but *ahimsa* is in it. What is perceived by a pure heart and intellect is truth for that moment. Cling to it, and it enables one to reach often enough; it is difficult to decide what is *ahimsa*. For instance, the use of disinfectants is *himsa*, and yet we cannot do without it. We have to live a life of *ahimsa* in a world of *himsa*, and that is possible only if we cling to truth. That is how I deduce *ahimsa* from truth. Out of truth emanate love, tenderness, humility. A votary of truth has to be as humble as the dust. His humility increases with his observance of truth. I see this every moment of my life.... It will make us magnify the mole-hills of our errors into mountains and minimise the mountains of others' errors into mole-hills."

In his famous statement at the Great Trial (1922), Gandhi said: "Nonviolence is the first article of my faith. It is also the last article of my creed."[27]

"Now, what is non-violence?"

Gandhi defined *ahimsa* as "uttermost selflessness. Selflessness means complete freedom from a regard for one's body. If man desired to realize himself, *i.e.* Truth, he could do so only by being completely detached from the body, *i.e.* by making all other beings feel safe from him. That is the way of *ahimsa*." But, "*Ahimsa* does not simply mean non-killing. *Himsa* means causing pain to or killing any life out of anger, or from a selfish purpose, or with the intention of injuring it. Refraining from so doing is *ahimsa*."[28]

For Gandhi's *ahimsa* "is not merely a negative state of harmlessness but it is a positive state of love, of doing good even to the evil-doer. But it does not mean helping the evil doer to continue the wrong or tolerating it by passive acquiescence. On the contrary, love, the active state of *ahimsa* requires you to resist the wrong-doer by dissociating yourself from him even though it may offend him or injure him physically."[29]

And "In its positive form, *ahimsa* means the largest love, greatest charity. If I am a follower of *ahimsa* I must love my enemy. I must apply the same rules to the wrongdoer who is my enemy or a stranger to me, as I would to my wrong-doing father or son. This active *ahimsa* necessarily includes truth and fearlessness. As man cannot deceive the loved one, he does not fear or frighten him or her. Gift of life is the greatest of all gifts; a man who gives it in reality, disarms all hostility. He has paved the way for an honourable understanding. And none who is himself subject to fear can bestow that gift. He must therefore be himself fearless. A man cannot practice ahimsa and be a coward at the same time. The practice of *ahimsa* calls forth the greatest courage."[30]

That the doctrine of *ahimsa* as propounded by Gandhi is active and militant in character should be always borne in mind. In a sense, the relevance of *Satyagraha* as a group technique of action is based on this dynamic and assertive character of nonviolence. That Gandhi's concept of nonviolence was farthest removed from meek submission to evil and quietism will be further evident when we shall attempt to find out the distinction between *Satyagraha* or nonviolent resistance on the one hand and passive resistance and nonresistance, as practiced by the group generally known as pacifists, on the other.

SELF-SUFFERING

'Love never claims, it ever gives. Love ever suffers, never resents, never revenges itself.'

'The test of love is *tapasya* and *tapasya* means self-suffering.'[31]

The classical Yogic law of self-restraint and self-discipline, and the precept of *tapas* which means penance or austerity are familiar elements in the Indian culture.

Self-suffering in the Gandhian ethic has several essential

characteristics which clearly mark it off from the practice of *tapas* or asceticism undertaken for its own sake. Self-suffering in *Satyagraha* is directed, first of all, towards the moral persuasion of one because of whom it is undertaken. It is not a substitute for inability to use violent means to achieve victory over an opponent; it is not, that is, a 'weapon of the weak'. Self-suffering is clearly of a different character from cowardice; nor is it to be exercised indiscriminately. Self-suffering differs from violence in that violence consists of doing injury to another.

"Suffering injury in one's own person is... of the essence of nonviolence and is the chosen substitute for violence to others. It is not because I value life so that I can countenance with joy thousands voluntarily losing their lives for *Satyagraha*, but because I know that it results in the long run in the least loss of life, and, what is more, it ennobles those who lose their lives and morally enriches the world for their sacrifice."[32]

The insistence upon self-suffering has, then, an element of expediency in it. The resort to self-sacrifice and voluntary submission to injury is a positive policy and is not merely a matter of last resort. Gandhi was careful to distinguish his method from that of passive resistance, which either suggests lack of capacity to employ violence or tends to be a preliminary step to violence. In his exposition of *Satyagraha* in South Africa, Gandhi reports the comments of a well-wisher in introducing him to a public audience. The speaker observed that the Indians had 'had recourse to passive resistance which is the weapon of the weak. Gandhi continued to refer to the 'nonviolence of the weak throughout his life whenever he wished to criticize his followers, or when he thought—as he tended to in the last months of his life—that he had failed to instil into others the full meaning of *Satyagraha* as the nonviolence of the strong. *Satyagraha* was at its height when those who practiced it were in a position, as they often were, to use violence effectively but refrained from doing so and invited suffering upon themselves.

'Passive resistance may be offered side by side with the use of arms. *Satyagraha* and brute force, being each a negation of the other, can never go together. In passive resistance there is always present an idea of harassing the other party and there is a simultaneous readiness to undergo any hardships entailed upon us by such activity; while in *Satyagraha* there is not the remotest idea of injuring the opponent. *Satyagraha* postulates the conquest of the adversary by suffering in one's own person.'[33]

Gandhi guarded against attracting to his *Satyagraha* movement those who feared to take up arms or felt themselves incapable of resistance. 'I do believe,' he wrote, 'that where there is only a choice between cowardice and violence, I would advise violence.' Nonviolent conduct, Gandhi insisted, is 'never demoralizing', whereas cowardice 'always is'.[34]

'Non-violence cannot be taught to a person who fears to die and has no power of resistance. A helpless mouse is not non-violent because he is always eaten by pussy. He would gladly eat the murderess if he could, but he ever tries to flee from her. We do not call him a coward because he is made by nature to behave no better than he does. But a man who, when faced by danger, behaves like a mouse, is rightly called a coward. He harbours violence and hatred in his heart and would kill his enemy if he could without being hurt himself. He is a stranger to nonviolence.'[35]

Throughout his teachings on self-suffering Gandhi emphasised the need for discrimination in inviting suffering and sacrifice. Submission was never an element of this concept. Submitting to humiliation should be strictly resisted and, where necessary, the greater self-suffering of the body, even unto death, should be invited. In every case a *Satyagrahi* must refuse to do that which his conscience forbids him to do and must preserve the dignity of the individual though it mean loss of property or even life.

The element of self-suffering in *Satyagraha* is, perhaps, of all three fundamentals, the least acceptable to a Western mind. Yet, such sacrifice may well provide the ultimate means of realising that characteristic so eminent in Western moral philosophy: the dignity of the individual. In proceeding to consider the role of the individual in the Gandhian ethic, one is reminded of the observation of a contemporary Western thinker:

> "There are two entirely different types of sacrifice. It is one of the tragic facts of life that the demands of our physical self and the aims of our mental self can conflict; that actually we may have to sacrifice our physical self in order to assert the integrity of our spiritual self. This sacrifice will never lose its tragic quality. Death is never sweet, not even if it is suffered for the highest ideal. It remains unspeakably bitter, and still it can be the utmost assertion of our individuality."[36]

THE ROLE OF THE INDIVIDUAL

Gandhi's own life is the best practical example of the role which the individual can play in society. In an age when the place of the individual is being challenged and the spectre of total mass-control is raised on every hand, Gandhi has insisted that no power on earth can make a man do a thing against his will. The technique of *Satyagraha* provided the means and suggested the discipline through which resistance could become an active force. The element of self-suffering or sacrifice provided the ultimate alternative. For Gandhi, freedom and preservation of individual integrity were the higher values.

"The bond of the slave is snapped the moment he considers himself to be a free being. He will plainly tell the master: "I was your bond-slave till this moment, but I am a slave no longer. You may kill me if you like, but if you keep me alive, I wish to tell you that if you release me from the bondage, of your own accord, I will ask for nothing more from you. You used to feed and clothe me, though I could have provided food and clothing for myself by my labour".[37]

Gandhi's concern for individual freedom does not seek the elevation of the individual ego. He is not the extreme anarchist position of freedom *per se.*

'If the individual ceases to count, what is left of society? Individual freedom alone can make a man voluntarily surrender himself completely to the service of society. If it is wrested from him, he becomes an automation and society is ruined. No society can possibly be built on a denial of individual freedom.'[38]

Nor is Gandhi's a strictly voluntaristic ethic. The human will may serve as the ultimate protection against an invaded freedom, but the will is not operating alone. However much voluntarism appears to dominate the Gandhian experiment, there are clear indications that Gandhi understood a certain undeniable influence of social institutions on the individual life. '*Goondas* (ruffians),' he wrote, 'do not drop from the sky, nor do they spring from the earth like evil spirits. They are the product of social disorganization, and society is, therefore, responsible for their existence. In other words, they. should be looked upon as a symptom of corruption in our body politic.'[39]

The element which leaves no doubt as to the distance of Gandhi's position from that of the determinist is his insistence upon the power of man's will together with his reason to effect change in his society.

THE RELATIONSHIP OF THE THREE ELEMENTS IN SATYAGRAHA

The truth concept as it functions in the Gandhian technique of *Satyagraha* has been shown to be that of relative truth. The objective standard by which truth can be judged is a human standard expressed in terms of human needs. The proper means for discovering truth in those terms cannot, then, result in human harm or frustrate rather than fulfil human needs—for in such a procedure truth would become travesty. The discovery of truth, or the resolution of conflict arising out of differences of opinion as to what is truth, must be prosecuted through non-violent action. Action based on the refusal to do harm often requires dealing with violence which may be instigated by the opponent in a conflict. Self-suffering is thus further means by which relative truth is tested.

To the three fundamentals of *Satyagraha* may be added certain corollary elements. Truth in *Satyagraha* leads to an ethical humanism. It follows that *ahimsa* (non-violence), which includes the concept of love, leads in turn to social service. Self-suffering not for its own sake, but for demonstration of sincerity, and flowing from refusal to injure the opponent while at the same time holding to the truth—implies sacrifice and preparation for sacrifice, even to death

THE ESSENTIALS OF SATYAGRAHA IN ACTION

If one were to lay out a handbook for the conduct of a mass *Satyagraha* campaign based upon the experience with *Satyagraha* in India, the three first chapters might well deal with (1) fundamental rules governing the campaign, (2) the code of discipline, and (3) the steps through which the campaign is to be pursued. Among the points which should enter into such a guide are those outlined below.

Fundamental Rules

(1) Self-reliance at all times. Outside aid may, in the proper circumstances, be accepted, but should never be counted upon.

(2) Initiative in the hands of the *Satyagrahis*. Through continuous assessment of the conflict situation *Satyagrahis* should, by means of constructive efforts where possible, by positive resistance where indicated, or by the tactics of persuasion and adjustment, press the movement ever forward.

(3) Propagation of the objectives, strategy and tactics of the

campaign. Propaganda must be made an integral part of the movement. Education of the opponent, the public, and participants must continue apace.

(4) Reduction of demands to a minimum consistent with truth. Continuing reassessment of the situation and the objectives with a view to possible adjustment of demands is essential.

(5) Progressive advancement of the movement through steps and stages determined to be appropriate within the given situation. Decision as to when to proceed to a further phase of the *Satyagraha* must be carefully weighed in the light of the ever-changing circumstance, but a static condition must be avoided. However, direct action is to be launched only after all other efforts to achieve an honourable settlement have been exhausted.

(6) Examination of weaknesses within the *Satyagraha* group. The morale and discipline of the *Satyagrahis* must be maintained through active awareness (by members and leaders alike) of any development of impatience, discouragement, or breakdown of non-violent attitude.

(7) Persistent search for avenues of cooperation with the adversary on honourable terms. Every effort should be made to win over the opponent by helping him (where this is consistent with the *Satyagrahi's* true objectives) thereby demonstrating sincerity to achieve an agreement with, rather than a triumph over, the adversary.

(8) Refusal to surrender essentials in negotiation. *Satyagraha* excludes all compromise which affects basic principles or essential portions of valid objectives. Care must be exercised not to engage in bargaining or barter.

(9) Insistence upon full agreement on fundamentals before accepting a settlement.[40]

CODE OF DISCIPLINE

The following points were laid down by Gandhi as a code for volunteers in the 1930 movement:

(1) Harbour no anger but suffer the anger of the opponent. Refuse to return the assaults of the opponent.

(2) Do not submit to any order given in anger, even though severe punishment is threatened for disobeying.
(3) Refrain from insults and swearing.
(4) Protect opponents from insult or attack, even at the risk of life.
(5) Do not resist arrest nor the attachment of property, unless holding property as a trustee.
(6) Refuse to surrender any property held in trust at the risk of life.
(7) If taken prisoner, behave in an exemplary manner.
(8) As a member of a *Satyagraha* unit, obey the orders of *Satyagraha* leaders, and resign from the unit in the event of serious disagreement.
(9) Do not expect guarantees for maintenance of dependents.

STEPS IN A SATYAGRAHA CAMPAIGN

The outline below is applicable to a movement growing out of grievances against an established political order. These steps could be adapted to other conflict situations. Dr. K.C. Shridharni in his *magnum opus* 'War without Violence' has discussed the techniques of *Satyagraha* in the following way[42]:

Negotiations and Arbitration

No avenue leading towards the peaceful settlement of a given conflict should be left unexplored before embarking upon a programme of *Satyagraha*, that is, non-violent direct action. Direct action, in order to be non-violent, should at the very start create an atmosphere of understanding. The preliminary action, therefore, should be limited to such activities as would not precipitate a crisis. Consequently the exercise of constitutional rights takes precedence in a programme of *Satyagraha*. *Satyagraha* is preferable to riots, street fights and violent revolutions, but not to parliamentary procedures or democratic processes where they obtain in the service of economic, social or political change. "Those only can take up Civil Disobedience," Gandhi has said "who believe in willing obedience even to irksome laws imposed by the state so long as they do not hurt their conscience or religion, and are prepared equally willingly to suffer the penalty of Civil Disobedience."[43]

The search for a peaceful solution as the indispensable first step in the strategy of *Satyagraha* has a two-fold significance. In the first place, it emphasizes the fact that, though unfortunately disrupted for the time being, the disputants have a fundamental unity. In other words, all men are brothers beneath their temporary differences and conflicts. No man, group or class is, beyond repair requiring the extreme Marxian prescription of liquidation. Hearts can be mended, groups converted, and nations revolutionized non-violently. It also emphasises that the unemotional attitude of give-and-take is the ideal condition for arriving at a settlement. In case this ideal condition is not obtainable at the critical moment, the *Satyagrahis* hope to create it as a result of their nonviolent direct action.

The prerequisite of an honest quest for a peaceful settlement before engaging in any of the *Satyagraha* activities clarifies, in the second place, the spirit of the programme. It brings forth in bold relief the reluctance the *Satyagrahi*s show towards starting direct action. The opponent is given to understand that the *Satyagrahis* look upon direct action only as the final weapon, as the last resort. They would not use it unless there was no other course open to them. Their attitude seems to say: we welcome a peaceful settlement now, and we will welcome it at any stage of the movement. This position gives them an aura of morality in the eyes of the opponent. It also makes it clear that they are not just "irresponsible law-breakers" but persons fighting for what to them seem to be the truth. Making the right first impression is half the battle won in *Satyagraha* which aims at "the winning over of the opponent by suffering, *i.e.* love."[44]

This first stage of *Satyagraha* includes various items. Over and above utilizing such legislative channels as are open to them, the *Satyagrahis* may enter into direct negotiations with the responsible party on the opposite side. Sending a deputation composed of influential and notable citizens to the proper authorities is another manoeuvre. Failing in either action, the *Satyagrahis* may seek arbitration by a third party acceptable to both the disputants. When even arbitration fails to satisfy the demands of the *Satyagrahi*s, the time is ripe for them to take the second step in the programme of non-violent direct action.

Agitation

Unable to get redress from the powers that be, the *Satyagrahis* launch their activities in the Opposite direction. They go to the people. They start, as the second step in the programme of violent direct action, a campaign of agitation among the people more directly affected by the dispute. Generating "cause-consciousness" becomes the supreme aim of *Satyagraha* leaders at this stage of the movement.

Issuing pamphlets which give a clear picture of all the implications of the "Cause", circulating books and papers on the same theme, are some of the numerous activities of the agitators. Catchy songs and slogans upholding the "Cause," personal contacts, speeches, group meetings, debates and discussions form a vital part of the propaganda activity. The use of modern means of communication such as the press, radio, television and the cinema is included as an integral part of the machine of mass propaganda.

For one thing, the agitation keeps the issue alive. The opponent can no longer consider it a thing of the past and assume an attitude of complacency. In case there is even an infinitesimal conflict in anti-*Satyagraha* ranks with regard to what stand their group or interest should take, that conflict is now increasingly aggravated by the constant activity of the *Satyagrahis*. And at this stage of non-violent direct action, as well as at many other stages, the *Satyagrahic* assignment is to disrupt the balance of personal and group loyalties in the opposition camp by psychological suggestions, by dramatizing moral factors.

Gandhi and other pioneer leaders of the National Congress party have had to utilize all these instruments in order to create on one hand what we call for want of a better name, "cause-consciousness" and a contagious spreading of the ideology of Swaraj (self-government), and turning from that, to expose the moral defaces of the ruling group. In addition to these techniques, Gandhi had time and again undertaken all-India tours from Bombay to Burma and from Kashmir to Cape Comorin. He had taken special pains to cover as many out-of-the-way villages as possible in order to enthuse the illiterate and unorganized peasantry. The all-India Congress party, under the inspiration of Gandhi, had posted a "village-worker" in practically every town and most of the villages of India. Until 1931 Gandhi was the editor-publisher of two now defunct weeklies: *Young India* in English, and *Navajivan* in Gujarati. Latterly he edited *Harijan* (a 'Man of God,' Gandhi's name for the untouchable). His policy was to make his publication, as inexpensive as possible so that even the poor could afford them.

In democratic countries, this stage of non-violent direct action is not likely to meet with serious obstacles. The agitators, nevertheless, have to be prepared to reckon with indirect pressure. For no government, however democratic, is likely to view with passive resignation a propaganda aimed against itself. In totalitarian countries and in colonies such as India once was, the battle has to begin at this early stage.

The *Satyagrahis* hope even at this stage that their agitation among the people concerned, and the widespread interest in the issue among sympathetic neutrals—the floating vote—may influence the decision of the opponent. But when they find no confirmation of their hope, they go ahead with their third step in the programme of non-violent direct action.

Demonstrations and the Ultimatum

'Cause-consciousness' now seeks expression. A vague sense of solidarity, the result of vigorous agitation, now tends to become organized. Public meetings grow larger and larger, and there is a buzz of discussion in the bazar and in the market place. Schools and colleges, though under the control of the government, become undercover centres of *Satyagrahic* thinking and planning. The more pervasive the cause, the more extensively felt is its consciousness.

When the *Satyagrahis* try to organize these loose ends of solidarity, when they try to divert them into manifest channels, the movement enters its third stage. Various kinds of demonstrations are next on the programme. There is a procession of one hundred people one day, of ten thousand the next. Public meetings clear the way for mass meetings, and they take place more frequently.

Resolutions are passed codifying the determination of the people to the finish. And then *Hartals* (complete cessation of all activities as a sign of mourning) are called.

Satyagraha at this point is colourful, and "colour" leads to good publicity. Publicity draws in more people. Party songs and party slogans are directed towards individuals who have not as yet been swayed. Uniforms are paraded and the youth of the community finds a new outlet for its energies. In India, this period of non-violent direct action was disproportionately long, mainly for two reasons. In the first place, the great distances of India coupled with an inadequate system of communications and transportation, were something of a drawback when it came to the element of "social-contagion" so necessary to a successful mass movement. Illiteracy distanted the distances even more. In the second place, the populace of India had not exerted itself in the mass direct action for the past hundred years—the last of such endeavours being the so-called Sepoy Mutiny. It was not surprising, therefore, that they lingered a little over the preliminaries and apparently enjoyed each moment.

In due time, however, the whole of India became a veritable ocean of snowy, handmade cloth — the simple and inexpensive uniform of the Gandhi movement. Congress party nuclei began to grow in village after village like mushrooms. There were more parades, and these in every corner of India. Resolutions embodying the determination of the people were hammered on plaster walls, and Gandhi's name was on every tongue. Even popular music was replaced by the songs of Gandhi and of Mother India.

Satyagraha is the precipitous step of issuing an ultimatum. In this document, drawn up by the leader with the consent of the party dignitaries, the needs of the people are listed without any exaggeration. A specific time limit is set for the government to grant these minimum demands. If the government does not change its position after the ultimatum, the people, confident that they can make government impossible, embark upon direct action. Thus the ultimatum amounts to a "conditional declaration of war," in this case a war without violence, at least on one side.[45]

Gandhi during his life had delivered two such historic ultimatums to the British Government. The first was delivered to Lord Reading, then Viceroy of India, in 1922, before starting the Non-cooperation Movement. The second was conveyed to Lord Irwin in 1930 as a prelude to the Civil Disobedience Movement. True to the spirit of nonviolence, Gandhi approached the authorities, according to his own words, on 'bended knees' and implored them to 'find a way out' before he had to resort to civil disobedience. In connection with the second instance Gandhi added a characteristic personal, human touch. He selected an English and Christian disciple of his to deliver his ultimatum to the 'English and Christian Viceroy'.

The people 'lay their cards on the table' at this point in *Satyagrahic* development and they fully expect their new move to have a sobering effect on the opponent. They aim to force issue and to remind the government that the threatened direct action will be a grave matter.

If this decisive phase of *Satyagraha* also fails to bring about a just settlement, the populace is then called upon to plunge into the more militant programme of direct action.

Self-purification

The mobilized energy of the people as a direct result of dynamic crusade for the 'Cause' is now ready to be moulded into action. The failure of all constitutional and lawful attempts has left revolutionary activity as the only alternative. Moral persuasion having proved ineffective, the *Satyagrahis* do not hesitate to shift their technique to compulsive force.

The illegality, the extra-constitutionality, of the use of force is obvious. At this point in the relentless advance towards direct action, democratic regimes adopt measures similar to those of autocracies and totalitarianisms in stamping out the growing danger. From here on, direct action is regarded as revolutionary. Nonviolent direct action, however, claims to be distinguished from revolutionary direct action. Although illegal, non-violent action is lent a certain overtone of justification and legitimacy by the introduction at this juncture of self-purification, the fourth phase of the *Satyagrahic* prospectus.

By taking upon themselves a part of the responsibility for 'the wrong' they are fighting against, the *Satyagrahi*s undertake a different line of attack from that of the revolutionists. In their eyes, the wronged are also to be blamed, however partly, along with the wrong-doers for allowing a conflict-situation to develop. Contending that—the wrong might not have materialized but for their own initial and progressive submission—the *Satyagrahis* begin to change their own behaviour and thought patterns. "The primary object," Gandhi has written, "is self-purification. Its direct result must be paralysis of a government which lives on our vices and wickednesses."[46] For the tyrant has the power to inflict that which we lack, strength to resist. Submission is but a smaller crime than perpetration.

Fasting and public prayers have been the two most universal self-purification phases of *Satyagraha* in India. Lest some people think that fasting and public prayers might not work as morale builders in the West as they do in India, let me quote Thomas Jefferson who commented on June 1st, 1774, the day on which the port of Boston was to be closed by the British: "We were under the conviction of the necessity of arousing our people from the lethargy into which they had fallen as to passing events; and thought that the appointment of a day of general fasting and prayer would be most likely to call up and alarm their attention... we cooked up a resolution... for appointing... a day of fasting, humiliation and prayer, to implore heaven to avert from us the evils of civil war, to inspire us with firmness in support of our rights, and to turn the hearts of the King and Parliament to moderation and justice. The people met generally, with anxiety and alarm in their countenance, and the effect of the day through the whole colony was like a shock of electricity, arousing every man and placing him erect and solid on his centre."[47]

In addition, the taking of vows of self-denial by individuals and by groups has been an important aspect of the Indian movement. Many denied themselves intoxicating drinks and drugs, and thereby bored a hole in the government income. Others gave up luxurious articles imported from foreign ports. Quite a few resigned from lucrative government posts to come down to the level of India's peasant and proletarian. It was significant that most of the ranking leaders of the National Congress party, including Gandhi, were formerly rich businessmen or legal practitioners. Moreover Gandhi's periodic fasts and his pledge "never to return home until India is free" became among the notable examples of the effective use of the instrument of self-purification." Other countries are likely to evolve different forms of self-purification, when and if they engage in a *Satyagraha*. For the forms of self-purification are conditioned by the nature of the wrong as well as by the folkways and mores of the community. Central idea of self-denial may seek different expressions in different cultures.

Self-purification is advanced by its adherents as an instruments for convincing the opponent that the *Satyagrahis* intend to struggle to the finish, and that they are ready to make any sacrifice in order to achieve their ends. It is also expected to assure the opponent that the *Satyagrahis* harbour no motive of revenge but are, on the contrary, prepared to suffer willingly. Furthermore, voluntary suffering and self-denial attract the attention of the people at large. Wavering members of the Indian community could seldom withstand the urge to join the movement made so appealing by its opportunity for sacrifice and martyrdom. The urge to be a hero is provoked in the participants.

The *Satyagrahis*, by emphasizing the spirit of self-sacrifice and suffering, endeavour to raise the level of the issue. It ceases to be a matter of wrangling. The issue revolves around the bringing about of a just settlement of the dispute. Thus the level of the fight is raised. The opponent is forced to operate at higher, less ruthless level.

Some even see in this an attempt to embarrass the opponent. But embarrassment is better than annihilation. The failure of this instrument of nonviolent direct action clears the way for sanctions.

Strikes and General Strike

From this point on, it is hard to present a progressive step-by-step development of *Satyagraha*. Many of the phases of *Satyagraha* that are to follow are not the direct outgrowth of one from the other, but are, on the contrary, distinct instruments to be utilised either simultaneously or separately.

The strike as such is labour's instrument for the acquisition of a desired standard of treatment and living from the employer. Its place therefore, in a political movement directed towards either amending or ending the government is not so obvious. But a closer scrutiny of our complex economic life will uncover a few places where modern forms of government are extremely vulnerable weapon of the strike. Attacking these vantage points through the instrument of strike, consequently, becomes *Satyagraha* strategy.

For one thing, there is hardly any distinction between big industry and the government in modern capitalistic societies. Big or extreme form of vested interest, generally aligns itself with the government in the time of a political crisis. Weakening the vested interests, therefore, amounts to weakening the political system under which they flourish.

Secondly, modern governments engage themselves in various activities relating to finance, industries and public utilities. These occupations and interests of the government provide the *Satyagrahis* with an opportunity to utilize the instrument of strike.

Picketing

Picketing is the natural consequence of a strike. It advertises the strike and it adds to its effectiveness. It is an appeal to the general public to withdraw its patronage from the shops and concerns picketed. In the programme of the Indian *Satyagraha*, however, a strike is not the only signal for picketing. The latter has been evident many times in

India independent of any strike. In most cases, picketing as a phase of *Satyagraha* has followed the boycott.

In 1921, for example, the law courts were picketed by the Non-cooperators and litigants were urged to go to Panchayats. Government schools and, colleges were also picketed, and the students were urged to go to nationalist institutions. Shopkeepers who carried British-manufactured goods came to dread the word "picket". Most of the government houses were assiduously picketed by women whose particular ambition was to embarrass the government officials for failing to sacrifice their lucrative Jobs in the cause of India's freedom. The 1930 movement repeated the entire performance with the addition of picketing in front of opium and liquor stores. Women clad in saffron *saris* (the Indian colour of sacrifice and self-immolation) proved to be the most effective pickets. At every rally, stress was laid on the winning of new converts by oratory and arguments which should be gently presented. The 1942 movement included the picketing of administrative offices, police stations and public transport.

The government retaliated with jailing and general harassing of the picketers. Some could even show teeth marks made by the police. The oppression, instead of crushing the movement acted against those who used it. Many policemen became disgusted with their duty of beating harmless people who never failed to do an act of kindness whenever it was possible. The public at large became enraged at the government action. As a result, picketing became more successful.

Dharna

Dharna, the father of all sit-down strikes is an ancient institution of India. Ever so often in the Middle Ages a money-lender, failing to receive his money back in due time, would sit in front of the house of the debtor, refusing to budge from place or to take any food until the client paid in full. Since the interesting situation always gathered a crowd of idle curious, the debtor would make a supreme effort to pay rather than suffer long-drawn-out siege with its attendant embarrassment. The Bhat (bard of the royal court) used a similar method when wanted his king to "be a man" and fight. When his ruler, out of sheer cowardice or other considerations, refused to meet an invading or offending king in combat, the Bhat would sit in the palace gate and start a hunger strike. In most cases, this compelled the king to fight.

In modern times, there have been sit-down strikes in the textile mills of the Punjab and in the jute mills of Bengal. In France, England, and especially in the United States, the weapon has proved highly effective. The success of the sit-down is due to the fact that no industry which sells its products (directly to the public) can afford to alienate public opinion. The general public is always opposed to violence and bloodshed in suppressing strikes, and unless these methods are utilised, it is almost impossible to break a sit-down strike. *Dharna*, therefore, is the most dramatic way of influencing public opinion both when the effort is successful and when it is crushed.

Sitting *Dharna* has assumed peculiar forms in India's *Satyagraha* operations. In 1922, the non-cooperation its sat down at the gates of Calcutta University and blocked the passage of their fellow students. The *Satyagrahis* implored the conformist students not to hesitate to step on their bodies if the latter felt justified in entering that way. They also assured the non-striking students that they would not raise a finger in retaliation and that they were prepared to bear the physical pain with smiling faces. Similar tactics were employed against those Indian government servants who continued to serve on administrative posts in defiance of the call for non-co-operation. There have been instances of people stretching themselves flat on the ground and inviting the official to tread on their bodies in order to go to his work. In quite a few cases, women are reported to have resorted to *Dharna* against their own 'loyal' husbands.[48]

In spite of the numerous successes of the instrument of *Dharna*, Gandhi has declared himself against the "barbaric" practice. Time and again he has exhorted his followers to "refrain from sitting *Dharna*."[49] The technique of sitting *Dharna*, however, has proved to be a powerful way of moulding public opinion. During the Quit India movement, there were cases of people lying down in front of trains carrying troops. There have been instances of *Dharna* against dock-workers unloading ammunition from ships. The extreme form of both strike and picketing, *Dharna* has goaded people still undecided to participate in direct action. It has often precipitated upheavals in the usual loyalties of the populace at large. Recourse to *Dharna* from time to time seems to signify that the movement in this respect has gone beyond the men who originated it.

Economic Boycott

Boycott, as an organised programme of withdrawing, and of including others to withdraw, from business relations with the opponent, is very effective weapon. The practice is old, but the name is relatively recent. Captain Boycott was one of the most hated of the landlords' agents during the agitation against the landlords by the Irish Land League. The name of a man stuck to a technique of social and economic pressure in 1880. The boycotts that have taken place in India in the past years have been of the international variety by which one nation refuses to buy the commodities of another. As such, there have been an effort on India's part to restrict the market of the opposing nation by putting into motion the consumer's power. By restricting or destroying the Indian market of Great Britain primarily a mercantile country, the *Satyagrahis* sought to destroy England's zeal for holding India.

A steady boycott of British goods had existed in India ever since the attempted "Partition of Bengal" some generations ago. This boycott Movement has been supplemented and greatly enhanced by Swadeshi, a programme of patronizing indigenous industries and of reviving cottage crafts. Gandhi's Spinning Wheel Plan has been both the symbol and the backbone of *Swadeshi*.[50]

Non-payment of Taxes

The call for non-payment of taxes ushers in nonviolent direct action in its purely illegal, unlawful and seditious stage. By refusing to fill the coffers of the state, the *Satyagrahis* attempt to cut the very life-line of the government. America's "no taxation without representation" campaign during the Revolutionary War falls within this category. Various have been the uses of the weapon in India. Sometimes it has been resorted to on a small regional basis, on the other occasions as a large provincial measure, and then again it has been wielded by the entire nation. In comparatively few cases, the city people have used it by refusing to pay their income and other taxes. In the majority of cases, however, non-payment of taxes has been resorted to by Indian farmers, mostly village-dwellers, who have refused to pay land revenue. In the last-mentioned form, "no-tax" campaigns had occurred, all over India quite frequently until 1947, the freedom year.

When a "no-tax" is attempted, the reactions of the state can easily be imagined. It strikes back at the *Satyagrahis* with arrest, confiscation of land plots and leases, confiscation of property, bank accounts and of cattle; beatings; terrorizing, and finally, by the command to shoot at sight whenever there is "mutiny."

To these forms of oppression, a *Satyagrahi* is pledged to turn a smiling face. He is honour-bound to receive these penalties willingly and without rancour; he is to suffer in silence. The suffering of the *Satyagrahi* enthuses other members of the community to follow his example. Officials start to resign when the general public begins to show sympathetic leanings towards the victims. Finally, it becomes difficult, if not impossible, for the opponent to muster up enough men to continue "the reign of terror." He is then compelled to import "scabs," hirelings from outside, a process which further alienates the general public. The newcomers in turn become disgusted with their job of torturing people who do not mean any harm to them but who, on the contrary, often reciprocate with a gracious act right on top of the worst kind of treatment. In the end, nonresistance breaks the momentum of the opposition. There is no immediate incentive for oppressive action; so it comes to a standstill.

It may well be argued here that the efficacy of non-violence on individuals cannot prove its influence on groups. A group as such never comes within the loving embrace of the non-violent resister or resisters. It has no personality and, therefore, it is not subject to experience. However, there is no getting around the fact that though the group has no personality, it always has personnel. Without the individuals, there would be no group, and individuals, from necessity, come in direct contact with *Satyagrahis*. Thus a group of a system, through its personnel, becomes subject to *Satyagrahic* influence. Conversion of individual members shatters the solidarity of the group. As evidence, it might be mentioned that the non-violent spirit of Gandhi's movement had won many friends from British ranks, both at home and in India, and consequently the die-hards and the vested interests could not present an entirely confident and solid front. In a way, the final renunciation of power by the British in 1947 can be described as the cumulative effect of conversions of a progressively greater number of Englishmen to the Indian point of view.

There is still another avenue through which *Satyagraha* works. The spirit of non-violence never fails to gain the sympathy of the general public which, most of the time, is opposed to violence and bloodshed. It becomes in this way a powerful instrument for influencing world opinion, a factor in public affairs which cannot be ignored since the growth of rapid transportation and communication.

Hizrat

A spontaneous though peculiar offshoot of India's numerous no-tax campaigns has been the practice of *Hizrat*. The word *Hizrat* is of Arabic origin, and it was used in its original form of *Hejira*, in connection with Mohammed's flight from Mecca to Medina. Instead of submitting to the tyranny of Mecca, the Prophet preferred emigration as Lord Krishna migrated from Mathura to Dwarka. Still further back in history, the instrument of emigrating from the oppressive region was utilized by the plebs in order to secure reforms from the ruling Patricians of the Roman Republic. Mass emigration as a protest against oppression has been resorted to frequently in modern Europe. The very foundation of the American Colonies was the result of the Puritan Fathers' mass emigration from England.

The farmers of the districts of Bardoli and Kheda in the Bombay Presidency perfected the technique of mass emigration during their no-tax campaigns of 1919, 1929, and 1930. When the government's oppression became unbearable, they emigrated en masse to adjoining territories of the State of Baroda, a native state over which the British government had no direct jurisdiction.

The employment of *Hizrat* is conditioned by the composition of the region where a *Satyagraha* takes place and of its surroundings. It is less practical in areas which are at a great distance from territories with a different sovereignty. But wherever and whenever possible, *Hizrat* is not merely an escape from hardships, but it is also an effective way of neutralizing the power of the opponent. For it becomes impossible to govern when there is none to be governed. In most cases, consequently, the populace is called back on its own terms.

Non-cooperation

"Even the most despotic government," Gandhi has said, "cannot stand except for the consent of the governed which consent is often forcibly procured by the despot. Immediately the subject ceases to fear the despotic force, his power is gone." Any political power, likewise, is paralyzed as soon as its source of supply, viz., the support of the community, is cut off. In the final analysis, cooperation of the people at large is the only reality for political authority.[51] The French philosopher, Rousseau, recognised this fact when he laid down his concept of the "general will" as the indispensable condition for the existence of the state.

It then follows that the withdrawal of public support must mean an end of a political system. The community, as distinguished from the state, can render the latter powerless by not cooperating with it. Thus the tenth stratagem of *Satyagraha*, viz., non-cooperation, constitutes a potent weapon in the hands of the people in order to end an oppressive rule.

The weapon of non-cooperation had been wielded continuously by a small-but powerful minority ever since the advent on India's political awakening. It attained threatening proportions, however, only when the public at large participated in the movement. The instances of the 1919-20, 1930-32 and 1942-45 movements are the most notable in this respect.

The programme covering the first period included:

(1) Surrender of all titles of honour and the voluntarily giving up all honorary offices. This action would, on one hand, shatter the prestige of the opponent government and, on the other, make the business of administration a difficult affair.
(2) Non-participation in government loans. This item of non-cooperation was aimed at unbalancing the monetary status of the government.
(3) Boycotting of law courts by Congress and by litigants. It would amount to the suspension of legal practice by lawyers and the settlement of civil disputes by private arbitration. It is conceived as a weapon for further lowering the prestige of government as well as a starting point for a new authority.
(4) Boycott of government schools and colleges. This step would provide the movement with a crop of youthful recruits and at the same time check the influence of academicians who are paid to instil loyalty in their charges.
(5) Boycott of the legislative councils. Outstanding and able

politicians would, as a consequence, come out to work among the people instead of wasting their time in impotent debates. By withdrawing from the legislatures, the leaders are likely to rob the government of such status as is bestowed by their participation.

(6) Withdrawal from government service. The refusal on the part of individuals of talent to accept or continue in any civil post would bring the entire administration to a standstill. From the tiniest village up to the capital city, there would be left only a few, if any, governmental officials to enforce the will of the state and to collect its revenues.

(7) Withdrawal of men from the army and the police. The state, without the indispensable assistance of coercion, would be virtually emasculated. Anti-militarism would further threaten the existence of the state a *coup d'etat* be attempted.

The non-cooperation programme for the period 1930-32 contained all these items together with that of withdrawing cooperation from British banks, shipping, insurance and other concerns. The "Quit India" movement of 1942 onwards embraced all these aspects within the fold of a general strike. Many more items can very well he added in response to new needs and different situations. Countries other than India, in case of a *Satyagraha*, might follow quite another series of stratagems of non-cooperation to meet their special conditions. The success of non-cooperation will always correspond to the degree of universality of its acceptance. When fully successful, "non-violent non-cooperation," to use Gandhi's words, "is the method whereby we cultivate the public opinion and get it enforced."[52]

When the established order is paralysed as a consequence of non-cooperation by the people, the *Satyagrahis* are ready to deal the final blow in their programme of non-violent direct action.

Ostracism

Ostracism, or social boycott, is a weapon of the community against its members who refuse to join in the general programme of non-cooperation with the opponent. Thus he who refuses to cooperate is non-cooperated in turn. It is generally justified on the ground that by siding with the community's opponent, he has forfeited all the privileges that are the result of community life. The technique, in a somewhat different form, has been used in the Western world by strikers against the "scabs." In the latter use, the weapon has been used generally as a form of intimidation. In India, this technique has its roots in antiquity. In fact, the birth of the institution of untouchability is ascribed by some scholars to the Hindu practice of social boycott or ex-communication of the offender. The ancient Athenians had also evolved the political institution of ostracism in order to rid the community temporarily of persons who were supposed to endanger its welfare by their very influence and prestige.

Ostracism as such is a spontaneous by-product of the general attitude of non-cooperation. The *Satyagrahic* use of it does not tend to penalize the dissenter but it reminds him of his unsocial attitude. Consequently, no physical harm is done to him or his relatives. *Satyagrahis* even see to it that the primary needs of the person ostracized—food, shelter, and clothing—are not interfered with. Otherwise, he is a political pariah beyond the pale of social intercourse. He has, however, a standing invitation to recant. Gandhi personally did not look upon this practice with favour. He had declared himself against its use. The move, however justified, has something crude about it and it goes against the democratic grain.

Civil Disobedience

A government paralyzed by organized non-co-operation awaits its destruction through the *Satyagrahic* manoeuvre of civil disobedience. What remains of a state after a successful onslaught of non-cooperation, is nothing more than a formal structure. It is up to civil disobedience to shatter that structure as a prelude to a new order. The phrase "civil disobedience" was coined by the American moralist, Henry Thoreau. According to the author of Walden, civil disobedience to unjust laws is the duty of all citizens. In Gandhi's hands, however, the technique outgrew its original import. It became a revolutionary weapon for destroying an undesirable political order.

By refusing to obey the statutes of the state, the *Satyagrahis* deny the existence of the established order. One by one, or simultaneously, the important laws and decrees of the state are broken, so that eventually the entire "rule" is uprooted. It is important, Gandhi insisted time and again, that only unpopular and obnoxious laws be broken at the beginning of a *Satyagraha*. This restriction ensures the eventual conversion of government employees who are at heart in agreement with the *Satyagrahis* as to the injustice of the laws in question. Only the breaking of unjust statutes attracts the sympathy of the general public and favourable world opinion.

Conforming to Gandhi's idea, only the Salt Law, the Forest Law, and the Revenue Law were included in the 1930 civil disobedience programme. These laws, moreover, touched and consequently affected the great majority of the people, so the active support of the populace was insured. A considerable part of the officialdom, both in India and in Great Britain, also thought the laws outrageous. James Ramsay MacDonald, to take only one example, had denounced the Salt Act in his books and public utterances before he came to power as the first Labour Prime Minister. It was the habit of Gandhi and other lesser leaders to quote MacDonald, who was then Prime Minister of Great Britain, in support of their opposition to the obnoxious law. Needless to say, the British Premier was not the only person who lent himself to the embarrassment that attends self-contradiction. This dulled the edge of the government's retaliation. In the later months of the movement, even the Press Act and the statutes governing prescribed literature was disobeyed. And then followed an attack on as many laws as possible.

After paralyzing the administration through non-cooperation and neutralizing the coercive agencies of the state through civil disobedience, the *Satyagrahis* embark on a programme of taking over the functions of the government one by one.

Assertive Satyagraha

When the *Satyagrahis* begin to gradually take over the functions of the paralyzed government, the twelfth stage of the strategy of nonviolent direct action is reached. During the operation of this measure, the *Satyagrahis* begin to discharge, partially at least, certain of the activities and functions of the state made stagnant by their own previous action.

During the 1930 movement which came nearest to this stage, volunteer corps were organised in certain cities to officiate as traffic-conductors and as policemen. The Bombay Congress committee in particular even worked out its own system of taxation over cooperating citizens. They also, in a few instances, punished those financial interests which attempted to go against the Congress commands. In a number of villages, the authority of the old *Panchayats* was restored. The programme of "national education" was executed with a remarkable degree of success by establishing schools in many communities. Quite a few forfeited Congress Houses were reoccupied by *Satyagrahis*. Unorganised attempts were made to capture Government Houses. The famous Vadala, and Dharasana incidents were precipitated by mass actions aimed at capturing government salt depots.

At this stage, however, a truce was made between the Congress and the British Government in the form of the Gandhi-Irvin Pact. Consequently, the validity of this manoeuvre has not been fully tested in India, although the stratagem had a greater play during the Quit India struggle.

Parallel Government

Parallel government is the full materialization of the programme of its immediate previous stage, viz., assertive *Satyagraha*. Herein the *Satyagrahis* establish a new sovereignty by replacing the established order. Parallel government is the community's act of taking over all the functions of the tottering government thus squeezing the established order out of existence.

None of the Indian *Satyagrahas* ever reached this stage. Consequently the ideology of parallel government has until now remained in its conceptual entity. It is implied in the programme of nonviolent direct action, but as yet it has never been tried. It goes without saying, however, that parallel government is the culmination of a *Satyagraha* carried through to its local conclusion.

A POSSIBLE EXTENSION OF THE PATTERN

The foregoing pattern of *Satyagraha* (Fig. 2.1) has from the very start presupposed a common area of action and interest for both the opponents; it has been the delineation of the direct action employed by a community in revolt against an already existing foreign rule. The factor of geography is thus operative here. What is more, in such a conflict confined to a country there is bound to be an area of common

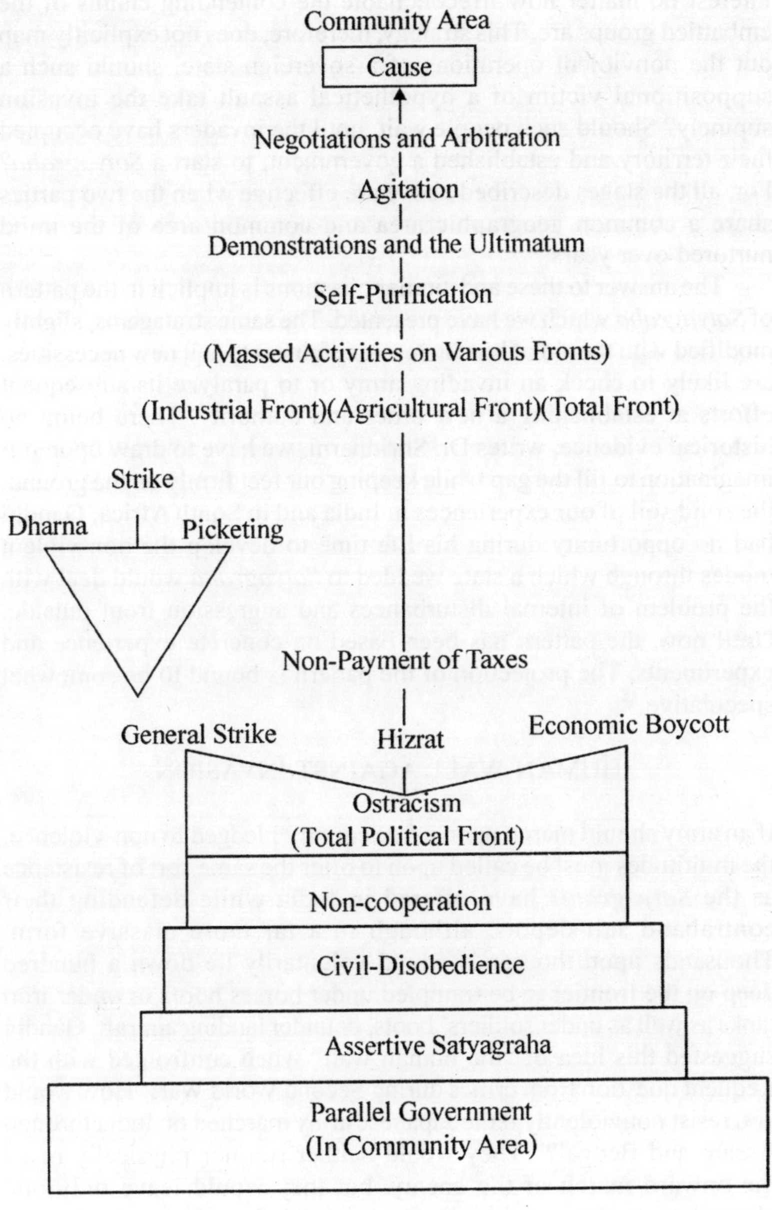

Fig. 2.1: Diagram of the Pattern of a Successful Satyagraha

interest no matter how irreconcilable the contending claims of the embattled groups are. This strategy, therefore, does not explicitly map out the nonviolent operations of a sovereign state, should such a suppositional victim of a hypothetical assault take the invasion supinely? Should such people wait, until the invaders have occupied their territory and established a government, to start a *Satyagraha*? For, all the stages described above are effective when the two parties share a common geographic area and common area of the mind nurtured over years.

The answer to these and similar questions is implicit in the pattern of *Satyagraha* which we have presented. The same stratagems, slightly modified with the aid of human resourcefulness to suit new necessities, are likely to check an invading army or to paralyze its subsequent efforts at establishing a new order and authority. There being no historical evidence, writes Dr. Shridharni, we have to draw upon our imagination to fill the gap while keeping our feet firmly on the ground, the solid soil of our experiences in India and in South Africa. Gandhi had no opportunity during his life time to develop the non-violent modes through which a state wedded to *Satyagraha* would deal with the problem of internal disturbances and aggression from outside. Until now, the pattern has been based on concrete experience and experiments. The projection of the pattern is bound to be somewhat speculative.[53]

HUMAN WALL AGAINST INVASION

If an army should march upon a free country pledged to non-violence, the multitudes must be called upon to offer the same sort of resistance as the *Satyagrahis* have offered in India while defending their contraband salt depots, although in a far more massive form. Thousands upon thousands would voluntarily lie down a hundred deep on the frontier to be trampled under horses hoofs or under iron tanks as well as under soldiers' boots, or under landing aircraft. Gandhi suggested this idea of "the human wall" when confronted with the frequent question from critics during Second World War: "How would you resist nonviolently if the Japanese army marched on India through Assam and Bengal?" They would neither run nor physically resist the onward march of the enemy, but they would leave only one alternative to the invaders: you can march in only over our dead bodies! The nonviolent soldiers would oppose the invasion with mass

Satyagraha to the point of mass death, if necessary, which would make the invasion a dreadful experience for all concerned. If the enemy's armed forces ride far above in airplanes to avoid an engagement with nonviolent resisters, the *Satyagrahis* would employ the same measures at airports when eventually they alight. For the invaders have to alight at some place, some time, to occupy the territory and to rule the people.[54]

Writing in his *Harijan* of June 22, 1940, a war year during which he received repeated inquiries as to the *Satyagrahic* form of stopping an invading army, he tackled the problem from another angle, the angle of a neutral country (because his questioner was a Swiss) through which an invader wants to pass. "It would be cowardly of a neutral country," he wrote, "to allow an army to devastate a neighbouring country. But there are two ways in common between soldiers of war and soldiers of nonviolence, and if I had been a citizen of Switzerland and a President of the Federal State what I would have done would be to refuse passage to the invading army by refusing all supplies. Secondly, by re-enacting Thermopylae in Switzerland, you would have presented a living wall of men and women and inviting the invaders to walk over your corpses. You may say that such a thing is beyond human experience and endurance. I say it is not so. It was quite possible. Last year in Gujarat, women stood lathi-charges unflinchingly and in Peshawar thousands stood hails of bullets without resorting to violence…the army would be brutal enough to walk over them, you might say. I would then say you will still have done your duty by allowing yourselves to be annihilated. An army that dares to pass over the corpses of innocent men and women would not be able to repeat that experiment."[55] Here, it seems, he was advancing the theory of the expendables. As in war, so in *Satyagraha*, some sacrifices are inevitable before the invader is placed in a position wherein his moral defences are exposed.

The power of such selfless, beatific and forgiving suffering has shown in India, that armed men cannot sustain their violence against *Satyagrahis* for a long time. The invaders are likely to turn back at this stage. In case they succeed in breaking through the human wall and enter upon the arduous task of establishing a new sovereignty and of enlisting the community's loyalty, all the measures described in our pattern would be used to offset these efforts. From here on, the course of the invaded peoples, counteraction would be more or less the same as outlined in our above pattern of a successful

Satyagraha, although perhaps the course of action would be upside-down. A nonviolent state overwhelmed by an invader's armed forces at the landing places may start its series with parallel government or whatever is left of it after the first shock. It may then adopt non-co-operation to be followed by non-payment of taxes, thus marching backwards in the pattern described already. For, an area of action and interest common to both the contending parties, shall have been established by this time. What is more revealing, the *Satyagrahis* do not have to fight against a well-established and organised rule. Their task is much simpler and easier. For they are only blocking the formation of a new authority which has still to enlist the loyalty and cooperation of at least a few representatives of the people violated in order to start the wheels of smooth government.

CONSTRUCTIVE PROGRAMME

By the late twenties, however, Gandhi came to stress on the positive role of Constructive Programme, as the most novel mode, of *Satyagraha.* As early as 1925, soon after a spate of essays on different aspects of *Satyagraha* appeared in *Young India,* he stressed the need for *Satyagrahis* to engage in silent, active, constructive work of reform and social service."[56] In 1928 he pointed out that votaries of *Satyagraha* must store up the necessary nonviolent energy that could set free an irresistible force in society, that "they will not become a nonviolent organisation unless they undergo a process of what may be called continuous corporate cleansing. This they can only do by engaging in carrying out a well thought out constructive programme requiring combined effort and promoting the common good."[57] He later pointed out that all this constructive work should be "for its own sake. And yet be sure that it will develop the quality required for nonviolent responsible government."[58] He felt that the energy spent in gaining political power means so much loss of energy required for urgent social reforms. In fact, the capacity to take political power will increase in "exact proportion" to the ability to achieve success in the constructive effort. "That is to me the substance of political power. Actual taking over of the government machinery is but a shadow, an emblem."[59] It is only through such a Constructive Programme that a system of nonviolent self-rule could emerge, that a new social order could be built.

In 1941, Gandhi wrote a pamphlet on the Constructive Programme, stressing in the Indian context the need for working towards communal unity, the removal of untouchability, a programme of adult education and village improvement, peasant uplift and the development of nonviolent labour unions, economic and social equality, decentralized economic production and distribution through the promotion of cottage and small-scale industries, and the abolition of various social evils. He pointed out that, whereas civil disobedience could be most-effective in the redress of local wrongs or in arousing of local consciousness or conscience, it could never be direct end for a general cause such as is possible with the Constructive Programme. Also, the "handling of civil disobedience without the Constructive Programme will be like a paralyzed hand attempting to lift a spoon."[60]

This would imply that civil disobedience would be ineffective in a communist society unless it were employed by those very cadres which engage in constructive social work. Civil disobedience is itself an aide to constructive effort, and a full substitute for armed revolt, but at the same time the best training for proper civil disobedience is through the Constructive Programme. Finally, three days before his assassination Gandhi declared that political freedom would not be meaningful to the individual citizen without the attainment of economic, social and moral freedom. "These freedoms are harder than the political, if only because they are constructive, less exciting and not spectacular. All embracing constructive work evokes the energy of all the units of the millions."[61]

Altogether, Gandhi elaborated and employed a wide range of methods, from the most negative and limited to the most positive and comprehensive, in his various campaigns of *Satyagraha.* It is not possible or necessary here to consider the different occasions on which he employed diverse devices of *Satyagraha.* He gave much thought to the tactics as well as the modes of *Satyagraha.*

In a *Satyagraha* campaign the mode of fight and the choice of tactics, *e.g.* whether to advance or retreat, offer civil resistance or organize nonviolent strength through constructive work and purely selfless humanitarian service, are determined according to the exigencies of the situation. A *Satyagrahi* must carry out whatever plan is laid out for him with a cool determination giving way to neither excitement nor depression.[62]

He also concluded from his early experience that every good movement passes through five stages: indifference, ridicule, abuse, repression and respect. He thought that every movement that survives repression, mild or severe, invariably commands respect "which is another name for success."[63]

Gandhi referred to a basic and distinctive feature of the application of *Satyagraha,* what he called the Law of Progression.

"My experience has taught me that a Law of Progression applies to every righteous struggle. But, in the case of *Satyagraha* the law amounts to an axiom. As the Ganga advances, other streams flow into it, and hence at the mouth it grows so wide that neither bank is to be seen and a person sailing upon the river cannot make out where the river ends and the sea begins. So also as a *Satyagraha* struggle progresses onward, many elements help to swell its current, and there is a constant growth in the results to which it leads. This is really inevitable, and is bound up with the first principles of *Satyagraha.* For, in *Satyagraha,* the minimum is also the maximum, and as it is the irreducible minimum, there is no question of retreat, and the only movement possible is an advance. In other struggles, even when they are righteous, the demand is first pitched a little higher so as to admit of future reduction, and hence the Law of Progression does not apply to all of them without exception.... The Ganga does not leave its course in search of tributaries. Even so does the *Satyagrahi* not leave his path which is sharp as the sword's edge. But as the tributaries spontaneously join the Ganga as it advances, so it is with the river that is *Satyagraha.*"[64]

Clearly, *Satyagraha* radically differs from the process of compromise and negotiation, as normally understood. Gandhi's antagonists found this to their cost and to his amazement—Smuts in South Africa over the Indian question[65], Lord Pethick-Lawrence in India over the Cabinet Mission proposals[66], Lord Mountbatten and Nehru over the issue of partition.[67] While bargaining is regarded as the very stuff of politics, in which expediency may combine with a strong sense of duty, the *Satyagrahi,* considering politics to be a matter of principle and of conscience, is willing to compromise in regard to details and self-interest but is adamant and increasingly insistent when he feels that "eternal principles" and his individual conscience are at stake. The difficulty between the *Satyagrahi* and the conventional politician is that on the former's, but not on the latter's, premises, it is both logical and inevitable that a battle for strictly limited objectives should grow into a battle for wider objectives. Like Lord Pethick-Lawrence, we could also desist from concluding that this difficulty is due to the fault of either party or of either conception of politics. The uncompromising radical can be tiresome especially if he elevates, what generally seems to be a concrete dispute, to the level of abstract principles, or if his preoccupation with his own conscience makes him insensitive to the sense of duty of other people and their own anxiety to come to a settlement. On the other hand, the pragmatist and gradualist can be intolerable when they reduce a grave matter of moral import, involving basic human needs and concerns, to the level of purely expedient or formal solutions.

It is, however, clear that the application of *Satyagraha,* despite the universality of scope claimed for it, is no simple matter. Individual instances of *Satyagraha* could be accommodated within a stable political system and a settled social order founded chiefly upon a liberal, democratic faith in compromise, bargaining and negotiation. Some techniques will be more awkward than others, some *Satyagrahis* and negotiators more tiresome than others, some occasions for *Satyagraha* or its repression more dubious than others. It is not possible to pronounce generally on the legitimacy or efficacy of *Satyagraha* in existing political systems; legitimacy may seem to be stronger under authoritarian regimes or in undemocratic systems and efficacy may seem to be greater under governments more or less sensitive to public opinion and to individual freedom or in societies which are tolerant in regard to all nonviolent methods of political action. But one can judge the merits of a method of *Satyagraha* in a concrete context only. It is not impossible, but it is difficult, to envisage a political system and a society in which the doctrine of *Satyagraha* is generally adopted and carefully applied. As long as human nature remains as unreliable as we now think it to be, such a polity and society may seem to us to be peculiarly unstable, anarchic and explosive. If, on the other hand, we are prepared to think that *satya* and *ahimsa* could be deeply instilled into the members of small communities, *Satyagraha* may be safe to employ, but the occasions for its use few and far between.

NOTES

1. M.K. Gandhi, *An Autobiography or the Story of My Experiments With Truth*, Ahmedabad, Navajivan Publishing House, 1988, p. 235.
2. M.K. Gandhi, *Satyagraha in South Africa*, Ahmedabad, Navajivan Publishing House, 1972, p. 102.

3. Joseph J. Doke, *M.K. Gandhi*, Varanasi, Akhil Sarva Sewa Sangh Prakashan, 1959, pp. 133-134.
4. *Young India*, 18-6-1925, p. 213.
5. *Ibid.*, 26-11-1919, p. 5.
6. *Ibid.*, 16-6-1920, pp. 3-4.
7. *Ibid.*, 11-8-1920, p. 3.
8. *Ibid.*, 16-4-1921, p. 108.
9. *Ibid.*, 16-6-1920, pp. 3-4.
10. *Ibid.*, 26-11-1919, p. 5.
11. *Indian Opinion*, 1914 (article reprinted in *Young India*, 3-11-1927, p. 369).
12. *Harijan*, 17-3-1946.
13. Raghvan Iyer, *The Moral and Political Thought of Mahatma Gandhi*, Delhi, Oxford University Press, 1973, p. 295.
14. *Young India*, 25-6-1925, p. 223.
15. *Harijan*, 11-2-1939, p. 8.
16. *Ibid.*, 17-3-1946, p. 45.
17. D.G. Tendulkar, *Mahatma*, Volume I, New Delhi, Publication Division, Ministry of Information and Broadcasting, Government of India, 1960, pp. 280-83.
18. *Young India*, 17-11-1921, p. 98.
19. *Ibid.*, 30-7-1931, p. 196.
20. D.G. Tendulkar, *op. cit.*, Vol. II, p. 249.
21. *Ibid.*, p. 312.
22. *Ibid.*, Vol. III, p. 176.
23. Joan Bondurant, *Conquest of Violence: The Gandhian Philosophy of Conflict*, Bombay, Oxford University Press, 1959, p. 17.
24. D.G. Tendulkar, Vol. I, *op. cit.*, p. 282.
25. *Harijan*, 18-7-1948, p. 170.
26. K. Kalelkar (ed.) *To a Gandhian Capitalist*, Wardha, Jamnalal Seva Trust, 1951, pp. 49-50.
27. *Young India*, 23-2-1922, p. 166.
28. *Ibid.*, 4-11-1926, p. 385.
29. *Ibid.*, 25-8-1920, p. 247.
30. *Speeches and Writings of Mahatma Gandhi*, Madras, G.A. Natesan and Co., 1933, p. 346.
31. *Young India*, 12-6-1922, p. 352.
32. M.K. Gandhi, *Non-Violence in Peace and War*, Ahmedabad, Navajivan Publishing House, 1944, p. 49.
33. M.K. Gandhi, *Satyagraha in South Africa*, Ahmedabad, Navajivan Publishing House, 1975, p. 175.
34. *Young India*, 11-8-1920, p. 3.
35. *Harijan*, 20-7-1935, pp. 417-18.
36. Eric Fromm, *Escape from Freedom*, New York, Rinehart, 1941, p. 268.
37. D.G. Tendulkar, Vol. VI, *op. cit.*, p. 199.
38. *Harijan*, 1-2-1942, p. 321.

39. M.K. Gandhi, *Non-Violence in Peace and War*, *op. cit.*, pp. 390-91.
40. N.K. Bose, *Studies in Gandhism*, Ahmedabad, Navajivan Publishing House, 1962, pp. 121-25.
41. D.G. Tendulkar, Vol. III, *op. cit.*, p. 17.
42. K.L Shridharni, *War Without Violence,* Bombay, Bharatiya Vidya Bhawan, 1962, p. 16.
43. M.K. Gandhi, *Autobiography*, *op. cit*, p. 347.
44. K.L Shridharni, *op. cit*, p. 17.
45. *Ibid.*, p. 20.
46. M.K. Gandhi, *Autobiography*, *op. cit*, p. 371.
47. K.L Shridharni, *op. cit*, p. 22.
48. *Ibid.*, p. 28.
49. *Young India*, 2-2-1921, p. 33.
50. Rashmi Sharma, *Gandhian Economics: A Humane Approach*, New Delhi, Deep and Deep, 1997, pp. 154-55.
51. Jai Narain Sharma, *Gandhi's View of Political Power*, New Delhi, Deep and Deep, 1987, p. 101.
52. *Young India*, 2-6-1920, p. 3.
53. K.L Shridharni, *op. cit*, p. 44.
54. *Harijan*, 6-7-1940, pp. 185-86.
55. *Ibid.*, 22-6-1940, p. 172.
56. *Young India*, 1-1-1925, p. 7.
57. *Ibid.*, 2-8-1928, p. 259.
58. *Harijan*, 24-6-1939, pp. 176-77.
59. *Young India*, 2-7-1931, pp. 161-62.
60. M.K. Gandhi, *Constructive Programme: Its Meaning and Place*, Ahmedabad, Navajivan Publishing House, 1975, Preface.
61. *Harijan*, 1-2-1948, p. 1.
62. *Ibid.*, 1-4-1939, p. 72.
63. *Young India*, 23-2-1921, pp. 89-91.
64. M.K. Gandhi, *Satyagraha in South Africa*, *op. cit.*, pp. 208-09.
65. W.K. Hancock, *Studies in War and Peace*, London, Cambridge University Press, 1961, pp. 74-75.
66. Raghvan Iyer, *op. cit.*, p. 308.
67. Pyarelal, *Mahatma Gandhi, The Last Phase*, Ahmedabad, Navajivan Publishing House, 1958, p. 238.

3

Satyagraha in Action

By a strange coincidence, it was in far off South Africa, several thousand kms. away from the land of his birth, that Gandhiji first experimented with his new method of nonviolent mass resistance against injustice—political and social. He perfected his technique in the course of long years of struggle by the indentured Indians against the South African Government in which ultimately he came out successful. A careful study of the development of *Satyagraha* during those weary years is very important and necessary. It was the seminal period for that particular way of fighting evil with purely moral weapons. Those were also the most formative years in the life of the unique originator of that path of non-violence which was later used in India for achieving freedom and which, in the end, proved to be his greatest gift to humanity

It was the lure of getting a little more money and the attraction of visiting a new land that first took Gandhiji to the shores of South Africa. He went there "prompted by self-interest and curiosity,"[1] as he puts it. He had been disappointed with his career as a barrister in Bombay and had gone to Rajkot after a six months' stay. But when a chance of going to Africa offered itself, he seized it. It was for a legal assignment on behalf of a rich Indian firm in Porbander. He set sail in April 1893.

But apart from his legal work, what did Gandhiji find there? On the very day of his landing he observed that the Indians, to put it very mildly, "were not held in much respect." The conditions of life for them were simply intolerable. All Indians except those who chose to call themselves "Arabs," were coolies', *i.e.* porters. He himself came to be called a 'coolie barrister'. On his first informal visit to the court, he was asked by the Magistrate to remove his Indian turban. Local newspapers chose to call him an 'unwelcome visitor'. He was thrown out of a railway compartment at Maritzburg for no fault of his except that he was an Indian. He was thrashed by the conductor of a coach for not agreeing to sit down at his feet though he was entitled to sit within the coach.

In Transvaal it was still worse. First and second class tickets ever issued to Indians. He was refused admission in the Grand National Hotel at Johannesburg. The Natal Law Society opposed his being enrolled as a barrister on the ground that he was coloured, though fortunately the objection was not upheld. There was thus no end to humiliation and persecution of Indians throughout South Africa.

After some of these preliminary experiences, "Should I fight for my rights or go back to India?" was the question that knocked at Gandhiji's heart. "To leave would be cowardly" was his conclusion. He decided to stay and fight. It was this decision which was responsible for his "most important experiments in South Africa."[2]

In South Africa at that time, there were a number of social and legal restrictions. Most of them were the result of race-prejudice, colour-bar, and the jealousy of the European settlers. In fact the Natal Law Society opposed him being enrolled as a barrister on the ground that he was coloured! However, the objection was not upheld. Indians were not allowed to enter railway stations by the main gates. Difficulties were placed in the way of their getting higher class tickets. If they got tickets, they would not get accommodation in the higher class compartments as few Europeans would tolerate them as fellow passengers. They were likely to be thrown out at any time or be asked to shift to the lower class. That they also had paid for the higher class was no consideration. They were not allowed even to stay at posh Hotels.

Then in addition to these prejudices and racial jealousies, there were the discriminatory 'black laws'. Every ex-indentured Indian labourer had to pay a poll-tax of 3 pouds if he wished to settle down there, and a similar amount for his wife and for every son and daughter above sixteen. None could trade without a licence. European, got licences merely for the asking while Indians experienced great difficulties in getting them. Then there was the Education Test, according to which an immigrant was obliged to pass a test in one of the European languages. Those who had settled three years earlier were, however, exempted from the operation of this Act. Even while agitation against the Asiatic Registration Bill of 1906 was on, the Transvaal Immigrants Registration Act was passed in 1907, which particularly closed the door on every new Indian immigrant even if he passed the language test.[3]

While agitation was being carried on through the Natal Congress, founded in 1894, and similar bodies in Transvaal and Cape Town, and through the columns of the journal, *Indian Opinion*, Gandhi had not neglected what may be called the 'internal improvement programme', of the Indian community. That was his constructive programme in those days. It included such items as domestic sanitation, separate buildings for residence and for shops, education, etc.

Ultimately the storm gathered round the Asiatic Law Amendment ordinance. Gandhi first read it in the Transvaal Government Gazette Extraordinary of 22 July 1906. Reverend Joseph J. Doke writes as follows about it:

> For some eighteen months, the Asiatic community which numbered about ten thousand throughout Transvaal, naturally a loyal and law-abiding community, has been in revolt against the Government. The Asiatic Law Amendment Act, which was based on the theory that the Asiatics had inaugurated a widespread fraudulent traffic in 'permits' and was consequently a criminal community, to be legislated against as criminals, awakened intense indignation amongst them. They clamoured for proof of this traffic, but were refused. They appealed to have the charges investigated by a Judge of the Supreme Court, but the appeal was ignored. They had no parliamentary vote, and no representative in Parliament, so nothing remained but either to give outward sign of the criminal in registration—which was the impression of the digits—or resist the law. They decided on resistance. Fortunately, their leader was a refined, gentle, chivalrous man, a disciple of Tolstoy and the resistance took the form of Passive Resistance.... I said yesterday to him, 'My friend, it is likely to be a long struggle. England is careless, and the Government here is like iron.' He replied, 'It does not matter. If the trial is long, my people will be purified by it, and victory is sure to come.'[4]

Commenting on this piece of legislation, Gandhi said: 'I have known legislation of this nature being directed against free men in many parts of the world.... There are some drastic laws directed (so-called) criminal tribes in India, with which this Ordinance can be easily compared.... Finger-prints are required by law only from criminals. I was, therefore, shocked by this compulsory requirement regarding finger-prints.'[5]

After deep thought and excited debates, the Indian community took the decision in a crowded meeting of three thousand delegates held in Johannesburg on 11 September 1906 to resist the insulting Ordinance. An oath was administered to each delegate to resist the law at all costs.

Preliminary to actual resistance, the usual petitions, deputations, interviews and correspondence were carried on. But Mr. Duncan, the Colonial Secretary, told them definitely that the Government deemed the Ordinance essential for the existence of the Europeans there.

Thus the stage was set. Refusal to register, to give finger-prints, and to receive permits was the form which *Satyagraha* was to take. *Satyagrahi*s were to get ready to suffer the consequences of their refusal to obey the law.

The 1st of July 1907 saw the opening of the permit offices of the Government, in accordance with the new Ordinance. Gandhi organized peaceful picketing of the offices. Even boys of twelve enrolled themselves as pickets. Though some five hundred persons registered and took permits, the Government could not proceed further and decided to arrest the organisers and resisters.

The crisis came in December 1907 when notices were issued against prominent members of the Indian community to appear before the Court and show cause why they had not yet registered. Many including Gandhi were sentenced to various terms of imprisonment. But on 30 January 1908, promises were given by General Smuts and as a result of some settlement, Gandhi, along with some other important members, was released. General Smuts promised to repeal the Ordinance and validate registration provided the Indians registered voluntarily. Indians did their part. The leaders did it even at the risk of being misunderstood by their followers. But General Smuts did not fulfil his part of the agreement and broke the promises he had made previously. The Ordinance was not repealed. He did not even give satisfactory replies to Gandhi's letters.[7] On the other hand, another bill was introduced effectively barring all further Indian immigration. That bill was later passed into law..

The resumption of the struggle became inevitable. A meeting of the delegates was called at Johannesburg on 16 September 1908, when a big bonfire of the certificates, which were taken voluntarily in pursuance of the settlement, was planned. Two thousand certificates were flung into the fire that day.

Then began the long and arduous struggle when fines, imprisonments, hard labour and hardships, harassment, insults, flogging and even firing were the resisters' lot. On 13 March 1913, a High Court judgement invalidated all Indian marriages as being not in accordance with the local law. This was a brazen insult to Indian women who were stung to the quick and joined the struggle. All those who were inmates of the Phoenix Park crossed over to Transvaal in a batch of sixteen and they were sentenced. Some Tamil ladies who were not arrested went to the mines and roused the labourers there against the iniquities of the 3–Pouds tax. This agitation finally culminated in the great march of 2,037 men, 127 women, and 57 children across the border of Transvaal on the morning of 6 November 1913. Then came the arrests of Gandhi, Polak and others. The 'invaders' of Transvaal were also arrested and sentenced, and made to work in the mines. In the meanwhile, the strike-wave spread to other mines. Hardships were heaped upon the *Satyagrahis*.

At last the position of the Union Government became untenable and they announced the appointment of a Commission to give relief to the Indian community. Gandhi, Kallenbach, and Polak were released on 18 December 1913. Other prisoners were released within the next few days. By the end of July 1914 the Indian Relief Bill was passed. It repealed the 3–Poud tax, validated Hindu and Mussalman religious marriages (only one wife being recognized as legal) and recognised the domicile certificate as conclusive evidence of citizenship.

Thus ended the struggle which was spread over a period of eight long years (1906-1914) and made new history by revolutionizing the method of fighting for social justice.

The story, however brief, would not be complete without a mention of the acts of chivalry which distinguished the conduct of the *Satyagrahis* during the struggle. In every step that he took the *Satyagrahi* had to consider the position of the adversary, said Gandhi. The opponents' difficulty was never the *Satyagrahi's* opportunity, and a *Satyagrahi* would go out of his way to help the opponent in his difficulties. *Satyagrahis* in South Africa acted up to this precept as the following instances will clearly show.

When labourers in the North Coast went on strike, the planters at Mount Edgecombe would have suffered heavy losses if the sugar-cane that had been cut was not brought to the mills and crushed. So twelve hundred Indians returned to the mills to finish this piece of work and then resumed the strike.

On another occasion when the Indian employees of the Durban Municipality struck work, those who were engaged in the sanitary services of the Borough or as attendants on the patients in the hospitals were sent back to their duties so that there might be no out break of epidemics in the city, and the sick might not suffer.

The most notable example of such chivalry was seen on the occasion of the great strike of the European employees of the Union Railways. The Government was really embarrassed. It was suggested to Gandhi to strike the blow which would prove decisive. But Gandhi refused to do so. It would be contrary to the spirit of *Satyagraha*, he argued. This decision was very widely appreciated and one of the secretaries to General Smuts said to Gandhi: 'I do not like your people and do not care to assist them at all. But what am I to do? You help us in our days of need. How can we lay hands upon you? I often wish you took to violence like the English strikers, and then we would know at once how to dispose of you. But you will not injure even the enemy. You desire victory by self-suffering alone and never transgress your self-imposed limits of courtesy and chivalry. And that is what reduces us to sheer helplessness.'[8]

There cannot be a better description of the psychological effect of *Satyagraha* upon an opponent. The *Satyagraha* in South Africa also brings out the important differences between mere passive resistance—which is admittedly the weapon of the weak—and *Satyagraha* proper, which springs out of the unswerving pursuit of truth through love even of the opponent and out of inner strength. Gandhi in this case insisted that truth and justice were on his side and that he would establish it without ill-will and by self-suffering. He never thought of harassing the opponent. A mere passive-resister would have acted quite differently.

CHAMPARAN

Champaran is a name to conjure within the history of *Satyagraha* in India. For the first time Gandhi disobeyed the fiat of the authorities and said that he would not be ordered about in his own country. That was the beginning of his new method in India. The statement he submitted to the Court at Champaran rings true today and will ever remain an inspiring document. 'That day', Gandhi says, 'was an unforgettable event in my life and a red-letter day for peasants (of Champaran) and for me'. It was India's first object lesson in Civil Disobedience.

It was during the session of the Congress in Lucknow in December 1916 that Gandhi came to know of the age-long sufferings of the Champaran peasants. A worker from Bihar, Kishore Babu, after acquainting Gandhi with the local conditions invited him to visit the place, which he did in April 1917.

Champaran, reputed to be the kingdom of the great king Janaka is a district of the north-western corner of Bihar. European planters who had reaped rich harvests from the indigo plantations there, had been exploiting the simple peasantry for nearly a century. They had practically set up a super-government with the aid of legislation and usage, and sometimes by naked force. The Executive of the government which was sympathetic to this planter-raj, turned down all pleas for relief made by local leaders on behalf of the peasants and even recourse to legal action proved ineffective in the face of Executive hostility. The planters, entrenched under the Bengal Tenancy Act and similar reactionary laws, exploited the poor peasants with impunity.

The main grievance of the peasants was in regard to the *tinkanthia* contract. *Tinkanthia*, which literally means 'three sticks', had an ominous significance to the peasantry. Each tenant was compelled to cultivate indigo in three-twentieths of his holding, whether it was profitable for him or not. Sometimes the proportion was raised to five-twentieths. This indefensible extortion was legalized by the Bengal Tenancy Act. When the cultivation of indigo became unprofitable on account of the advent of the synthetic substitute, the planters entered into new agreements with the peasants, relieving them from the obligation to grow indigo, but on condition that they paid enhanced rents. Here too the Bengal Tenancy Act came to the aid of the planters who quoted sections in the Act in support of their action. This procedure was adopted only in places where the planters had permanent lease of the lands, and thus would be entitled to the increased rent for ever. In the interior, there were places where the European planters were only temporary lessees. In such places, the permanent owners stood to benefit by an increase in rents as they would also get it when the period of temporary lease was over. To avoid such a contingency, European planters extorted cash payments from the tenants to release them from the obligation to grow indigo. The fact that in most of the villages the barbarous *tinkanthia* contract had no legal existence did not prevent the planters from extracting the money.

The methods they adopted to extort money out of the peasants would blacken any civilized record. Beating and shutting up the peasants in temporary prisons, impounding the cattle, looting houses, stopping the service of barbers, washermen and chamars, preventing people from getting in or out of their houses, were only some of the ways which the planters adopted to terrorize the recalcitrant. Many illegal levies were collected on various occasions. There was a tax on marriages, a tax on oil-mills and a tax on every house. If the 'Sahib' chose to go to a hill-station to escape the sweltering heat of the plains, the peasants had to meet his master's fare, and tax called '*paparhi*' had to be paid by each tenant. If the Sahib needed a car, a horse or an elephant, it was the peasant who had to pay for it through a tax. Besides these, heavy fines used to be imposed on peasants, if any offence was committed against any of the Sahibs. The influence of the planters with the Government and the officials was so great that the peasants dared not approach either the judicial or the executive authorities.

It is said that the planters made about twelve lakhs of rupees through these iniquitous levies, and thus, at the cost of the poor peasant, made good the losses they suffered during the slump in the indigo trade.

The peasants direly needed deliverance from the tyranny of the planters but knew not from where it could come.

It was in these circumstances that Gandhi was invited to visit Champaran.

He reached Motihari, the headquarters of the district, on 17 April 1917. Immediately on arrival, he saw the authorities and told them what he had planned to do. He saw the Secretary of the Planters' Association as well. Both of them were, of course, unsympathetic. However, as was his wont, Gandhi wanted to study the case in detail and on the spot. He wished to assure himself of the truth of the grievances and of the allegations against the planters. He was about to proceed to a village for this, when he was served with an order under Section 144 of the Criminal Procedure Code to quit the district, on the obviously false plea that there would be a disturbance of peace if he remained in the district.

Who was the magistrate to order him about in his own country? Gandhi asked himself and decided to disregard the order. He courteously intimated to the magistrate his intention. He wrote to him to say that he had come in search of information—he wanted to inquire into the grievances of the poor peasants and he had no intention of leaving the district before finishing his task. He said he would stand his trial for disobeying the order, but the burden of removing him from the people whom he had come to serve would fall on the Government. He was summoned to the Court and he submitted a statement pleading guilty of the charge of disobedience of the magisterial order. He said he was obeying a higher law, the law of his conscience. Judgment was never delivered against him and later the case was withdrawn.[9]

Meanwhile he had continued with his inquiry. The C.I.D. staff were generally in attendance when statements were being taken. As many as twenty thousand statements were submitted, and the case for the peasants was based on them. Their demands were formulated. Later the Governor of the Province took interest in the inquiry and the Government appointed a Commission of Inquiry with Gandhi as the member representing the peasants. The Commission came to the unanimous conclusion that the 'tinkanthia' and all other illegal levies should be abolished, and recommended a partial refund of exactions from tenants.

In the early stages of the inquiry, the planters were hostile and the Government backed them. But Gandhi's readiness to disobey the magistrate's order and his persistence in following his own course to find out the truth surprised them and to a great extent confounded them. No occasion arose for the peasants to resort to *Satyagraha*. The *Satyagraha* of a single individual, of Gandhi, was sufficient to rouse the conscience of India and to open the eyes of the provincial Government to the iniquities involved. The peasants, it must be said to their credit, kept peace, came up boldly and gave evidence, and above all, prepared themselves to follow Gandhi wherever he chose to lead them.

What was it that Gandhi demanded in the first instance? He insisted on his simple right to inquire into the grievances of his fellow countrymen, the suffering peasantry of Champaran. The Government could neither suppress such a simple right nor could they neglect the inquiry once it had begun.

It is interesting to study how Gandhi proceeded in this case. He was very cautious at the beginning. He did not readily consent to go.

But once he made up his mind, he went into the struggle whole heartedly, and risked his liberties from the outset. When some people suggested that he should seek legal remedies against the planters, he brushed aside the suggestion saying that law courts were no good and not useful in the circumstances. Instead of avoiding the planters, he straightaway interviewed the Secretary of their Association and explained to him his mission. He civilily disobeyed the magistrate's order and went about as if no order existed. When he saw that he would be spending some time there for the ensuing fight, he took the opportunity to do some constructive work as well. He caused some six primary schools to be started in villages and made arrangements for medical relief. He wanted to teach the villagers to live better and healthier lives. When teachers and doctors were not available locally, he got them from outside and laid the foundation for further constructive activity and disinterested village service. He warned the teachers and doctors not to concern themselves with the economic and political problems. He cared more for the moral fibre of his teachers than for their intellectual attainments—for instance, he enrolled Kasturba as one of the teachers. When she pleaded that she could not teach reading and writing, he exhorted her to teach cleanliness and better manners rather than the three Rs, which were not, after all, the most important thing. He had become convinced that work of a permanent nature was impossible without village education.

The campaign lasted for about six months, by which time the labours of the Inquiry Committee came to an end. The recommendations of the Committee were embodied in an Act which swept off the iniquities of a century. Later when indigo went out of vogue, most of the European planters left the district and the few that remained began to live like any other local landholder.

'Today', writes Babu Rajendra Prasad, 'the peasant of Champaran is as free as any other man in India can be in the present conditions to develop and improve himself and his surroundings'.[10]

THE KHEDA SATYAGRAHA

In Champaran, Gandhi was able to achieve results comparatively easily. In Kheda, where peasants were struck by famine, they had to launch a regular civil disobedience campaign with all the sacrifices such a movement involves, even to attain a limited objective. This happened in 1918.

The district of Kheda or Kaira is in Gujarat. The crops had failed and semi-famine conditions prevailed. The peasants were unable to pay the assessment for the year. They were entitled to a suspension of the tax under the rules which laid down that if the annewari estimate of the crops showed that the peasants could realize only one-fourth of the normal yield, they should be relieved from the obligations of paying the assessment that year. But the Government refused to grant this legitimate relief. Petitions, representations, and resolutions in the Provincial Council were of no avail.

Gandhi then appeared on the scene. After studying the situation, he advised the people to withhold payment. The people responded nobly and took an oath that they would rather lose their land than pay what was not rightly due. Even those who could afford to pay refused to pay the taxes, in sympathy with their poorer brethren.

Gandhi put before the public and the Government the peasant's case and appealed for justice. He enlisted volunteers to work in the district and keep up the morale of the peasants. Vallabhbhai Patel, then a rising barrister in Ahmedabad, joined the struggle.

A systematic education of the peasantry began. Their fear of officialdom was wiped away. They were taught that officials were really their servants and they had no business to order them about. This emboldened the peasants to stand up to the officials and defy threats of coercion and intimidation. The peasants, however, were asked to be civil in the face of the gravest provocation. They faced all attachments of property and notices for forfeiture of their land with equanimity.

An occasion for civil disobedience was provided by the Government. An onion-field was attached. The attachment was bad in law. So Gandhi advised one Mohanlal Pandya and some seven or eight of his followers to reap the crop. They did so, and were arrested and imprisoned. This only strengthened the morale of the people and all fear of imprisonment disappeared.

When the officials saw that the people refused to yield, they began to beat a hasty retreat, but without openly announcing any concession for or negotiating with the peasants. They ceased to press those who were unable to pay. The attachments and notices stopped. Thus they tacitly recognized the contention of the people that relief should be granted to those who were unable to pay.

In principle, the *Satyagraha* was successful but lacked the essentials of a complete triumph. The Government did not meet in full the demand of the peasants, but by partial relief satisfied some of them. The people did not feel the glow of immediate success nor did they realize the benefit they had gained. Gandhi remarked that 'the end is worthy only when it leaves the *Satyagrahis* stronger and more spirited than in the beginning'. He saw that the people felt frustrated and dejected and that they were not civil enough towards the authorities. Moreover, the Government had succeeded in dividing the ranks of the people by discrimination in realizing the assessment.

But the indirect results that followed were valuable. There was widespread awakening among the peasantry in Gujarat. In fact, they shed their lethargy and they learnt the lesson of self-reliance and self-confidence. For the first time they realized that they had certain fundamental rights which they could enforce by mass action.

Referring to this campaign Gandhi says in his autobiography: 'The lesson was indelibly imprinted on the public mind that the salvation of the people depends upon themselves, upon their capacity for suffering and sacrifice. Through the Kheda campaign, *Satyagraha* took firm root in the soil of Gujarat.' [11]

It was the first occasion on which Gandhi called upon the masses of India to face hardships and sufferings and educated them on the lines of *Satyagraha*, and they did that very successfully.

After the campaign, Gandhi saw the necessity of training volunteers to educate the people in the science of *Satyagraha* and he also felt that the peaceful side or the constructive aspect of *Satyagraha* had not yet become sufficiently attractive to the people. But he could not get enough men immediately to do that type of work, so that the actual progress in that direction was not up to his expectation.

AHMEDABAD MILL STRIKE

While Kheda was still engaging Gandhi's attention a dispute between the textile millowners and labourer force come to a boiling point. Though the difference between the parties concerned began with the dispute about the grant of a bonus, ultimately the issue revolved round the percentage of dearness allowances. When both the parties approached Gandhi, he studied the whole case and persuaded them to agree to arbitration. That was done, but unfortunately after few days some misunderstanding arose amongst some of the mill hands and they went on strike. This angered the millowners who were waiting for an excuse to get out of the agreement. They declared a lock-out on 22 February 1918. Gandhi pleaded with the millowners as well as the workers but to no avail. He saw that the labourers were, on the whole, in the right. When the lock-out became an accomplished fact, he advised the labourers to demand a 35 per cent increase in the allowance which he to considered reasonable.[12] The mill- owners had, however, decided not go beyond 20 per cent. Then began a regular strike from the 26th of February 1918 in which thousands of labourers were involved. [13]

The labourers took a simple oath: They would not go to work in the mills till a 35 per cent increase was given to them on their July pay. They would not create any trouble during the days of lock-out and would observe perfect nonviolence. They would not indulge in any assault or looting. They would not harm in any way the property of the millowners. They would not allow any indecent words to escape their lips. They would maintain absolute peace.

During the lock-out, Gandhi kept himself and his co-workers busy. His co-workers visited the quarters of the labourers and gave instructions regarding clean and healthy living, and rendered medical aid and other help. Everyday educative bulletins were issued for distribution among the labourers. There were also daily meetings where the day-to-day problems were tackled.

Gandhi is very strict about monetary help. He does not believe in a campaign run on the strength of money. He exhorted everyone to find work for himself and to live on his own earnings. Many were temporarily employed for building the dam which was under construction. At the same time Gandhi assured the labourers every day that if it should happen that starvation was in prospect, he would starve first, and not they.

The morale of the labourers remained splendid for about a fortnight. In the meantime some of the millowners were trying their tricks. Numerous rumours were circulated, and the mill-hands seemed to be wavering and losing morale. It was at this time that Gandhi took one of those sudden decisions which was at once striking and original. He said he would neither take food nor use a car till he saw the end of it all.

Here are his own words: 'Instead of five to ten thousand blooming faces full of the luster of iron determination, I saw but a thousand or two who seemed worn out and dejected.... I am one of those who believe that one has to stick to his vow in any circumstances. I cannot even for a moment tolerate the idea that you should violate the solemn pledge you have taken. Till such time as you would all get your 35 per cent increment or you are all completely defeated in your object, I am not going to touch my food nor am I riding a car.'[14]

This turned the scales. The labourers again became adamant. The fast brought an indirect pressure on the millowners and Gandhi said that to that extent it had an element of coercion in it. But he said that he could not help it as that was the only remedy he could devise for saving the labourers from a fall.

It was finally decided that Professor Anandshanker Dhruva should act as the sole arbitrator. After a period of three months he decided that an increment of 35 per cent on their July pay should be given to the mill-hands.[15]

In this case, Gandhi's active non-violence, that is his love for the cause of the mill-hands of Ahmedabad was so intense that he risked his own life for it. After about a fortnight's struggle, when he took to fasting and thus maintained the morale of the labourers and hastened the settlement, Miss Ferring, a Danish lady in a telegram to Gandhi said: 'Greater love knoweth no man than that he lay down his life for the sake of his fellowmen'.[16]

Gandhi remarked at the end of the struggle that there was no place for hatred or ill-will in it and that he was as much the servant of the millowners as of the labourers. Mahadev Desai has characterized the strike as one conducted with the cleanest means, on the strength of sheerest determination, and with least bitterness on both sides. The result too was beneficial to both parties.

ROWLATT ACT SATYAGRAHA

The policies of the Government during First World War had pushed him from the area of local conflicts to all-India political arena. The occasion of this transition from local to national scene was the *Satyagraha* against the Rowlatt Bill which he took as an attack on national self-respect. The Government appointed a committee headed by Justice Rowlatt, to review the situation during War in December 1917. The Committee recommended that the Government should have emergency power to deal with any area, officially proclaimed subversive. Among the powers it suggested were the trial of seditious crimes by benches of three judges, sitting in camera, if necessary, without juries. The Government decided to legislate these recommendations. Politicians of all shades of opinion saw this bill as a blow to their type of politics. Gandhi worked actively to give organised expression to this popular resentment. He undertook an extensive tour of the country to demonstrate the popular feelings against the bill. He told Srinivasa Sastri that he thought the bills were not "just a stray example of lapse of righteousness and justice, but evidence of a determined policy of repression."[17] He decided not to obey these laws if passed and to offer *Satyagraha* against these laws. Gandhi now saw a national wrong which could possibly be righted only by the technique of *Satyagraha.* In a letter to C.F. Andrews he assured him that *Satyagraha* against the Rowlatt Bills would 'purify the atmosphere and bring in real *Swaraj*.'[18] He decided that *hartal* would be a form of protest. The extent of the *hartal* varied considerably between regions and between towns and countryside. Several Indian leaders opposed his action. But this did not dishearten him. He announced the plans for civil disobedience. He issued public advice to *Satyagrahis* to disobey laws dealing with prohibited literature and the registration of newspapers. He decided to visit Delhi and Amritsar but he was removed from the train at Palwal Railway Station as his entry into the Punjab territory was banned and he was sent back to Bombay.[19] When news of Gandhi's arrest became public, unrest in Bombay and Ahmedabad led to mob-violence, killing and burning of Government property. The worst occurrences were in the Punjab and Amritsar in particular. When Gandhi came to know about all these happenings, he admitted it a 'Himalayan Miscalculation' in offering civil disobedience to public insufficiently prepared by the discipline of *Satyagraha.*[20] He had to suspend *Satyagraha* not once but twice. He was criticized by both *Satyagrahis* and the Government. The Rowlatt *Satyagraha* as a political campaign on the lines which its author conceived, was a manifest failure. It did not obtain its objective, *i.e.* the repeal of the Rowlatt Act. It resulted in the eruption of violence. Nevertheless, as Gandhi's first essay in all-India leadership, it was remarkably instructive to those who could read it correctly, since it showed both his strength and weakness in politics. Thus the Rowlatt *Satyagraha* showed Gandhi as an all-India leader of immense potential. His personality, ideology, approach to politics and techniques of *Satyagraha* enabled his campaign to become the focus for multifarious grievances and gave him access to the power they generated.[21]

NON-COOPERATION MOVEMENT

Gandhi announced the inauguration of the nonviolent non-cooperation movement on the 1st of August 1920, as contemplated by the Khilafat Committee in June. While writing about the beginning of the second nationwide *Satyagraha*, he wrote in the *Young India* of 28 July 1920. 'The first of August will be as important an event in the history of India as was the 6th of April last year. The 6th of April marked the beginning of the end of the Rowlatt Act.... The power that wrests justice from an unwilling Government... is the power of *Satyagraha*, whether it is known by the name of civil disobedience or non-cooperation.... As in the past, the commencement is to be marked by fasting and prayer... suspension of business and by meetings to pass resolutions praying for the revision of peace terms and justice for Punjab, and for inculcating non-co-operation until justice has been done. The giving up of titles is to begin from that day.... But the greatest thing is to organise and evolve order and discipline.'[22] He again stressed the necessity of absolute nonviolence.

Then the Special Session of the Congress on the 4th of September 1920, passed the non-cooperation resolution by 1886 to 884 votes. The objects were declared—to get redress for the injustice done to Panjab and the Khilafat and the establishment of *Swaraj*. The Nagpur Congress which met in December 1920 was one of the biggest sessions, and it was attended by 14,582 delegates including 1,050 Muslims and 169 ladies. The Congress passed the resolution on non-cooperation amidst scenes of great enthusiasm. Those who were against the resolution in Calcutta had been completely converted. C.R. Das proposed it and Lala Lajpat Rai seconded it at Nagpur.[23]

The movement was called progressive nonviolent non-cooperation. In the first place, there was the five-fold boycott of titles and honours, of elections and legislatures, of schools and colleges, of courts and tribunals and of foreign clothe. There was also a constructive side to it. National schools and institutions were to be started, arbitration courts and Panchayats were to be established, spinning on *charkhas* was to begin. Then Government levies, durbars and all semi-official or official functions were to be boycotted, sale and use of drinks and drugs were to be prevented through peaceful picketing. People were asked not to offer themselves as recruits for civil or military services.

Never before was the country so awakened, so active, so united and so determined as during the eventful months of 1921-22. Hindus and Muslims seemed to have been welded into a single community. The movement which began with a simple hartal, fasting, and prayer spread like wild fire. The masses took up the campaign of prohibition spontaneously. There was some sporadic mob violence, but on the whole, the campaign was nonviolent, vigorous and effective. National schools sprang up by the hundreds. The Bezwada drive pushed up the Congress membership to fifty lakh. The Tilak Swaraj Fund was over-subscribed and went up to 115 lakhs. About 20 lakhs of charkhas began to ply in India.

Arrests were being effected on a fairly large scale. Prominent workers were not spared. Yet, in November 1921, the Government made it plain that they had instructed local Governments to take action only against those persons who had gone beyond the limits originally set by the organisers of the movement and had by speech or writing openly incited the public to violence or had attempted to tamper with the loyalty of the army or the police.

But this instruction was not always obeyed by the local Governments. Shootings took place at Dharwar and at Malegaon. Nor were the mass arrests and false prosecutions at Dharwar of all Congress workers in any way in consonance with the above policy. In most of the provinces, important Congress leaders had been either convicted or bound over. The success of the Bezwada programme, the successful boycott of the Prince of Wales' visit and similar activities had made the Government lose its balance. Most of the workers had offered no defence and were behind bars by the end of the year. By December 1921, the Government had set in motion the Criminal Law Amendment Act under which they could arrest Congress workers. They declared the Volunteer Organization in the U.P. and Bengal unlawful. That became a fruitful source of civil disobedience which really had not yet formed part of the general Congress programme. But Government itself showed the way by its repressive action. By the end of December, therefore, the number of prisoners had swollen to 30,000. The lathi, however, was not much in evidence in those days.

An unfortunate incident upset the Congress programme. On 5 February in far off Chauri Chaura in the district of Gorakhpur in U.P. some Congress volunteers, in a fit of anger, were responsible for the murder of some 20 constables and a sub-inspector. There were some small riots in Madras on 13 January 1922, when the Prince of Wales visited the southern capital. Gandhi felt that it would be wrong to proceed with Civil Disobedience in the face of such violence. So he induced the Working Committee, in spite of opposition, to suspend mass civil disobedience. It drew up instead a comprehensive Constructive Programme. The A.I.C.C. met at Delhi on the 24th of the same month and practically endorsed the stand taken by the Working Committee except that it allowed individual civil disobedience whenever necessary.[24]

CIVIL DISOBEDIENCE FOR SWARAJ 1930-31

The next step was civil disobedience not for the removal of any specific grievances but for *Swaraj* itself. Although the years 1924–29 were years of constructive activity on the part of the Congress, there was a growing feeling, particularly among youth, that the time was ripe for a declaration of Indian Independence. Hitherto, Congress had talked in terms of Dominion Status, but at the December 1927 session, a resolution was passed declaring "the goal of the Indian people to complete independence."[25] As a countermove to the unwanted and boycotted all-white Simon Commission on political reforms (1928-29), Congress appointed its own Committee to draw up a Dominion Status Constitution for India; this was adopted by the All Parties Conference held at Lucknow at the end of 1928. The Calcutta session of the Congress, December 1928, undertook to adopt the constitution recommended by the All Parties Conference, provided it was accepted by the British Parliament in its present form before December 31, 1929.

But in case it was rejected, the Congress would be free to organise a campaign of nonviolent non-cooperation, to advise the country to refuse taxes, and to carry on civil disobedience in such other manner as might be decided upon. Government paid no heed to this resolution, and hence the Lahore Session of the Congress, December 1929, changed the Congress creed from Dominion Status to Complete Independence. It instructed Congress members of the legislatures to resign and the people to take no part in the elections. It appealed to the nation "zealously to prosecute the constructive programme of the Congress" and authorized the All India Congress Committee to launch a program of civil disobedience, including non-payment of taxes, whenever it saw fit.[26] This was the formal beginning of the Civil Disobedience Movement of 1930.

The Working Committee of the Congress decided to observe January 26, 1930, as Independence Day throughout the country, and in February authorized Gandhiji to start civil disobedience in the manner he thought best. It said that civil disobedience for the purpose of obtaining complete independence should be initiated and controlled only by those who believed in nonviolence as an article of faith.

Gandhiji opened the campaign with his dramatic march from Sabarmati to Dandi for the purpose of breaking the Salt Laws. The 200 mile foot journey was completed on April 5, and on April 6, Gandhiji picked up a pinch of untaxed salt and broke the law. The All India campaign was on. Though Gandhiji was arrested on May 4, leadership of the campaign passed to a succession of others each relinquishing command as he was led to jail. Salt raids continued, and the repressive measures of Government became more and more severe. India became a vast prison-house.

During this movement, the lathi was brought into full play by the police and the number of firings that took place in a number of towns showed that the Government was trying to deal with the situation in a ruthless manner.

Mass raids on salt works and depots at different places in three or four provinces were a special feature during this movement. The Dharasana raid was witnessed by a number of foreign correspondents and by impartial observers in India. The volunteers there wrote new history with their blood. The marvellous endurance and discipline of the non-violent raiders at Dharasana and Wadala drew unstinted and unqualified praise from eminent foreigners like Henry Brailsford[27] and George Slocombe.[28] On the 21st of May, 2,500 volunteers raided the salt pans at Dharasana. Two hundred and ninety were injured by lathi charges. Two of them subsequently died. Fifteen thousand people, volunteers and non-volunteers raided the Wadala pans. About 150 were injured by lathis. At Sanikatta, ten to fifteen thousand people, in a mass, raided the salt depot and carried away hundreds of maunds of salt. But the point in a *Satyagraha* raid is not the amount of material removed but the bold, defiant, open action resorted to by the masses without the idea of using violence or counter violence, but with a clear idea about the suffering involved and of the right vindicated.

Mr. Webb Miller of New Freeman wrote about Dharasana as follows: "During eighteen years of reporting… I have never witnessed such harrowing scenes as at Dharasana. Sometimes the scenes were so painful that I had to turn away momentarily. One surprising feature was the discipline of the volunteers. It seemed they were thoroughly imbued with Gandhi's, nonviolent creed."[29] There was not a single case of retaliation or counter violence or even cursing. And this went on for days.

Though people showed such exemplary patience, and conducted themselves quite nonviolently, the police and the military acted most brutally and inhumanly against unarmed thousands that were ready to sacrifice themselves and shed their blood for their country. Many times even the innocent spectators were hit hard and hundreds of them were injured.

During the whole year a number of ordinances were promulgated. Lathi charges and belabouring by police became the order of the day. During the months of April and May alone, firing was resorted to at nineteen places killing 111 and injuring 422. But the people kept calm and suffered without violence on their side. Women in large numbers took part in this movement and persisted in spite of very harsh treatment.

In the meantime, attempts were being made by Messrs Slocombe, Sapru, Jayakar and Horace Alexander, to negotiate a settlement but all of them failed. The Round Table Conference, which had been convened in spite of the happenings in India, helped to speed Gandhiji's release.

On January 26, 1931, Gandhiji and twenty-six colleagues came out of jail to begin negotiations which ultimately resulted in the Gandhi-Irwin Pact of March 5, 1931. Mutual goodwill or, the part of Lord Irwin and Gandhiji, was responsible for the successful termination of the negotiations. The pact was a moral victory for the Congress and its principle of nonviolence. But Government parted with no real political power. The pact offered a breathing spell rather than a real peace.

The 1930-31 movement lasted a complete year. Nationalist India waged a relentless struggle, facing hardship and losses cheerfully, with no thought of resorting to violence. The British government, armed to the teeth with all modern weapons, sought to crush the spirit of India with ordinances, the lathi and other methods of terrorism. The main forms of *Satyagraha* current during the struggle were civil breach of Salt Laws, non-violent raids on salt pans and depots, breach of the ordinances, no-tax campaigns in certain parts of the country, civil breach of the press laws, boycott of foreign articles, special boycott of British cloth and British concerns, general non-cooperation with Government, and boycott of the legislatures. The campaign marked a distinct moral victory, which created self-confidence among the people and confidence in the weapon of *Satyagraha*. The pact that came at the end led the way to Congress participation in the Round Table Conference.

CIVIL DISOBEDIENCE FOR SWARAJ 1932-34

This was really a continuance of the struggle begun in 1930 with a break of nine months during which Gandhiji attended the Round Table Conference in London without any success.

The Gandhi-Irwin Pact, which was signed on 5th March 1931, was broken almost before the ink was dry. Lord Willingdon, who had succeeded Lord Irwin as Viceroy, was in no mood for compromise. When Gandhi returned from England from the Round Table Conference, he found India under Ordinance-Raj, with leading Congressmen under arrest. Although Gandhiji endeavoured to present the Congress point of view, the Viceroy was unyielding and Civil Disobedience had to be resumed. Gandhiji, and some fifteen thousand other prominent Congressmen throughout India, were picked up and arrested and detained without trial. Congress property was seized and Congress and allied organizations declared unlawful. Ordinance rule was the order of the day, with the lathi and baton very much in evidence. Soon the jails in the country were filled to capacity, with more than a hundred thousand prisoners. Repression was thorough and ruthless.

On 12th September 1932, the country suddenly heard the news that Gandhiji was going to fast unto death over the question of the Communal Award, which had proposed separate electorates for the *Harijans*. Gandhiji commenced the fast on September 20, and broke it when the Poona Pact, which restored joint electorates to the *Harijans*, was signed on the September 26. Civil disobedience was continuing, but the removal of untouchability came to receive more serious attention. Ultimately, after a meeting of Congress workers in Poona on 12th July 1933, mass civil disobedience was given up and only individual civil disobedience continued. Attempts at reconciliation with Government failed. On 7th April 1934, all civil disobedience was suspended.

INDIVIDUAL SATYAGRAHA 1940-41

1934–39 was a period during which the Congress decided to enter the legislatures and at the same time to carry on constructive activities among the masses. September of 1939 saw the coming of the Second World War. Britain declared war on behalf of India as well without consulting her. That gave occasion to the Congress legislators to resign their seats.

Individual *Satyagraha* campaign was of a type by itself. The life and death struggle in which England was engaged during the Second World War and the general non-embarrassment policy followed by the Congress decided the form of *Satyagraha*. Gandhiji in his speech initiating the movement said that the virtue of waiting was becoming a vice. Several alternatives had been suggested to Britain. It was asked to declare Indian independence but that question was evaded. It was asked to give India a constitution framed by a Constituent Assembly. The idea was laughed out. Full armed cooperation was offered if India was recognised as free. That was rejected. The exercise of restraint was good so long as it helped the spirit to live but it turned into a vice as soon as it threatened to kill the very spirit. He said, "I am not only speaking for the Congress but for all who stand for national freedom, unadulterated independence. I should be untrue to all of them if I said now: 'No embarrassment to the British....' therefore, if I exercised that self-suppression at this critical moment, it should be suicidal." He further said, "We cannot sit still. It is not *Satyagraha* to watch the people being marched to jail in the exercise of their right to freedom of speech. If we looked on, the Congress would disappear and with it the national spirit."[30]

Gandhiji hit upon individual *Satyagraha* as the most appropriate method of expressing its dissatisfaction it was the contention of the Congress that India should be free "to carry on nonviolently and openly anti-war propaganda" and "to preach non-cooperation with the Government in their war effort."[31]

Gandhiji interviewed the Viceroy on September 27 and 30, 1940. But the Viceroy could not concede his demand for freedom to preach the war policy of the Congress in a non-violent manner or to tell people not to help the war effort, on the grounds that all war was evil and destructive in nature. The Viceroy said that he would allow the same freedom that was given to conscientious objectors in Britain to Congressmen in India, but could go no further.

Then followed the inauguration of the *Satyagraha* campaign. Gandhiji laid down very strict rules and drew up a pledge. He wanted "quality" on this occasion. The campaign was opened at Paunar, October 17, 1940, when Vinoba Bhave, selected by Gandhiji for this honour, made a public speech in which he preached the Congress war policy and exhorted the people not to help the war effort, as all war was immoral and bad. He was arrested after he had been making speeches for four days and sentenced to three months' imprisonment.

Gandhiji then directed chosen Congressmen to march on foot towards Delhi, explaining the Congress war policy as they went. Hundreds started, but many were arrested and sentenced before leaving the bounds of their own provinces.

Later Gandhiji prescribed that instead of speeches and statements, *Satyagrahis* should repeat a slogan that it was wrong to help the British war effort with men and money and that nonviolence was the best way of resisting all wars. On this issue about thirty thousand people courted jail. It is significant that most of the Congress representatives in the Legislatures, Central and Provincial, in District Boards and Municipalities, in Congress organisations, and in public life found themselves in jail in this campaign. Eleven members of the Working Committee, 176 members of the All India Congress, 29 ex-Ministers, 22 members of the Central Legislature and 400 of the Provincial Legislatures courted jail. This campaign continued until the end of 1941, when the imminent invasion of India by the Japanese led Government to release the *Satyagrahis* in an attempt to secure co-operation in the war effort.

QUIT INDIA 1942-44

In December 1941, Japanese planes swooped on Pearl Harbour and forced America into the war. The soldiers of Nippon, however, marched with incredible speed and stepped from island to island in the Pacific. They were marching across Burma and Japanese bombs had already fallen on Indian soil. The prestige of the British was at its lowest.

It was at this time that Sir Stafford Cripps brought his proposals to India which were rejected by all parties because they had no substance. Cripps left India angered and bitter, and anti-British feeling ran the highest. Gandhiji saw that the parting of ways had come if India were to defend herself. She must free herself from the enervating influence of British Imperialism that was his feeling. He had no objection to the armies of United Nations being here but he said that it must be with the consent of Free India.

In July 1942, the Congress Working Committee passed a resolution calling upon Britain to withdraw from India. The resolution said that if the appeal failed, Congress would then be reluctantly compelled to utilize all its nonviolent strength for the vindication of the political rights and the liberty of India, under the leadership of

Mahatma Gandhi. The All Congress Committee, meeting in Bombay, August 7 and 8, endorsed this action, resolving "to sanction for the vindication of India's inalienable right to freedom and independence, the starting of a mass struggle on the widest possible scale, so that the country might utilize all the nonviolent strength it has gathered during the last 22 years of peaceful struggle." It declared that such a struggle must inevitably be under the leadership of Gandhiji.

Before the next day dawned, Gandhiji and all the Working Committee members were arrested. Within a week everyone who mattered in the Congress organisation was in jail. Then followed rule by ordinances, firings, lathi charges—even bombings from airplanes were reported from some places. At some centres people, driven to desperation, retorted in kind, attacking railways and the police. Government reported that 56 people succumbed to mob fury. It is estimated that more than 2,000 unarmed and innocent people were shot down and about 6,000 were injured by the police and military. Tens of thousands were wounded by lathis, about 150,000 jailed, and about a million and a half of rupees were imposed as collective fines. There is no record of tortures, burning of houses, looting, and other atrocities by the police and the military.

This struggle, which continued to 5th May 1944, was truly remarkable and incomparable with anything in past history. The few acts of unorganised violence can detract in no way from the mass awakening and mass revolt witnessed throughout India and the predominantly nonviolent manner in which the masses conducted themselves. What shape the movement would have taken in Gandhiji's hands is a matter for conjecture. But even without his guidance, or without the guidance of any top rank leader, the struggle continued unrelently and paved the way for final victory.

A Theoretical Statement of Satyagraha

Satyagraha refers, not to an end-product, but to a means for achieving agreement. It is dynamic, not static. It allows for the fullest realization that means are ends-in-the-making, or ends in process. Analysis of *Satyagraha* suggests that its essence may be cogently described in terms of dialectic.[32]

Gandhian dialectic does not refer to any phenomenal or notional system; it does not describe a metaphysical order. The Gandhian dialectic, which lies at the heart of *Satyagraha*, is a process to be made explicit by human action, not to be found as implicit either in the nature of things or the progress of time. It partakes of prescription, rather than description. These distinctions are essential if one is to understand 'dialectic' as applied to the action technique of Gandhi. The contrast between the Gandhian dialectic and that of Marx or his forerunner, Hegel, is striking. Each deals with a different level of abstraction and by comparing them the dynamic quality of *Satyagraha* may be illuminated.

Sidney Hook, in discussing criteria of dialectical thinking, remarks:

'Only when that whole or unit or continuity which has been destroyed by the presence of conflicting factors has been restored or re-established in another whole... can we claim validity for our procedure.'[33]

And he proceeds to define the heart of the Marxian dialectic thus:

'For Marx any material, which is the subject of man's activity generates its own normative ideals in relation to the way it succeeds in fulfilling human needs. From the reciprocal influence and interaction between the ideal and the actual a new subject matter is produced out of which in turn are born the means by which it will be changed.'[34]

Marx was critical of the Hegelian dialectical method because it did not allow for empirical approach. He believed that he had answered the problem by interpreting the dialectic in such a way as to allow the dialectical process to control both the thought and the action. Marx retains the dialectic as a system of logic and applies it to human activity solely as an interpretation. The interaction is expressed in terms of social environment on the one hand, and human-needs on the other. For Marx, the class struggle results.

Whether or not Gandhi would have accepted the Hegelian dialectic or the Marxist critical adoption and interpretation of the dialectic, is not our present concern. There is much in Hegelian dialectical idealism which Gandhi might well have accepted, had he been given to formulations and interpretations of systematized philosophy. He could, no doubt, have accepted the criterion for a dialectical approach as stated above, recognizing its applicability to his method of *Satyagraha*. He could also have accepted the Marxian assertion of dialectic as a social relation. But Gandhi could not have travelled far with either Hegel or Marx.

Gandhi could agree with Marx that the dialectical concept must have a social orientation, must relate to human action. He could accept the convenient structure of thesis and antithesis as expressing elements in the continuing process of growth through conflict and, again, the idea of synthesis as the welcomed result. But, inherent in the Gandhian approach, is a rejection of the Marxian (as well as the Hegelian) development of dialectic in the direction of predetermining the content of both thesis and antithesis—a development which, in Marx, defines class struggle and anticipates a synthesis in the realization of a classless society where, of course, the dialectical process must, for Marx, end.

The dialectical materialism of Marx bends the dialectic in a direction which, at first glance, might appear to gratify the Gandhian approach. The dialectic is projected beyond the realm of logic into the field of social and political action. The Marxist dialectic as a process involving social action is relieved of the Hegelian philosophical system, which obscured it as a method. But, again, with Marx the dynamic quality of the dialectic is only partially retained, for the content of the process is supplied through the dogma of the class struggle. It is here—at the point where Marx introduced content—that Gandhian *Satyagraha* strikingly departs. The method loses its true dynamic, creative quality when it becomes entangled with historicism.[35] The dialectic as a method relating directly to conflict is shorn of its dynamic character when the substance of conflict is specified. With Marx, conflict is inevitably class conflict, and the direction in which such conflict can move is irrevocably determined.

We may say, then, that Hegelian dialectic is a system of logic describing inherent, natural processes; Marxian dialectic is a method embracing not only man's original nature, but his class relationships, an historical method by which both the direction and the structure of conflict are predetermined. Gandhian dialectic, as distinct from Hegelian logic, on the one hand, and the Marxist adaptation on the other, describes a process resulting from the application of a technique of action to any situation of human conflict—a process essentially creative and inherently constructive.

HOW THE GANDHIAN DIALECTIC OPERATES ?

The dialectic implicit in the Gandhian method of *Satyagraha* is not dependent upon Gandhi's metaphysical assumptions, nor upon his Hindu-based theology. It could operate in non-Hindu societies, as it did among the Muslim Pathans of the Northwest Frontier Province.

Despite the tremendous faith Gandhi had in divine power, the technique of *Satyagraha* is based upon the admission of relative truths and the rejection of absolutes, which are not knowable for mortal man. God was, in Gandhi's definition, even the atheism of the atheist. There was no insistence upon an objective absolute. Absolute truth cannot be known absolutely to mortal man. Yet, *Satyagraha* means clinging to the truth. The problem was practical, for Gandhi—as it was for Marx. For both, criteria of truth lay in the meeting of human needs. But whereas Marx accepted a philosophy of history which defined the content of those needs and indicated their satisfaction, Gandhi perceived the necessity for developing an approach, a tool, a form whereby the content (substantial human needs) could be met and the truth (relative truth in terms of substantial human needs) of any situation could emerge. Gandhi could reject the Hegelian concept of reality and reason to agree with Feuerbach that 'man is the measure of reason'.[36] For, despite the ever-present overtones of religion in Gandhian thought, concern for human needs lies at the core of Gandhian teaching.

Perhaps the most persistent element in Gandhi is the recurring theme that non-violence is truth-creating. Here again, we find an expression not of absolutes and substance, but of relatives and process. By non-violence Gandhi means, as we have seen, the technique of conducting social relations characterized by constructive, peaceful attitudes, and infused with the determination to enlarge areas of agreement and to achieve resolution of conflict by persuasion.

Means and ends in Gandhian *Satyagraha* are distinguishable only temporally. Both means and ends partake of a continuous process. The means precede the end in time, but there can be no question of moral priority. Truth is inseparable from non-violence, and the method of achieving and clinging to the truth is non-violence. Non-violence becomes both the means and the end, and the terms become convertible. Non-violence is the heart of a technique—the Gandhian philosophy of conflict accepts the Hegelian position that 'every relation may be viewed from two opposite aspects, *i.e.* from the point of view of the two terms it relates. Each term regards the relation as internal to itself and the other term as external to itself. An antinomy results which can be solved only by reinterpreting the situation and by looking at both terms and their relation from the point of view of a wider relation… But one antinomy is solved in order to make way for another. Opposition breaks out between the terms on a higher level.[37] Hegel, however, made his interpretation and left the rest to the inexorable march of history and, in the last analysis, to formulation by historicists. The Gandhian philosophy, accepting the dynamics of the dialectical situation, and taking man as the measure of reason, centres upon a technique whereby one or both sides in a conflict can resolve the antinomy into a reinterpretation (which, in turn, gives rise to another antinomy). The technique, for Gandhi, necessarily involved an active exercise of nonviolence.

Again, Gandhi could agree with Marx that through action alone can beliefs be tested. Gandhi went further to supply the empirical control, which Marx sacrificed to historicism. Where Marx introduced subject and content, where he predetermined the structure and direction of conflict, the Gandhian philosophy insists that the process and technique must suffice. A technique such as *Satyagraha* could only lead to solutions yet unknown.

The inference in all that has been said above is that Gandhian *Satyagraha* assumes the rationality of man. This is not to say that *Satyagraha* denies large areas of non-rationality in human motivation and behaviour. It requires simply the assumption that man is endowed with reason, that man can utilize reason to direct his actions, and that a technique for conducting conflict can appeal to the rational in man.

The first step for any *Satyagrahi* is an analysis and a reflection upon the character of the total conflict circumstance. He must clarify his understanding of his own position and his own immediate objective and consider these carefully in the light of the total situation. Whatever the subject of a specific conflict, understanding the nature of conflict in general and of the objective to be attained in the given conflict situation is the prerequisite. The force within any dialectical situation is derived from the clash of opposing elements within that situation. In every case of *Satyagraha* the conflict is to be understood in dialectical terms. The immediate objective is a restructuring of the opposing elements to achieve a situation, which is satisfactory to both the original opposing antagonists but in such a way as to present an entirely new total circumstances. This is, in Hegelian terms, an aiming at synthesis out of the conflict of thesis and antithesis. The claim for *Satyagraha* is that through the operation of non-violent action the truth as judged by the fulfilment of human needs will emerge in the form of a mutually satisfactory and agreed upon solution.

The *Satyagrahi* must recognize that elementary to his technique is the first step of a full realization that his immediate goal is not the triumph of his substantial side in the struggle but, rather, the synthesis of the two opposing claims. He does, then, all he can to persuade the opponent of the correctness of his own position, but, while he carries on his own persuasive activity, he allows the opponent every opportunity and, indeed, invites him to demonstrate the correctness of his (the opponent's) position and to dissuade him of his own position. He is at all times prepared to depart from his own position and to embrace the opponent's position should he be persuaded, by the opponent, of his error. This may, of course, be achieved totally or partially; the *Satyagrahi* may be persuaded to abandon certain parts of his original position. He recognizes, and attempts to demonstrate to his opponent, that he recognizes the desirability of a resulting synthesis, and that he is not seeking a one-sided triumph. His effort is to allow for the emergence of the best restructuring of the situation. He seeks a victory, not over the opponent, but over the situation in the best (in the sense of the total human needs of the situation) synthesis possible.

Satyagraha *Versus* Compromise

It was Feuerbach's view that 'That is true in which another agrees with me—agreement is the first criterion of truth; but only because the species is the ultimate measure of truth.'[38]

Agreement is an essential element in the objective of Gandhian *Satyagraha*. In a conflict situation agreement is achieved through nonviolent persuasive action, possibly involving aggressive non-violence. Agreement, in the Gandhian philosophy, is in the nature of adjustment and is of a quite different character from compromise in the usual sense of that word. Gandhian philosophy does not exclude compromise as a device for the accommodation of differing positions at a point where conflict has not become explicit and basic principles have not been challenged. But once conflict materializes, the Gandhian technique proceeds in a manner qualitatively different from compromise. What results from the dialectical process of conflict of opposite positions as acted upon by *Satyagraha*, is a synthesis, not a compromise. The *Satyagrahi* is never prepared to yield any position which he holds to be the truth. He is, however, prepared and this is essential—to be persuaded by his opponent that the opponent's position is the true, or the more nearly true, position. In the working out of the Gandhian dialectical approach, each side may, of course, yield through dissuasion any part of its position. But this is not compromise. When persuasion has been effected, what was once the opponent's position is now the position of both antagonist and protagonist. There is no sacrificing of position, no concession to the opponent with the idea of buying him over. Nonviolent resistance must continue until persuasion has carried the conflict into mutually agreeable adjustment. Such adjustment will be a synthesis of the two positions and will be an adjustment satisfactory to both parties in the conflict. There is no victory in the sense of triumph of one side over the other. Yet, there is no compromise in the sense in which each side would concede parts of its previous position solely to effect a settlement. There is no 'lowering' of demands, but an aiming at a 'higher' level of adjustment which creates a new, mutually satisfactory, resolution.

NOTES

1. M.K. Gandhi, *An Autobiography*, *op. cit.*, p. 117.
2. *Ibid.*, p. 129.
3. M.K. Gandhi, *Satyagraha in South Africa*, *op. cit.*, pp. 89-94.
4. R.R. Diwakar, *Saga of Satyagraha*, New Delhi, Gandhi Peace Foundation, 1969, p. 119.
5. *Ibid.*, pp. 119-20.
6. M.K. Gandhi, *Satyagraha in South Africa*, *op. cit.*, p. 101.
7. *Ibid*, pp. 173-8I.
8. M.K. Gandhi, *An Autobiography*, *op. cit.*, pp. 482-83.
9. *Ibid.*
10. Rajindra Prasad, *Satyagraha in Champaran*, Ahmedabad, Navajivan Publishing House, 1951, p. 7.
11. M.K. Gandhi, *An Autobiography*, *op. cit.*, p. 513.
12. Mahadev Desai, *Righteous Struggle*, Ahmedabad, Navajivan Publishing House, 1951, p. 7.
13. *Ibid.*, p. 6.
14. *Ibid.*, p. 26.
15. *Ibid.*, p. 35.
16. R.R. Diwakar, *Saga of Satyagraha*, New Delhi, Gandhi Peace Foundation, 1969, p. 119.
17. *The Collected Works of Mahatma Gandhi*, Vol. XV, New Delhi, Publications Division, Ministry of Information and Broadcasting, Government of India, 1961, p. 87 (Herein after as *CWMG*).
18. *Ibid.*, p. 104.
19. M.K. Gandhi, *An Autobiography*, *op. cit.*, p. 386.

20. *Ibid.*, pp. 391-92.
21. Jai Narain Sharma, *Gandhi's View of Political Power*, *op. cit.*, p. 54.
22. *Young India*, 28-7-1920.
23. Jai Narain Sharma, *Gandhi's View of Political Power*, *op. cit.*, p. 61.
24. R.R. Diwakar, *Saga of Satyagraha*, *op. cit.*, p. 163.
25. A.M. Zaidi and S.G. Zaidi (ed.) *The Encyclopaedia of Indian National Congress*, Vol. 9, 1925-1929, New Delhi, S. Chand and Co. Ltd., 1980, p. 308.
26. *Ibid.*, pp. 565-80.
27. Henry Brailsford, *Rebel India*, London, Leonard Stein, 1931.
28. D.G. Tendulkar, *Mahatma*, *op. cit*, Vol. III, p. 41.
29. *Ibid.*
30. R.R. Diwakar, *Satyagraha in Action*, Calcutta, Signet Press, 1949, p. 96.
31. *Ibid.*
32. K.L. Shridharni, *op. cit.*; p. 316.
33. Sidney Hook, *From Hegel to Marx: Studies in Intellectual Development of Karl Marx*, London, Victor Gallancy Ltd., 1936, p. 72.
34. *Ibid.*
35. Karl Popper, *The Open Society and Its Enemies*, London, Routledge and Kegan Paul, 1949, Vol. !I, p. 78.
36. Joan Bondurant, *op. cit.*, p. 193.
37. Sidney Hook, *op. cit.*, p. 67.
38. Ludwig Feuerbach, *The Essence of Christianity* (translated by Marion Evons), London, John Chapman, 1954, p. 157.

4

Theory and Practice of Satyagraha

The political experience in *Satyagraha* that Gandhi conducted in South Africa and later on in India constituted a total challenge to the conventional power politics and its basic assumptions. If his techniques repudiated any thing very clearly, it was the need for a 'conventional power criterion in the political struggle'. The traditional patterns of political behaviour are altered in his politics. His technique of *Satyagraha*, since the beginning of its evolution in South Africa during 1906-14, has had valuable evidence on this matter. When Gandhi found that General Smuts did not implement the agreement in 1913, he planned a protest march of the *Satyagrahis* from Durban on January 1, 1914. The plan was in preparation, and all efforts were being made to make it a success. In the meanwhile, Gandhi went to Pretoria with C.F. Andrews. But there he learnt of a great strike of the European employees of the Union railways which made the position of the government extremely delicate. Gandhi was faced with a potential dilemma. It was open for him to bargain with his opponent, when he was in difficulty by exploiting his weakness as is usually done in the conventional power politics. Here was an excellent opportunity waiting for him. In fact, Gandhi admitted that some of his colleagues urged him to take advantage of the situation and strike the iron as it was very hot. But he was guided by the ethics of his nonviolent technique alone which required that he should not press his demands at a time when the government was confronting a genuine difficulty. He resisted all types of pressures from his colleagues and decided to postpone the contemplated march. Gandhi wrote about this decision, "But I declared that Indians could not thus assist the railway strikers, as they were not out to harass the Government, their struggle being entirely different and differently conceived. Even if we undertook the march, we would begin it at some other time when the railway trouble had ended."[1] This is the difference between his techniques based on truth and non-violence, and the other techniques based on the power politics. The working of the nonviolent technique is not affected by the consideration of power. This decision was greatly appreciated by the Britishers. This gesture of cordiality amidst an acute conflict evoked a natural response from the adversaries. "This decision of ours, "Gandhi added, 'created a deep impression,' and was cabled to England by Reuter. Lord Ampthill cabled his congratulations from England. English friends in South Africa too, appreciated our decision. One of the Secretaries of General Smuts jocularly said: "I do not like your people, and do not care to assist them at all. But what am I to do? You help us in our days of need. How can we lay hands upon you? I often wish you took to violence like the English strikers, then we would know at once how to dispose of you. But you will not injure even the enemy. You desire victory by self-suffering alone and never transgress your self-imposed limits of courtesy and chivalry. And that is what reduces us to sheer helplessness."[2] In 1914, Gandhi presented a pair of chappals, he had himself made, to General Smuts. After 25 years the general returned the chappals to Gandhi saying that he was unworthy of standing in the chappals of such a great man.[3] Here is a testimony from the enemy about the impact of the nonviolent technique. The adversary was not humbled or outwitted but was enabled to take the right course. This was because Gandhi always sought a genuine reconciliation and settlement, and not a one-sided victory. Even when the 'Smuts-Gandhi agreement' embodying the substantial acceptance of the demands of the Indian settlers in South Africa was signed on January 30, 1914, Gandhi was urged by his associates to press for more demands. But he declined this plea as it would be contrary to the spirit of *Satyagraha*. Referring to this question Gandhi wrote in the *Indian Opinion* of February 11, 1914: "It needs to be understood, once and for all, that the path of truth is not meant for ends, not consistent with truth. It is our belief that raising our demands will amount to untruthfulness."[4] And this rare spirit is usually uncommon to the power politics.

During the Ahmedabad Mill strike in 1917 when certain workers suggested to increase the demands beyond 35 per cent hike in allowances, he refused to do so by saying, "I say you can demand even a 100 per cent increase. But it would be unjust if you do so. Be content, in the present circumstances, with what you have demanded. If you ask for more, it will pain me. We cannot demand anything unreasonable from anybody." He reminded the workers of their own, shortcomings. When he noticed signs of their weakening in the face of hardships, he undertook an indefinite fast to demonstrate his readiness to die for their cause. Later on, when the employers yielded, he refused to take full advantage of the situation and press for a complete acceptance of the workers' demands. His stand possibly antagonized a section of workers for a while, but he pacified them. The conclusion of the struggle embodied the true spirit of *Satyagraha*—where no advantage was taken from the difficulties of the opponent.

The Gandhian technique in the Indian national movement developed these characteristics to a great extent. The method of nonviolent resistance was easily conspicuous among them. It grew out of the historic challenge of the Indian nationalism. At the time of Gandhi's advent in the Indian politics, the Indian National Congress represented two major attitudes on the question of fighting the foreign government. They were divided between the extremist view and the liberal wings of the Congress. The extremist view was completely opposed to the British power which it sought to replace by the nationalist power. The liberal or moderate view was equally opposed to the power of foreign government, but it was conditioned to share this power gradually in the process of transition from foreign rule to the self-government. Both the extremists and the liberal nationalists were unanimous on the objective of national power though their methods of obtaining it varied. But it was the nonviolent technique of Gandhi alone that made a real difference of two sections of the Indian National Congress by projecting an alternative to the power of that kind. Nonviolent resistance to the British Government emerged as a valid alternative to the previous methods of national agitation that were based upon the customary sanctions of violence and power.

The Gandhian technique, as it was operated by the Indian National Congress, was marked by a positive rejection of power. When the Congress demonstrated its faith in the nonviolent movement by implementing its programme with unprecedented enthusiasm in 1919-21, the whole nation seemed to vindicate Gandhi's leadership. Romain Rolland wrote in his biography of Gandhi, "In 1921 Gandhi's power was at its apogee. His authority as a moral leader was vast, and without having sought it, almost unlimited political authority hds been placed in his hands."[6] The nonviolent 'non-cooperation movement was thoroughly shaken by the tragedy of Chauri Chaura on February 1922, when mob violence claimed many casualties. Gandhi was again on the horns of a dilemma. If Gandhi was keen on attaining power, he could have continued the movement despite the happenings in Chauri Chaura. In view of the mounting popular participation, he might not have been deterred by usual norms, from the course he took, as an unquestioned leader of his people. But he immediately suspended the non-cooperation movement after Chauri Chaura incident, and made a public confession of his mistake. Writing in *Young India* of February 16, 1922, he explained his unexpected move thus: "Suspension of mass civil disobedience and subsidence of excitement are necessary for further progress, indeed indispensable to prevent further retrogression. I hope, therefore, that by suspension every Congressman or woman will not feel disappointed but he or she will feel relieved of the burden of unreality and of national sin."[7]

The entire body of workers in Bardoli, young and old, who were getting ready for mass civil disobedience, told Gandhi that if—he retreated after throwing out a challenge to the Government, the whole country would be disgraced before the world.[8] Jawaharlal Nehru mentioned his reaction to this decision of Gandhi in his Autobiography in the following words: "Suddenly… we in prison learnt, to our amazement and consternation, that Gandhiji… had suspended civil resistance…. We were angry when we learnt of this stoppage of our struggle at a time when we seemed to be consolidating our position and advancing on all fronts."[9] What Nehru voiced on this matter was also the common criticism amongst the national leadership of the Congress of this aspect of Gandhi's politics. But Gandhi stood firm, however, in the midst of the storm he refused to lead a movement 'half violent and half nonviolent, even though it might result in the attainment of so called Swaraj'[10], for it would not be real Swaraj as he had conceived it. The withdrawal of a political movement when it was deviating from the main principle was basic to Gandhi's notion of politics without conventional notion of power. It was not an aimless measure, but an implicit ethic, involved in his techniques. The nonviolent movement was also withdrawn several times in 1932–34.

But the premature suspension of a movement is also viewed by some as a political strategy. If the suspension of civil disobedience movement 1932–34 is analysed, some possible explanations can emerge. In the first place, it was not possible to keep these struggles going effectively for more than a year with almost all the leaders in prison. Then, no great empire with its power intact, is likely to yield to a rebellion, violent or nonviolent, while it is still going on. The 'conversion' Gandhi expected might happen gradually, in favourable circumstances. Even then, there must be a pause, an interval for reconsideration and this suspension period can be this much needed interval. Gandhi might not have planned this but in fact the series of movements, he led wave after wave with intervals for recovery in India and reflection in England, was the best strategy he could have followed. It is very useful politically to suspend a movement when the circumstances are not favourable and things have gone out of control and then again relaunch that during the favourable time.[11]

Gene Sharp has listed three possible broad processes or mechanisms, by which the *Satyagrahis* can influence the behaviour of their opponents. These are conversion, accommodation and nonviolent coercion.[12] Conversion means that there is a genuine change of heart of the opponent and he comes around to the point of view of the *Satyagrahi*. Gandhi's own statements provide good illustrations of this objective of conversion. In a letter to the Viceroy, Lord Irwin, in 1930, he wrote. "For my ambition is no less than to convert the British people through nonviolence, and thus make them see the wrong they have done to India. I do not seek to harm your people. I want to serve them even as I want to serve my own people."[13] On another occasion he wrote that it is not the intention of a *Satyagrahi* to embarrass the wrong doer. The appeal is never to his fear; it is, must be, always to his heart. The *Satyagrahi's* object is to convert, not to coerce the wrong doer.[14] In line with this attitude the *Satyagrahis* are supposed to emphasize that they intend no personal hostility towards the members of the opponent group. He added that he wished by non-cooperation to induce the opponent to cease inflicting the evil or harm so that cooperation could be possible on a different basis. This aim of conversion in certain situations had significant effect on the opponent group. Replacement of hostile personal attitudes by positive attitudes can reduce the pressure on the opponent group to be defensively aggressive.

Practically, the complete conversion of the opponent is very rare. Also the conversion of the opponents may contribute to change by accommodation or by nonviolent coercion.

Accommodation as a mechanism of *Satyagraha* falls in middle position between conversion and nonviolent coercion. In accommodation the opponent is neither converted nor nonviolently coerced but resolves to grant the demands of the *Satyagrahi*. He considers some other factors more important than the issues at stake in the conflict and the opponent is, therefore, willing to yield on the issue rather than to risk or to experience some other condition or result regarded as still more unsatisfactory. But there may be opponents who are not willing to concede the demands of *Satyagrahis*. Even if they know that they may be finally defeated, they prefer to remain firm to the end, *Satyagrahis* may resort to nonviolent coercion.

In nonviolent coercion, the opponent has not changed his mind on the issues and wants to continue the struggle, but is unable to do so, as the source of his power and means of control have been taken away from him without the use of violence. The concept of coercion is not limited to the effects of threats or use of physical violence. On the contrary, coercion is defined as "the threat or the application of force, physical or non-physical, in order to persuade some person or group to take some decision or perform some action which otherwise they would not be likely to do."[15] It is often made clear that coercion can be effected by non-physical pressure including moral compulsion.[16] The will of the opponent is blocked despite his continued efforts to impose it. Thus the opponent is coerced, though nonviolently. Jawaharlal Nehru also believes that nonviolence coerces as well as violence, sometimes even more terribly. But there is, however, vast difference between nonviolent coercion and violent coercion.[17] As Bondurant points out: "The difference between violent coercion in which deliberate injury is inflicted upon the opponent and nonviolent coercion in which injury indirectly results is a difference of such great degree that it is almost a difference of kind.[18] Deliberate intention of inflicting physical injury is involved in the former while the nonviolent coercion largely arises from non-cooperation, a refusal from the *Satyagrahis* to submit despite repression and at times removal of the opponent's ability to inflict violence.

The crucial point involved here is the question of whether *Satyagraha* is a coercive force. Gandhi himself had time and again refused to see any element of coercion in it and advocated it to be a method of conversion. In the light of events in India as well as in the light of some of Gandhi's own activities however, it becomes apparent that *Satyagraha* does contain an aspect of nonviolent coercion, if in a somewhat modified form. The self-purifying phase of *Satyagraha* does not allow nonviolent coercion to be a part of the compulsion of nonviolent action. It is misleading, therefore, to describe *Satyagraha* as a form of nonviolent coercion. But it is equally misleading, on the other hand, to call *Satyagraha* a pure and simple process of conversion as Gandhi and some of his followers would have it. Krishanlal Shridharni rightly puts it "as a process of conversion in a special sense of the term; special because there is always present in it what for the lack of a better name we will call the compelling element."[19] To be more fair, it can be then called moral compulsion.

A critical analysis of the working of any method of *Satyagraha* can make the issue clear. The methods of *Satyagraha* can be broadly classified into four categories: purificatory devices; forms of non-cooperation, methods of civil disobedience, and Constructive Programme. The division is mainly for conceptual clarity and convenience of presentation. There is an inevitable overlap in practice as well as in theory between these four categories. In the first category of purificatory devices pledges, prayers and fasts can be included while in the second category of non-cooperation techniques, *hartal*, boycott, *hijrat* and fasting up to death can be listed. Picketing, marches, nonpayment of taxes and deliberate defiance of a specific laws comes under the third category. The fifteen points constructive programme offered by Gandhi is illustrative of the constructive side of *Satyagraha*.

Leaving aside the constructive programme, fasting is the mildest tool of *Satyagraha*. This creates the minimum inconvenience to the opponent. But not to speak of other techniques, fasting can also compel the opponent. A detailed analysis of some fasts undertaken by Gandhi corroborate this line of argument.

Gandhi undertook a great many fasts in his life. But in the present study oniy three of his famous fasts will be focussed; the fast against the communal award in 1932, the Rajkot fast in 1939 and the 'Epic Fast' of Communal Award 1943 against the policies of the British Government.

The British Government had announced the communal award of 1932. Under this scheme the depressed classes were recognised as a minority community entitled to the separate electorate. Gandhi strongly opposed the demand for the separate representation of the untouchables and declared his determination to fast unto death from September 20, 1932, unless the communal award was meanwhile revoked. But the British Government took the stand that the separate electorates were demanded by the depressed classes themselves and the decision of the British Government could not be altered unless the minority communities concerned agreed to do so. In a meeting on September 19, 1932, the Hindu leaders including Pt. Madan Mohan Malaviya, Sir Tej Bahadur Sapru, M.R. Jayakar, C. Rajagopalachari etc., tried to persuade Dr. B.R. Ambedkar to withdraw the damand for separate electorates, but he refused to do so without knowing Gandhi's terms. On September 20, 1932, Gandhi started his fast. Informal negotiations started between Dr. Ambedkar and the Hindu leaders. When Dr. Ambedkar refused to give in, Sir Tej Bahadur Sapru suggested a scheme of primary and secondary election for a limited number of seats which, while maintaining the principle of joint electorate, would enable the depressed classes to choose their own candidates. Dr. Ambedkar accepted this proposal. Then came the question of period after which the system of primary and secondary elections would come to an end. Dr. Ambedkar suggested a referendum at the end of 15 years but the other leaders rejected it. Meanwhile Gandhi's condition had been deteriorating rapidly. After some discussion over this issue, Gandhi suggested a period of five years for referendum but Ambedkar did not agree. Gandhi's condition deteriorated further; Ambedkar offered to reduce the period in question to ten years. But Gandhi replied, "Your's logic is irrefutable. But let the referendum be at the end of five years. Surely, five years is a sufficient period to prove the *bona fides* of the caste Hindus. But if you insist on postponing the referendum further, I would begin to suspect that what you want is not to test the *bona fides* of the caste Hindus, but time only to organize the depressed classes for an adverse referendum." Ambedkar, however, remained adamant on the ten years period, until Gandhi terminated the interview by saying, "There you are. Five years or my life."[20] Gandhi's condition had now become quite critical. On the same evening after the interview, Ambedkar had a prolonged discussion with his associates, at the end of which he declared that he was unable to change his position regarding the ten years period. Nocturnal discussions with the caste Hindu leaders followed, until finally Ambedkar responded to the appeal of the latter in the small hours of the morning, to postpone the question of the period concerned until a future date when it would be decided by a mutual agreement. Gandhi expressed his satisfaction over this. Thus on September 25, a Conference of the leaders took place at Poona, where Poona Pact was signed. Gandhi informed the British

Government telegraphically that he would break the fast if the latter would accept the Poona Pact in full. The British Government did so promptly, and on the evening of September 26, Gandhi broke his fast.

Undoubtedly, Gandhi had caused the necessary change in the stand of Dr. B.R. Ambedkar. We can also say that Gandhi exercised his power of pursuation over him. But in order to prove that this exercise of power was completely free from coercion, it would be necessary to show that Ambedkar underwent a genuine change of heart. When Gandhi declared his intention to fast unto death, Ambedkar issued a statement in which he totally rejected Gandhi's case against the communal award stating, "I however trust the Mahatma will not drive me to the necessity of making a choice between his life and the rights of my people."[21] The facts of the case briefly narrated above indicate that Ambedkar was most reluctant to change his position throughout the negotiations, that Gandhi very definitely placed before Ambedkar the clear alternatives of accepting his terms or the responsibility for his death and the former made each concession most reluctantly with the progressive deterioration of Gandhi's condition. Long afterwards, Ambedkar still maintained that he had signed the Poona Pact against his best judgement. In his own words, "I had to make a choice between two different alternatives. There was before me the duty, which I owed as a part of common humanity, to save Gandhi from sure death. There was before me the problem of saving for the Untouchables the political rights which the Prime Minister had given them. I responded to the call of humanity and saved the life of Mr. Gandhi by agreeing to alter the Communal Award in a manner satisfactory to Mr. Gandhi.'[22] Thus if Ambedkar's own statement about his reaction to Gandhi's fast is correct and analysed carefully then it follows that he remained convinced about the correctness of his original stand, and yielded against his wishes and was merely compelled by Gandhi to change his original stand. It was a pact signed under moral compulsion.

Several other explanations can also be given which influenced Dr. Ambedkar's decision of signing the pact. It was almost sure that if Ambedkar had not altered his stand, Gandhi would have died. The death of Gandhi could completely eclipse the political career of Ambedkar since he would have been held responsible for the death of the Mahatma who was very much popular among the depressed classes also. Ambedkar had clearly anticipated the reaction of the death of Gandhi and so he signed the pact.[23]

RAJKOT FAST

The Rajkot fast, too, is not free from the element of coercion: A *Satyagraha* struggle had been going for some months between the people and the ruler of Rajkot, a state on the Western coast of India near Bombay. Sardar Vallabhbhai Patel was leading the people. In the course of the struggle an agreement was arrived at between the ruler and Sardar Patel. But the ruler repudiated the agreement almost immediately afterwards. At this stage Gandhi intervened and pleaded with the ruler and his advisers to honour the agreement. The efforts failed. Thereupon, Gandhi decided to resort to fast on March 3, 1939, in order to arouse the ruler's conscience. Several friends and colleagues pleaded with him to have mercy upon himself and give up the fast but with no result. The following morning Gandhi dictated a letter to E.C. Gibson, the Resident, requesting him to transmit a message to the Viceroy, Lord Linlithgow, calling for "the immediate intervention of the Paramount Power so as to induce the promise made by the Thakore Saheb."[24] This appeal to the Viceroy succeeded. Lord Linlithgow intervened, with the result that the matter was referred to the arbitration of Chief Justice of India, Sir Maurice Gwyer. To Gandhi this seemed to "provide a basis for breaking the fast,"[25] which he actually did at 2 P.M. on March 7, after assuring himself of the Thakore Saheb's "immediate order for the release of prisoners."[26] Sir Maurice Gwyer gave the award in favour of the *Satyagrahis*. The ruler had no alternative left but to yield.

One would expect that, a direct *Satyagraha* method having been choosen, it would have been carried to its logical sequence. The ruler would have yielded, or come to some other agreement, or allowed Gandhi to die. But this was not done. Rather the help of Viceroy was sought. It consisted in seeking the help of the Viceroy, as a sort of additional weapon in aid of the weapon of fast. Later on Gandhi himself realized his mistake. In a statement to the press, he said, "My fast to be pure should have been addressed only to the Thakore Saheb and I should have been content to die if I could not have melted his heart or rather that of his adviser, Durbar Shri Virawala."[27] The ruler yielded not because of the fast. If Thakore Saheb had decided to flout the award, the Paramount Power would have, assuming that it would have acted honestly, compelled him to abide by it, if necessary by the use of force. It was thus a victory of the Viceroy and not of the fast. Gandhi admitted that "this was not the way of *Ahimsa* or conversion."[28]

It was the way of *himsa* or coercion. If it was open to Gandhi to try the constitutional method of appealing to Viceroy for the redressal of grievances, it might well be questioned whether it was proper to resort to direct action at all, until all other methods had been exhausted. If on the other hand, there was a perfect case for direct action, why did he seek the Viceroy's intervention? Thus on both grounds his position was inconsistent with the principle of *Satyagraha.* But as soon as this became clear to Gandhi, he at once repented publicly and as a practical proof of repentance renounced the fruit of his victory.[29] He had realized that it was his moral weakness that had prompted him to appeal to the Paramount Power and seek adventitious aid unbecoming of a true *Satyagrahi.* He apologized to the Viceroy and Sir Maurice Gwyer for having in his weakness thrust on them a needless burden.

EPIC FAST (1943)

Gandhi undertook another fast for 21 days on February 9, 1943, against the policies of the British Government towards himself and the Indian National Congress, in Aga Khan Palace in Poona where he was detained. Again some fundamental questions regarding fasting as a technique to coerce the opponent to change his behaviour were raised by both the sides, which more or less represent the two opposite view points. In a letter to the Viceroy, Lord Linlithgow, dated December 31, 1942, Gandhi declared that he would start a fast after 6 months of detention (that is, in February 1943) if the attitude of the government towards him and the Congress did not change, because as a *Satyagrahi* he had no other remedy left but to "crucify the flesh by fasting."[30] He still did not want to do it if it could be avoided. In another letter to the Viceroy, Gandhi communicated in the following Words, "If then I cannot get soothing balm for my pain, I must resort to the law prescribed for the *Satyagrahis*, namely, a fast according to capacity.... For my wish is not to fast unto death, but to survive the ordeal, if God so wills. This fast can be ended sooner by the Government giving the needed relief."[31]

On the other hand, the Viceroy wrote to Gandhi, "I would welcome a decision on your part to think better of it, not only because of my own natural reluctance to see you wilfully risk your life, but because I regard the use of a fast for political purposes as a form of political blackmail (*himsa*) for which there can be no moral justification, and understood from your own previous writings that this was also your view."[32] Similarly on February 15, 1943, Sir Reginald Maxwell, the Home Minister, speaking on an adjournment motion on the fast in the Central Legislative Assembly observed: "I must confess that speaking for myself, it is certainly repugnant to the Western ideas of decency to exploit against an opponent his feelings of humanity, chivalry or mercy, or to trifle with such a sacred trust as one's own life in order to play on the feelings of the public for the sake of some purely mundane object."[33]

Even if one does not agree with the official attitude of the British Government, there is no denying the fact that fasting as a technique to pressurize the opponent contains coercion in it in one form or the other. Fasting can be practiced only in a liberal socio-political set up. It can be practiced only against a sympathetic adversary. In case of communal award fast, one is tempted to speculate that had the adversary been M.A. Jinnah instead of Dr. Ambedkar, who was uncompromisingly critical of the Gandhian method and rather adamant in his views, and against whom significantly Gandhi never resorted to a fast although he had more conflicts with this individual in his life than with any other person, the results of the fast might have been quite different.[34] It is again highly doubtful whether this form of *Satyagraha* can be practiced in a political system where opponents of the Government can disappear at midnight never to be heard of again. It may not always lead to the opponent yielding ground. Even when the opponent makes necessary concessions. There is no certainty that he has done so out of conviction or of a change of heart. There is also the danger of fanatical or otherwise irresponsible persons motivated by political expediency or religious orthodoxy, using the technique of fasting for serving vested interests or even personnel ends.

The resort to fasting may be very inconvenient and irritating to the person or authority against whom it is used particularly if the person fasting is more popular than the person or authority against whom the fast is directed, and his cause logically answerable and sympathetically looked upon by those whose goodwill the person in authority cannot altogether ignore. He may find himself on the horns of dilemma, if, on the one hand, he does not wish to grant the fasting man's demand, and on the other, does not want to take the odium of allowing him to die. He does not want to be in the wrong box in the eyes of the world and does not know how to avoid it, without being obliged to do right. But if the invitation of suffering upon oneself is *himsa* or blackmail, as Lord Linlithgow termed it, then decidedly every form of *Satyagraha* is coercive and every demand accompanied by a threat to resort to self-suffering is blackmail. For there is no *Satyagraha* except for gaining some point, with preparedness to suffer for it until it is gained. Being a moral substitute for violent methods of achieving the same purpose, what is being sought in violence by inflicting suffering on the opponent is sought in *Satyagraha* by inviting suffering on oneself. And blackmail or coercion is never expected to invite self-suffering or to be done with a feeling to do or be good to the opponent. What is more the exact term for the effect of *Satyagraha* on the opponent is not nonviolent coercion. The term 'moral compulsion' or 'moral pressure' can demonstrate this effect rather more specifically. Gandhi himself preferred this form. Referring to his Rajkot fast he said, "If my fast which I hope will be avoided, is to be interpreted as pressure, I can only say that such moral pressure should be welcomed by all concerned."[35]

So this much pressure is always there when an attempt is made to exercise power over others. Hence when Gandhi talked of 'complete coercion free power' and when actually he exercised power, there seems to be an element of nonviolent moral pressure in his exercise of it. On this basis it will be wrong to conclude that there is some difference between his theory and practice. As stated earlier, what actually is, there are two Gandhis—Gandhi the idealist and Gandhi the realist statesman. In his idealism Gandhi dreamt of a complete pressure free political power, where there is no coercion, violent or nonviolent. But actually when he himself exercised power, there was definitely some pressure over others. But this is the contradiction between the abstract and the concrete, the ideal and the real and not between his theory and practice.

Gandhi was very well aware of this coercive element of political power and that is why he suggested complete diffusion of it. He was of the opinion that when power is concentrated at one place or around one person or group of persons, it may lead to violence, but when it is diffused, power loses its teeth and the element of coercion in it is neutralized. Repeatedly, he argued that no man however highly placed he may be, should have absolute power in his hands. But it is alleged in certain quarters that although Gandhi advocated complete diffusion of power and bitterly criticised its concentration, he himself exercised immense political power. Rather he had become a source of power himself. On the one hand, he tirelessly advocated for the decentralisation of power but on the other, the concentration of immense political power around him, hints at the existence of some gap between his theory and practice about the nature and role of political power. Let us examine this controversy in its true perspective and see whether actually there is some gap or not.

Right from the Nagpur session of Indian National Congress in 1920 till his death, Gandhi remained the main arbitor and policymaker of the Congress Party. The way in which he suspended the Non-cooperation Movement in 1922 after the tragedy of Chauri Chaura, the suspension of civil disobedience movement several times in 1932–34 and the handling of Quit India Movement in 1942 speaks volumes of the political power Gandhi exercised.His opponents have argued that he tolerated the views of others so long as his own power in the Congress was not touched. They say that when Subhas Chandra Bose successfully contested for the second term in 1939, despite the opposition of Gandhi, he showed great intolerance and consequently, Subhas Chandra Bose had to resign. Gandhi, who always went on advocating the decentralization of power but when someone challenged his own power, he became restless and managed to oust the legally elected president. This gives ample proof of a wide gap between his theory and practice. Tolerance of the view of the opponent is very essential for the decentralization. Further, his subsequent differences with the Congress Working Committee in the early forties and the stiff attitude he showed towards the then Congress President Maulana Abul Kalam Azad, showed that Gandhi always acted on his own and whenever there was a difference of opinion, the opponent either had to bow or had to go. But when the power is decentralized, equal weight should be given to the views of others and sometime one has to accept the views of others even if this is contrary to his own viewpoint. Consequently, it is argued that Gandhi had no real love for the decentralization of power when his own power was challenged. But if all these events are studied in their true perspective a more satisfactory conclusion can emerge.

As for his relation with the Indian National Congress is concerned, he was a father figure to the most of Congress men and had the power to decide all the matters alone. But actually, he never embarked on a new departure from the established policy without the consent of the Congress Working Committee. Even in 1922, when the tragic incident took place at Chauri Chaura, he summoned a meeting of the Congress workers at Bardoli on February 10,1922 and discussed with them the propriety or otherwise of starting civil disobedience in the face of terrible happening at Chauri Chaura.[36] In its meeting on February 11 and 12, the Congress Working Committee, at his instance suspended the movement and subsequently All India Congress Committee endorsed the Bardoli resolution after a heated discussion. There was a great resentment over it in the Congress circle. Pt. Motilal Nehru, Lala Lajpat Rai, C.R. Das, Subhas Chandra Bose, Pt. Jawaharlal Nehru and many other Congress leaders criticised this action of Gandhi. He, too, was aware of the fact that the drastic reversal of the entire programme was likely to appear to his followers politically unsound and unwise. But he took the step because he considered it to be morally sound and sought to justify it. Gandhi had also realised that there was 'a strong undercurrent of violence in the country. The incident of Chauri Chaura was just like a straw indicating the direction in which the wind was blowing; it was symptomatic of the general temper of the mass mind, which was steeped in violence and had not yet imbibed to any appreciable extent, the spirit of nonviolence. He did not regard it as an isolated event. Subhas Chandra Bose and Jawaharlal Nehru did not seem to realize that the non-cooperation movement was losing its nonviolent character. He had the uncanny insight to see the writing on the wall which other leaders lacked. When he realised that the movement was going out of the track, he applied the brake and cried a halt. There is nothing like concentrating the power around himself. Rather suspending the movement at the height of its popularity should be viewed as rejection of conventional power politics which assume concentration of power as its basic assumption.

Gandhi also suspended the civil disobedience movement in 1933-34. It is true that no duly elected body sanctioned the suspension of civil disobedience in 1933 for a good reason. The Congress was then an illegal organization, whose committees could not meet. But he did, even then consult a gathering at Poona of the few leading Congressmen who were not in prison. The movement was showing sign of exhaustion and also with a view to creating an atmosphere favourable for opening negotiations with the Government, he advised the Acting Congress President to suspend the movement for six weeks. But when the Government did not yield there was no option left to Gandhi but to resume civil disobedience. But what was resumed was individual and not mass civil disobedience. However, in March 1934, he again advised all Congressmen to suspend the movement. In the observance of democratic procedure few leaders have been more scrupulous. He never bullied, never asserted himself, never even raised his voice. The fact was, nonetheless, that his prestige was so immense, his magnetism so compelling, and the affection men bore him so genuine, that few dared to oppose him when once he had made up his mind.[37] The suspension of the movement does not give the impression that Gandhi always acted on his own and did not care to consult his fellow colleagues. But even in this instance there is nothing like concentration of power by Gandhi and if analysed in the proper context, there appear to be no gap between his theory and practice.

The controversy over the election of Subhas Chandra Bose as the Congress President in 1939 for the 2nd time also gave air to the belief that Gandhi never tolerated any challenge to his leadership. In a straight contest Bose had defeated Pattabhi Sitaramayya although Gandhi had put his whole weight in favour of Sitaramayya. In a statement to the Press, Gandhi admitted, "I must confess that from the very beginning I was decidedly against his re-election for reasons into which I need not go.... And since I was instrumental in inducing Dr. Pattabhi not to withdraw his name, a candidate when Maulana Saheb withdrew, the defeat is mine more than his."[38] The last sentence from this quote is unfortunate, the opponents of Gandhi argue that it introduces a personal element and makes the result of election a question of confidence in Gandhi. The fact was that the defeat of Sitaramayya was not actually the defeat of Gandhi. For Sitaramayya was only the covering candidate and was hardly known especially in the North. The unexpected withdrawal of Azad created the difficulty. The electors were not aware that by electing Bose, they would be abandoning Gandhi. They simply elected the more known and popular who had earlier the support of Gandhi. They wanted to have both Bose and Gandhi, but more Gandhi than Bose as the subsequent events proved. There was no personal element in this struggle. It was a matter of privilege. For Gandhi knew that Bose was more inclined towards violence than nonviolence and so with Bose at the helm of affairs the Congress could convert itself to violent means, which could be harmful to the Congress as well as to the country.

Whatever might have been the intention of Gandhi in making the above statement, it had an ominous significance. It resulted in the subsequent crossing of the floor by an appreciable number of delegates and consequently, Bose had to resign. Thus, it is argued in certain quarters that Gandhi should have shown the respect for the will of majority. Bose was duly elected and there was no bungling in the election. All the times Gandhi's will prevailed in connection with the election of presidents of the Congress and if someone was duly elected against his will he ought to bow. Tolerance and acceptance of the opinion of others is a basic assumption of the theory of decentralization. On the one hand, he is arguing a complete decentralization but on the other he is not accepting the will of others. So all this, according to these circles, gives a clear indication that Gandhi considered the election of Subhas Chandra Bose as a serious challenge to his leadership and this observation also is sufficient to point out a gap between his theory and practice.

But if the other side of the picture is analysed, a different conclusion emerges. This is true that Gandhi put all his weight behind Pattabhi Sitaramayya. There was a fundamental difference between the approaches of Gandhi and Bose. Even Bose did not make secret of his plans and policies. So, if one does not agree with the opinion of other, one has every right to criticise him. In the proper functioning of democratic institutions constructive criticism has a very important role to play. Criticism, rather checks the despotic functioning of the opponent. Gandhi did not approve Bose's methods and policy, so he had every right to criticise him. What is more, whenever Gandhi differed from anyone, he differed openly and unlike a conventional politician, he did not hide his feelings. He believed in the openness of every thing. And to conclude that Gandhi had no faith in decentralization of power, when his own power was challenged on the ground that he criticised Bose, is not a satisfactory approach. If the Congressmen followed him blindly, it is not because he pressurized them to follow but because everyone among them had realised that the surest way to keep the ranks united and to hold the masses together was to follow Gandhi loyally. Ever since Gandhi entered the political arena in India, the Congress began to preach his doctrines and other leaders were reduced to the secondary position. But all this does not mean that he did not care for the opinion of others. On the contrary, he gave due weight even to his political opponents. Several times, in order to accommodate the viewpoint of others, he modified his original stand. It is known to everybody that Gandhi was deadly against the partition of India in the beginning. But later on he gave due weightage to the opinion of others and kept quiet.

THE NATURE OF SATYAGRAHA: A SURVEY OF OPINIONS

We have seen above that the professed aim of *Satyagraha* is to persuade the opponent, to evoke the best in him and consequently to convert him, and as such there is no place of coercion in *Satyagraha*. The whole philosophy of *Satyagraha* is based on the fundamental assumption that man's nature is not beyond redemption and is perfectible. *Satyagraha* is active, constructive and synthesizing. But it is at the same time assertive. What does this assertion or 'aggression' amount to?

Scholars and interpreters differ in their opinion as to the nature of *Satyagraha*. A good number of them—all of them are not hostile critics, and some of them are pronouncedly sympathetic—have termed *Satyagraha* as a form of nonviolent coercion. We shall not try in this present study to judge the question whether coercion itself is intrinsically moral or immoral. We shall limit ourselves to considering the question as to whether *Satyagraha* contains elements of coercion or not. Important contributions being made on this point earlier, only a brief survey is deemed advisable.

Achariya J.B. Kripalani denies any motive of coercion in nonviolent resistance.[39]

Dr. B.S. Sharma observes: "If we represent the resistance through *Satyagraha* by the phrase 'moral coercion' then it gives the impression that *Satyagraha* is indistinguishable from violent resistance because of the association of the word coercion with violence. It would be better, therefore, to describe it as 'moral pressure' as Gandhi has suggested."[40]

The term 'coercion' is generally understood in terms of the application of physical force as its primary characteristic. But as has been defined above, it can be physical as well as moral or psychological.

In a pioneer study on the subject, Clarence Marsh Case contrasts violent and nonviolent coercion in the following terms:

"The nonviolent coercion is, and ought to be, a two-edged sword. In other words, it causes, and it is well that it should cause, inconvenience and suffering to those who wield it, as well as to those against whom it is invoked. In this it is exactly contrary to violent methods; for a principal reason accounting for the appalling growth of terrorism in modern times, is the unfortunate fact that the development of fire-arms and high explosives carries no automatic check and penalty for all who use them. As for the methods of nonviolent coercion, particularly the strike and the boycott, the public usually stands more or less in a position to determine which way the blow shall fall, that is, which party in the controversy shall suffer the greater loss. It is well that this should be so, for it is not in the interest of the general good that any group of men should exert irresponsible power… we hold that there is a most vital, salutary, and socially necessary connexion between the open, truthful, self-denying spirit of passive resistance and the constructive use of non-violent coercion in any of its forms…."[41]

Professor Case denies a contradiction in the term non-violent coercion, and he comments, at the outset of his essay, that the combination of nonviolent and coercion "is not the outcome of a preconceived notion, but represents a working arrangement, to which the writer came naturally during the course of a prolonged effort to find separately the working efficiency of these two principles of human conduct, neither of which was found functioning rightly alone."[42]

Dr. Bondurant approvingly quotes Professor Case and argues:

"Despite the protestations of a few followers of Gandhi that *Satyagraha* is always persuasive and never coercive, the method does contain a positive element of coercion. Non-cooperation, boycott, strike—all of these tools which may be used in *Satyagraha* involve an element of compulsion which may effect a change on the part of an opponent, which initially was contrary to his will and he may suffer from the indirect results of these actions. But there remains a significant difference between nonviolent and violent coercion." ("a difference of such great degree that it is almost a difference of kind.")

"*Satyagraha* allows for several stages of winning over an opponent. The first stage is characterized by persuasion through reason. The subsequent stages enter the realm of persuasion through suffering wherein the *Satyagrahi* attempts to dramatize the issues at stake and to get through to the opponent's unprejudiced judgement so that he may willingly come again into a level where he may be persuaded through rational argument. Finally, if persuasion by reason or by suffering does not succeed, the *Satyagrahi* may resort to nonviolent coercion characterized by such tools as non-cooperation or civil disobedience."[43]

In an article on "The Nature and Methods of Nonviolent Coercion", Anthony De Crespigny attempts a scientific analysis of the concept of nonviolent coercion. Nonviolent coercion is defined by Crespigny as an attempt to limit or destroy freedom of choice, which does not involve the threat or use of physical force, whether directed against persons or against property. This nonviolent coercion may be both direct and indirect.[44]

Reinhold Niebuhr does not draw any absolute line of demarcation between violent and nonviolent coercion. But he holds it to be important to make an analysis of the issues involved in the choice of methods of coercion in the social process and refers to Gandhi's nonviolent resistance in this regard. In his opinion:

"The distinguishing marks of violent coercion and conflict are usually held to be its intent to destroy either life or property. This distinction is correct if consequences are not confused with intent. Nonviolent conflict and coercion may also result in the destruction of life or property and they usually do. The difference is that destruction is not the intended but the inevitable consequence of nonviolent coercion. The chief difference between violence and nonviolence is not in the degree of destruction which they cause, though the difference is usually considerable, but in the aggressive character of the one and the negative character of the other. Nonviolence is essentially non-cooperation.

"Non-cooperation, in other words, results in social consequences not totally dissimilar from those of violence. The differences are important; but before considering them it is necessary to emphasise the similarities and to insist that nonviolence does coerce and destroy.

"The use of truth-force or soul-force, in the purer and more exact meaning of those words, means an appeal to the reason and goodwill of an opponent in a social struggle.

This may be regarded as a type of resistance, but it is not physical coercion. It belongs to the realm of education. It places no external restraints upon the object of its discipline. It may avail itself of a very vivid and dramatic method of education. It may dramatise the suffering of the oppressed, as for instance Mr. Gandhi's encouragement to his followers to endure the penalties of their civil disobedience 'long enough to appeal to the sympathetic chord in the governors and the lawmakers.' But it is still education and not coercion."

Niebuhr adds that education may contain coercive elements."[45]

Arthur Moore criticizes the high spiritual claim made for the theory of nonviolent non-cooperation, "because it drew a spiritual distinction between physical and mental violence." According to him, "It is a method of fighting which is open to unarmed people, and is on a par with the boycott and the strike, which are indeed part of its technique... But it is not a distinctively spiritual weapon any more than is armed rebellion or war....Bluntly stated, the economic object of boycotting Lancashire goods was to provide work, wages and food for one set of people in India and to deprive another set in England of work, wages and food. Between starving and killing, there is no notable moral difference."[46]

Roland H. Bainton says: "...non-violent resistance has two objectives. The first is to coerce the opponent into compliance through pressures mainly economic. Gandhi's boycott of British cotton goods was of this order. It differed not in principle from any other boycott and resembled also the strike as a weapon. Nonviolent resistance of this sort is preferable to war because it is more amenable to moral control, and less likely to produce those passions, which impede and preclude a generous peace. The other object is to persuade. Gandhi's fasts sought to persuade his followers to be disciplined and his opponents to yield."[47]

Dr. K. Satchidananda Murthy alleges that the Gandhian technique was not a case of "genuine nonviolence" since it "cannot be founded on national interests, or patriotism, but only on universalism" and that "the desire to overwhelm and coerce the minds of opponents seems to have been at work in many of the Gandhian movements and fasts."[48]

Professor Morris-Jones observes: "It constitutes, of course, a form of coercion or force—in the sense that it is designed to bring about change in actual political positions. But its nonviolent style is intended to make the change as a spontaneous consequence of changes in the minds of men. Its purpose is not capitulation and conquest but genuine agreement. Yet to describe it simply as a form of persuasion is to omit a great deal. Persuasion for one thing tends to be aimed in one direction only—against the opponent—whereas *Satyagraha* operates to at least the same extent on those who participate in the movement. The two effects are, of course, related: the rulers change their views about the ruled in part because the ruled have really changed; it is different to continue to despise men who have ceased to be despicable. As Gandhi once put it: 'We-the-people make the rulers what they are.' Moreover, persuasion has an air of the study circle and a movement of intellectual agreement, whereas *Satyagraha* appeals beyond the head to the conscience."[49]

An eminent British Marxist theoretician, Dr. John Lewis, who frankly acknowledges the legitimacy of social coercion, distinguishes Gandhi's *Satyagraha* from absolutist pacifism. According to him, the strength of nonviolent methods does not lie in their pacifism, but in their value as methods of coercion under certain conditions.

Speaking of Gandhi's technique of nonviolence, he comments as follows:

> "It is a form of compulsion, and as such will arouse resentment, especially where the nonviolent resisters have aroused public opinion, and thus beaten their opponents. R.B. Gregg even argues that the authorities will give way because they fear nonviolent resistance. This also suggests that its primary aim is not the conversion of its opponents at all, but their coercion.
>
> Nonviolent resistance may be useful tactics under certain conditions, but it partakes of the nature of war. Moral coercion becomes, in fact, a form of violence, even if it is not physical violence."[50]

In a discussion about Gandhi's nonviolent resistance, Jawaharlal Nehru posed the question, 'Conversion or Compulsion', and himself gave the answer as follows:

> "Whatever the motives of conversion behind it, in practice it has been a powerful weapon of compulsion as well, though that compulsion is exercised in the most civilised and least objectionable manner."[51]

He added: "...is the line between violence and nonviolence, compulsion and conversion, so obvious? Often enough, moral force is a far more terrible coercive factor than physical violence."[52]

Dr. Krishnalal Sridharani contended the thesis that *Satyagraha* is a form of nonviolent coercion though he acknowledged that "*Satyagraha* does contain an aspect of coercion, if in a somewhat modified form." He argued that the word 'coercion' has numerous connotations, and there is also in it a trace of punishment. The self-purifying and self-suffering phase of *Satyagraha*, on the other hand, does not allow punishment to be a part of the compulsion of nonviolent direct action. Hereon perhaps is founded, he argued, Gandhi's refusal to acknowledge the element of coercion as a part of his ideology of nonviolence.

He continued to add: "It is misleading, therefore, to describe *Satyagraha* as a form of nonviolent coercion as Clarence Marks Case has done in his book bearing that title. But it is equally misleading, on the other hand, to call *Satyagraha* a pure and simple process of conversion as Gandhi and some of his followers would have it. There is an element of what, for want of a better term, we shall call compulsion in it, if not of coercion, since the latter implies revenge and punishment."[53]

Dr. Paul F. Power concurs with the view of Sridharani.[54]

According to Richard Gregg, "Nonviolent resistance acts as a sort of moral jiu-jitsu. The non-violence and goodwill of the victim act like the lack of physical opposition by the user of the physical jiu-jitsu, to cause the attacker to lose his moral balance. He suddenly and unexpectedly loses the moral support, which the usual violent resistance of most victims would render him."[55]

As a technique of action, *Satyagraha* employs force. But the force employed in *Satyagraha* is not physical but moral. A moral weight is placed upon the adversary so that he yields. But the intent is never to score a victory over the opponent but to arrive at the truth. From the point of view of the *Satyagraha*, the technique is adopted to persuade the opponent and to wean him from error. No serious difference exists among the majority of the interpreters about the moral sincerity and nobility of Gandhi in his adoption of the technique. The difference lies in the assessment of the effect or consequence of the 'moral pressure' exerted on the person or the group against whom *Satyagraha* is directed. Moral pressure in certain circumstances. especially when employed on a mass level, is not so far removed from compulsion. Gandhi, it may be recalled, actually used the word 'compel' in his earlier writings.' One reviewer suggests that the use of the word 'compel' is unfortunate. We cannot agree to this opinion.

The assertive nature of *Satyagraha* is best expressed by the term 'compel'. And is compulsion very much different from coercion, if the term is understood in its wider sense, as has been defined above? Is this not a case of semantic quibble? The dictionary meaning of the term 'coerce' is to compel, to constrain. Nehru interchangingly used the terms, coercion and compulsion. To draw a line of distinction between the two terms, as had been drawn by Sridharani, may be justified on the ground that the odius connotation of coercion should not be associated with a moral weapon like *Satyagraha*, which should be sharply distinguished from the coercive war. It may be argued that coercion being usually associated with employment of physical force should be avoided in an exposition of *Satyagraha*. But in a scientific analysis the distinction between the two terms should not be overemphasized.

To close the discussion. We should like to observe that *Satyagraha*, while expressing the ideal of love and the spirit of moral goodwill, contains an element of coercion which is wholly dissimilar from overt expression of physical violence, 'coercion whose setting is drawn by its nonviolent qualifications.'

SATYAGRAHA—ITS FUTURE

To speak about the future of *Satyagraha* may be a journey into the regions of speculation, but it is not an idle or useless job. Those who think about the future of humanity have also to think about the way humanity will decide its disputes. A human community without wars is the only hope of survival for mankind, but it may yet take centuries before such an order comes into being.

Mahavira, Buddha, Jesus and many other saints have come and gone. They preached the doctrine of non-injury, of love. They have profoundly influenced humanity by setting up high ideals. Two thousand years have rolled away. And yet what do we find today? There are, no doubt, individuals here and there inspired by the highest ideals of love and charity, but beyond their personal lives, they often seem to be powerless in substantially moulding group-life or social life. The ultimate sanction in group-life and social conflicts is still violence. Even if negotiations and arbitration seem to succeed many times, they do so because of the fear of war and destruction, rather than as a result of reason or love of peace.

It is in a world like this that Gandhi passionately pleaded for the abolition of all violence and duplicity in the affairs of men and nations. He declared with uncompromising firmness that if truth and nonviolence were good for the individual, they were good for the group as well. He went further than Tolstoy and all others in this field by demonstrating the working of nonviolence in social conflicts of great magnitude.

Truth was his greatest love. He called Truth his God. He saw no safer and better approach to it than through innocence, nonviolence, love. This arose out of his perception of the truth that 'all life is one'. Moreover, he argued, erring mortal as man is, he ought not to be dogmatic about the truth he sees. If others see the same truth in the same way as one sees it, then what other things can make their relation sweeter than love? But even when others do not see eye to eye with him the lover of truth fights a winning battle if he takes to the path of love and suffering and refuses to force it down the throat of others by infliction of pain. He does not merely meditate, on love or nonviolence but lives it. His love translates itself into service, suffering and sacrifice for others. His love does not stop at saying, 'Love thy neighbour as thyself'. It goes beyond that and makes him look upon all creatures as his neighbours and makes him love the neighbour more than himself. He would not perhaps die for himself because that would take away the very motive for dying. But he would die for others. Thus his life becomes consecrated in the pursuit of truth through loving service and sacrifice with goodwill unto all.

Out of this kind of life of Gandhi arose the doctrine of *Satyagraha*, the doctrine which seeks to solve social conflicts through self-suffering. For the first time he applied what is called Christian ethics by European writers to public affairs and political conflicts. Whether the Christian masters in Africa and India appreciated it or not, he stuck to his methods to the last. Will Durant in his Case for India says: 'The Indian situation represents the most extensive efforts ever made to test the practicability of Christianity. If India should succeed, the stock of Christianity (by which we mean the ethical ideals of Christ) would rise throughout the world; courtesy and peace would be in good repute unparalleled.' For an unbroken period of twenty-five years Gandhi used the same weapon for the solution of the Indian problem—the attainment of her freedom.

Even before India attained success in achieving her objective of Swaraj, through the use of *Satyagraha* she travelled a long way towards it. *Satyagraha* achieved many a signal and unqualified success in fighting local wrongs, some of them very old and obstinate.

Some who speak with doubt and hesitation seem to think that once Gandhi was removed from the scene, *Satyagraha* had no future. It was his immense faith, his remarkable personality that had been responsible for the success of *Satyagraha*, they would say. It is to a great extent true that his personality was the base on which *Satyagraha* stood for years. But at the same time, the stature his personality attained was itself due to his having been a staunch *Satyagrahi*. It was not Gandhi who made *Satyagraha* but it was *Satyagraha* which made Gandhi. His personality was not something separate and foreign to *Satyagraha*. It will not be right to say that Gandhi was, as it were, a patron of *Satyagraha*. If it was a matter of obligation between the two, it is *Satyagraha* which obliged Gandhi rather than the reverse. *Satyagraha* would stand or fall by its own merits, only the extent of its application and popularity would depend upon personalities from time to time. The main question is whether it supplies a really felt human need. If it does; it is bound to live and prosper, Gandhi or no Gandhi. The principle is always greater than the person who discovers it or applies it. So too is *Satyagraha* far greater than all Christs and Gandhis. *Satyagraha* is eternal. Gandhi too would be eternal only to the extent that he was able to reflect it and live it in his own life.

Another argument that the sceptics put forward is that it is only the helpless and the weak that would think of *Satyagraha* and not the strong ones of the earth. They would say that it has no future so far as the strong and the mighty are concerned. Thus, they would not accept the statement of Gandhi that *Satyagraha* is a weapon of the strong. Even so, if according to them it has a great future only with regard to weak peoples, it is not a small thing, because it is often the weak that require a way out. The world is full of the weak. If they were all feeling helpless so long, and if now they feel they can do something to improve their lot and add to their self-respect, it is a great achievement. It is like finding a remedy for the anaemic of the earth. Feeling helpless is itself a mental disease that cripples people. Hope and faith, therefore, are always tonics and if in addition people have a weapon with which to fight and come out of their helplessness, such a weapon is bound to have a great future. Nor can it be said absolutely that the strong and the mighty who have weapons and who can wield weapons would never take to it. If in India *Satyagraha* had appealed only to 'the weak and the meek Hindu' of the plains, it would have been another matter. But now we have seen that the warlike Sikhs could and did wield *Satyagraha*, and that too in a masterly way. We have also seen that the sturdy and strong Mussalman Pathan of the mountainous frontier of India fell in love with it, discarded his sword and the spirit of revenge, and took to nonviolence. These two instances show that the statement that it is a weapon of the weak has no basis. My plea is that the adoption of *Satyagraha* does not and should not merely and always depend upon the strength or weakness of body or mind. One has to weigh its use from the point of view of the ultimate good, of ends and means, of higher culture, of human trends, of practicability, of profit and loss. If one feels, after full consideration, that violence is a better way, then one is free to use it, nay it is one's duty to take to it. But if one feels that nonviolence is a better way, then whether one is weak or strong, armed or unarmed, one has to prepare oneself for that path and follow it at all costs.

This is the background and we have now to peep into the future. It is certainly difficult to speak of the future. There is no doubt that the past of *Satyagraha* is brilliant, its present is interesting and its future promising. But the future will depend upon certain concrete factors, if all goes well.

Unless the world is really war-weary and the people disgusted with the barren results of mutual slaughter, and until they are free from the spell of war-mongers, they are not going to be interested in the doctrine of love and peace. The main attraction in *Satyagraha* is that it is able to give results, better results than war and at a lesser cost and with a high moral coefficient. But unless there is hunger for peace and peaceful methods this attraction is likely to prove fruitless. No doubt, great thinkers, philosophers and spiritual leaders are hankering after peaceful methods. But theirs is yet a sentimental or reformist endeavour. They are not willing to put themselves against the forces that stand for violence. They are yet trying very feebly to organize themselves against the war-makers in their own countries. But the number of protestants against war is increasing and that is certainly a good sign. It goes without saying that unless such people organize and are willing to go to the extent of taking to direct action, they will not be able to dislodge those who stand for and resort to violence.

Once there is a real demand for peaceful direct action, then the spread of the doctrine is easy. It has been sufficiently demonstrated. These demonstrations have been known throughout the world, though better publicity may be necessary. The technique has been sufficiently developed to be understood by intelligent as well as illiterate people. One wishes that Gandhi the originator, the experimenter, the demonstrator, the expert, were still alive to dispel any doubts, correct any mistakes and to guard against misinterpretations. That could not be. But Vinoba was there, and Dr. Martin Luther King Jr. by his martyrdom, has left a blazing trail for the world to see and follow.

Possibly the western countries with their more vigorous and active life may be able to develop this science of *Satyagraha* much more rapidly than India, the land of its birth. It might be that India by her spiritual traditions and by her age-long culture was a congenial place to give rise and shape to this great doctrine. But once the method has been evolved, it can be used by all who wish to go along that path and there is nothing in it that bars others from following it. It is based on human psychology and the human mind is everywhere almost the same.

If one were to look at human evolution and the evolution of human institutions, one sees that man has been averse to violence and is proceeding progressively towards nonviolence. If that trend continues, there is no reason why in the next few decades *Satyagraha* should not get a more honoured place in the institutions that go to solve human conflicts. *Satyagraha* as a way of life has for long had a permanent and prominent place in the lives of men. There is no doubt about it. But what we are mainly concerned with here is *Satyagraha* as a social weapon, a means for social change. Even if it gains a foothold in western societies as an intra-national weapon for solving social conflicts, it would go a long way towards advancing the cause of nonviolence. Today in Europe only impotent liberalism or helpless violent extremism unable to organize itself is in evidence as a method of combating evil. No violent organization worth the name can be tolerated for long by any well-armed government. Thus when all the institutional procedures and constitutional methods have failed, the reformers have no remedy today except fretting and fuming. If the reformers make bold to take to this nonviolent direct action after preparation, they are sure to bring due moral pressure on any group of men on any institution, or any government.

It is a good sign that great thinkers like Romain Rolland, Albert Einstein, C.E.M. Joad, Aldous Huxley and Gerald Heard have also thought along the lines of nonviolent resistance. There are many chapters in Aldous Huxley's book, *Ends and Means,* which are an excellent commentary on the Gandhian method of *Satyagraha*. It well repays reading at any time. Richard Gregg's *Power of Nonviolence* is a regular treatise on *Satyagraha*, its implications, its technique, and its discipline. Mulford Q. Sibley's *The Quiet Battle* is illustrative of the nonviolent battles waged since the dawn of history. These books show that the western mind is already applying itself to the study of this important subject. But one need not be too optimistic. We must ultimately depend upon the full success of that method in India even after *Swaraj*, and that alone can ensure the future of *Satyagraha* as an effective, efficient weapon in the armoury of the ardent reformer, the restless revolutionary, and the fighter for good and great causes.

NOTES

1. M.K. Gandhi, *Satyagraha in South Africa*, *op. cit.*, p. 295.
2. *Ibid.*
3. Jai Narain Sharma, "Gandhi: The Millennium Man", *The Times of India*, October 2, 2000.
4. *CWMG*, Vol. XII, p. 350.
5. *Ibid.*, Vol. XIV, p. 217.
6. Romain Rolland, *Mahatma Gandhi: The Man Who Became One With the Universal Being*, New Delhi, Publications Division, Ministry of Information and Broadcasting, Government of India, 1990, p. 93.
7. *CWMG*, Vol. XXII, p. 418.
8. *Ibid.*, p. 377.
9. Jawaharlal Nehru, *An Autobiography*, London, The Bodley Head, 1958, p. 81.
10. *CWMG*, Vol. XXII, p. 351.
11. Jai Narain Sharma, *Gandhi's View of Political Power*, *op. cit.*, p. 128.
12. Gene Sharp, *The Politics of Non-Violent Action: The Dynamics of Non-violent Action*, Part III, Boston, Porter Sarget Publishers, 1973, p. 706.
13. *CWMG*, Vol. XLIII, p. 6.
14. *Harijan*, 25-3-1939, p. 64.
15. Geoffery, K. Roberts, *A Dictionary of Political Analysis*, London, Longman, 1971, p. 34.
16. Horace M. Kallen "Coercion" in R.A. Edwin (ed.) *Encyclopaedia of Social Sciences*, Vols. 3 & 4, New York, Macmillan, 1956, pp. 617-19.
17. Jawaharlal Nehru, *op. cit.*, p. 539.
18. Joan V. Bondurant, *op. cit.*, p. 9.

19. K.L. Shridharni, *op. cit.*, p. 263.
20. D.G. Tendulkar, Vol. III, *op. cit.*, p. 173.
21. B.R. Ambedkar, *What Gandhi and Congress Has Done to the Untouchables*, Bombay, Thacker and Co. Ltd., 1946, pp. 322-28
22. *Ibid.*, p. 88.
23. Jai Narain Sharma, *Gandhi's View of Political Power*, *op. cit.*, pp. 134-35.
24. *CWMG*, Vol. LXIX, p. 22
25. *Ibid.*, p. 32.
26. *Ibid.*, p. 33.
27. *Ibid.*, p. 270.
28. *Ibid.*
29. *Ibid.*, p. 273.
30. *Ibid.*, Vol. LXXVII, p. 51.
31. *Ibid.*, p. 56.
32. Quoted from "*Gandhiji's Correspondence with the Government*," 1942-44, Ahmedabad, Navajivan Publishing House, 1975, p. 28.
33. D.G. Tendulkar, Vol. VI, *op. cit.*, p. 213.
34. Jayanti Bandyopadhyaya, *Social and Political Thought of Mahatma Gandhi*, Bombay, Allied Publishers, 1969, p. 244.
35. *Harijan*, 11-3-1939, p. 46.
36. *CWMG*, Vol. XXII, pp. 377-78.
37. H.S.C. Polak, H.N. Brailsford and Lord Pethick, Lawrence, *Mahatma Gandhi*, London, Odham Press Limited, 1949, p. 211.
38. *CWMG*, Vol. LXVIII, p. 359.
39. J.B. Kripalani, *Gandhi: His Life and Thought*, New Delhi, Publications Division, Ministry of Information and Broadcasting, Government of India, 1968, p. 149.
40. Bishan Sarup Sharma, *Gandhi As A Political Thinker*, Allahabad, Indian Press Pvt. Ltd., 1956, p. 60.
41. C.M. Case, *Non-Violent Coercion*, London, George Allen and Unwin, 1923, pp. 404-405.
42. *Ibid.*, p. 3.
43. Joan Bondurant, *op. cit.*, pp. 9, 11.
44. Political Studies, London, Vol. XII, No. 2 June 1964, pp. 256-65.
45. Reinhold Niebuhr, *Moral Man and Immoral Society*, New York, Charles Scribner's Sons, 1947, pp. 240-45.
46. Arthur Moore, "The evolution of Mr. Gandhi", in S. Radhakrishnan (ed.) *Mahatma Gandhi: Essays and Reflections*, Allahabad, Kitabistan, 1944, pp. 174-75.
47. Ronald H. Baiston, *Christian Attitude Toward War and Peace*, London, Hodder and Stoughton, 1961, p. 257.
48. K. Satichidananda Murthy and A.C. Banquet, *Studies in Problems of Peace*, Bombay, Asia Publishing House, 1960, p. 197.

49. W.H. Morris Jones, "Mahatma Gandhi-Political Philosopher?" *The Indian Journal of Political Science*, Vol. XXXI, No. 3, July-September 1960, pp. 221-22.
50. John Lewis, *The Case Against Pacifism*, London, George Allen and Unwin, 1939, pp. 110-111.
51. Jawaharlal Nehru, *op. cit.*, p. 540.
52. *Ibid.*, p. 539.
53. K.L. Shridharni, *op. cit.*, p. 264.
54. Paul, F., Power, *Gandhi on World Affairs*, London, George Allen and Unwin, 1961, p. 86.
55. Richard B. Gregg, *The Power of Non-Violence*, Ahmedabad, Navajivan Publishing House, 1960, p. 41.

5

Conflict Resolution: Meaning, Causes and Typologies

Conflict Resolution is a comprehensive concept to cover all ideas and a actions that help resolve various kinds of conflicts. It is a term which has its roots in international law, and theory of conflict, cooperation and integration. During the 1990s it took, more significant and central meaning. Systematic study is found only from the middle of 1980s, and the literature has grown in recent years.

Lest it be construed that conflict resolution is a recent concern, it would be worthwhile reiterating that conflicts and the ways to resolve them have been one of the main preoccupations of man and copious literature exists on how man through the ages fought and resolved his problem. The conflict resolution processes that have now evolved are effective only to the extent that parties to disputes are helped to cost accurately the consequences of change or no change.

Within these limitations it can be claimed that we are moving towards insights and processes in which bargaining of needs against interests can be avoided, and in which the parties concerned can define needs and interests and cost the consequences of preserving interests at the expense of needs. It is, furthermore, a process, unlike change by organised violence, to enable parties to move from point A to point B, conscious of the outcomes. In this way, change can be more than merely the substitution of one ruling elite for another which will also pursue sectional interests at the expense of human needs.

Translated on to the global scene and the relations between the Great Powers, this is a significant discovery. Both sides fear change lest it prejudice their relative power positions. Yet both sides know that change in every political system is not merely inevitable, but also desirable. The United States does not particularly desire to defend repressive feudal systems in Central America and elsewhere throughout the globe; but it fears the consequences of unpredictable political change. The former Soviet Union, if we could deduce its position from reactions by scholars there, was astonished and dismayed by the high level of violence that followed change in Ethiopia. If there were a means of reliably bringing about change with desired outcomes, many situations in world society would no longer attract Great Power interventions.

These considerations direct attention to what is probably the most serious problem in global politics, for it constantly leads the great powers into conflict: the deformities of domestic systems. These deformities are not confined to smaller and underdeveloped states. The United States has its share and they make it most defensive against the introduction of more egalitarian systems anywhere in its sphere of influence. Russia is self-conscious of its non-participatory society and becomes anxious when there are demands in bordering states for increased participation, even if only at the work level.

Before we can proceed further, there is a need to establish a preliminary definition of conflict resolution. Conflict resolution is a situation where the conflicting parties enter into an 'agreement that solves their central incompatibilities, accept each other's continued existence as parties and cease all violent action against each other. This means, of course, that conflict resolution is something that necessarily comes after conflict. It means that we first need to have concepts and tools for the analysis of conflict. This is what conflict theory is all about.

Let us scrutinize key elements in this definition. The agreement is normally a formal understanding, a document signed under more or less solemn conditions. However, there can be more informal, implicit understandings worked out between the parties. Such agreements may exist in secret documents, for instance, a crucial promise made as a precondition for the formal arrangements, or as deals about which the parties have been more or less explicit. Many cases are likely to see as much dispute around such informal understandings as over the formalized documents. Furthermore, such informal pacts require considerable trust between the parties. They are, most likely, not made without there being a formal arrangement. Thus, the formal document is important for any peace process.

The definition talks about the parties accepting each other's continued existence as parties. This is an important element as it is meant to distinguish a peace agreement from an agreement of capitulation. An agreement of capitulation is the strongest agreed expression of victory and defeat. It means that one side lays down its struggle, dissolves its organisation, departs from the disputed territory and, in short, ceases to be an actor of influence and significance. An example is a withdrawal agreement. This is an arrangement where one side agrees to remove its troops from an area of dispute and where this is the only matter the agreement regulates. The withdrawing party is not likely, however, to see it as a matter of capitulation, although the essence of the agreement is to end the party's participation in the conflict. An example is the soviet withdrawal from Afghanistan that was agreed in 1988 and implemented by 1989. It ended the dominant role of the Soviet Union in internal affairs. Another example is the resignation of a party leader from the government, where he/she also leaves the country. This was the case with the departure of General Raoul Cedras from Haiti in 1994, ending military rule of the democratically elected government of Mr. Arstide.

However, the conflict resolution agreements of interest here are more complex than such arrangements. Peace agreements refer to situations in which the fighting parties accept each other also as parties in future dealings with one another. It means that nobody wins all that there is to win, but no one loses all that there is to lose. Such arrangements are more difficult to maintain, no doubt, but they are more frequent than may perhaps be imagined. Of course the word 'accept' in the definition does not imply that the parties agree to everything or that they like each other. It only means that they accept the other as much as they need for the agreement to be implemented by the opposing sides.

The formulation that the parties cease all violent action against each other is most important. It is normally part of the same treaty but it can be done as a separate undertaking. Often the cessation of violence is made public at about the same time as the peace agreement is concluded. To the public at large, it means that the war ends and the dangers of being killed are reduced. Sometimes, however, cease-fire agreements can precede the actual conclusion of the agreement regulating the incompatibilities between the parties. There is debate whether cease-fires should precede, be parallel to, or come after the more political agreements. There are a number of truce agreements that have lasted a long time, without resulting in peace accords. The armistice lines drawn in 1949 separating Israel from its Arab neighbours were used in the agreements with Egypt 30 years later. The same territorial divisions are relevant for a final agreement between Israel and Palestine. The lines have existed for more than 50 years. The separation lines between Korea's two states in 1953 have reached the same respectable age.

Cease-fire agreements, in other words, are closer to conflict management, a way of freezing a military status quo, and do not necessarily result in peace efforts. It is to conclude that a peace agreement, solving the central incompatibilities between the parties, which does not include a simultaneous undertaking to cease fighting, is not likely to be credible. Thus, the agreements included as conflict resolution measures are those which both solve incompatibilities and end fighting.

A strong statement is that conflicts are solvable. This is not necessarily an idealistic or optimistic position. Most actors in conflicts will find themselves in need of negotiations at one time or another. Even if a conflict results in war and destruction, there may have been other options and alternative paths for the conflict. There are frequent statements on the inevitability of conflict, violence and war. Indeed, finding solutions may often be difficult. This difficulty not only arises out of political constraints, but can also be due to a lack of insight or imagination. There are also views of the desirability and even necessity of violence and war. Unbearable conditions or impossible threats may make such opinions understandable. Too often, however, the results of war negate the very hope for a better future that may initially have motivated the war. Few wars follow the paths anticipated by the actors. Short wars may avoid such pitfalls, but who is to guarantee that a war will be short? Many wars have started from this premise. Afterwards, it will be asked: were all avenues used to find a peaceful solution prior to the initiation of war? Only after this can be convincingly proven to the arguments of inevitability and desirability approach validity. Thus, the determined search for a solution is not only a moral question; it is also a rational one. This is the sole way in which a free society will be prepared to accept the strains of war. Indeed, if conflicts are exposed to such early challenges, solutions may actually be found, even in unexpected situations. Thus, conflicts are solvable and there are many and varied experiences of such solutions.

If conflicts are solvable, is it also true that conflicts—sooner or later—will be solved? Clearly, once a conflict has developed into a war the options are fewer. At that moment, the primary actors will pursue victory rather than a joint solution. The victory of one side over the other is, then, a possible outcome, even to the point of the other's capitulation, dissolution and disappearance as an actor. The record shows that this is what happens in some conflicts, but by no means all conflicts will come to an end at some point in time.

The term conflict has variety of meanings. To some, it refers to behaviour or action. There is conflict when a trade union goes on strike or an employer locks out its employees. It is also conflict when two states are at war with one another, and where battlefield events determine their relations. The actions constitute the conflict. If this were all, however, it would mean that a conflict ends this behaviour. Few would agree to this. A cease-fire is not the conflict. Even the cession of verbal statements, non-violent actions, the mobilization of petitions, demonstrations, boycotts and sanctions may only indicate that there is an interlude in the conflict. Actions may resume at some later stage. There may still be dissatisfaction. Obviously, conflict is more than the behaviour of the parties.

A closer look indicates that the parties in an industrial dispute will not cease their actions until there is some movement on the issues which sparked the dispute. The 'issue' refers to the incompatible positions taken by the parties, motivating their actions. This, then, is a deeper understanding of what a conflict is. It contains a severe disagreement between at least two sides, where their demands cannot be met by the same resources at the same time. This is incompatibility. Positions are incompatible. There is some form of scarcity. If there is an abundance of resources, the demands from the various sides may easily be met. The incompatibility can be solved. If there are limited resources, however, problems will arise. The easy solutions are no longer available and more ingenious ways have to be found. When the parties adjust their demands so that there is no longer scarcity, the conflict disappears. The incompatible demands have been handled. Incompatibility appears to be a key existence of conflict. If there are no actions although it is possible for an outsider to point to incompatibilities, there is a latent conflict. Manifest conflicts require both action and incompatibility.

'Conflict' does exists, even if there are no actions taken or demands formulated. The conflict is internal to the system. Similar descriptions also can be found for the interstate system. It is argued that sovereign states are inevitably locked into conflict with one another. States are continuously preparing to defend themselves from possible attack in order to protect their own survival. Such preparations lead others to believe that there are real dangers, thus they do the same. These are dynamics of the well-known security dilemma.[1] This perspective suggests that the existence of one state is a danger to any other state. As long as there is unpredictability in the system, there will be fear and thus conflict. For our purposes, it means that actors or parties are fundamental for conflict to exist. If the actors are formed, and if they make an analysis where their needs for survival are in conflict with others, then there is conflict built into the system. This means that the history of the actors, the actors' understanding of their own role and their resources are important elements in conflict analysis.

From this, one can conclude that conflict consists of three components: action, incompatibility and actors. Combining them, we arrive at a complete definition of a conflict as a social situation in which a minimum of two actors (parties) strive to acquire at the same moment in time an available set of scarce resources. This definition brings together essential elements from a number of commonly used definitions. It includes the actors or 'parties' in the definition which, as we have just seen, is basic.[2]

The synonym for incompatible or irreconcilable, for example, we often refer to conflicting values, beliefs or loyalties. A conflict starts when there exist two different sets of interests, aims, values, and beliefs. In other words, a conflict is a state of affairs characterized by the existence of incompatible aspect of relationship. But a conflict exists only when the incompatibility of interest and value is perceived by both the parties concerned. Fear of future injury can also operate as powerfully as the perception of a present injury. At the initial stage, a conflict is called only a latent or covert conflict. This means that the conflict exists only at the initial level at which both the parties perceive their interests as incompatible. But a latent or covert conflict becomes an overt conflict when both the parties concerned decide to resolve it by a behaviour that is likewise incompatible or mutually injurious. In other words, a latent conflict exists when the incompatible interests are perceived and it is transformed into an overt conflict when incompatibility of interests is sought to be resolved by incompatible means.

A distinction should also be made between a non-identified conflict and identified conflict. By the former it meant the conflict based on the existence of mutually perceived incompatible interest that are taken as residing in one or few definite areas of dispute, while an identified conflict is one which is identified with the self of a state and which may exist even in the absence of definite areas of dispute. However, there is no definite law according to which a latent conflict develops into an overt conflict and a non-identified conflict transforms itself into an identified conflict. Perhaps it depends to a considerable extent upon what Robert North calls a "States' threshold of tolerance" or what Chester Barnard calls, "the zone of indifference". In other words, the process of transformation of conflict is at rest only so long as the injured party tolerates the injury. But the extent of tolerance is itself dependent upon the calculation of many factors.

In any case, the concept of conflict applies to almost all its forms, economic, national or international. In his brilliant study of conflict, Kenneth Boulding has applied his theory of economic conflict to international conflict and he states a few peculiar characteristics of international conflicts. One such characteristic of international conflict is that the competition of states is marked by dramatic alternation of peace and war. This alternation can also be called an alternation between latent conflict and overt conflict. In the case of latent conflict, the means used are threats, promises and pressure, where as the means used in the case of overt conflict is war

Social life is always an admixture of conflict and peace. In society, "in every state of peace the condition of future conflict, and in every conflict the conditions of peace are framed."[1] In contemporary as well as historical societies, from primitive to civilized, perhaps we cannot find even a single instance in which a society exists or has ever existed without social conflict in its system. Cleavages and consensus are simultaneously present in all human relations.[2] As Max Weber says: "Conflict cannot be excluded from social life."[3] Therefore, social conflicts are ubiquitous, come in many forms, and involve vastly different kinds of parties, ranging from individual persons to large macro units such as nation states. Some are dramatic and well published, whereas others are much more subtle and hidden from public view.

Living beings everywhere compete for the means of existentence. Competition takes the more intense form. We call it conflict or when instead of merely using available resources for production or consumption purposes, contender try to hamper, disable or destroy rivals.[4]

Conflict can occur within state as civil wars, insurrections, or terrorism or it can occur among states as wars or outside-supported insurrections. Appropriate activities from another, can be within or among states.

Conflict may assume myriad forms and may influence a vast array of human activities. In politics, conflict may be over a party's nomination or the votes to win an elected office, or it may arise from rent seeking. Rent seeking involves an agent or collective expending resources to obtain a return that results in no net gain to society, that is, rent seeking concerns actions to gain a transfer of resources.[5]

Conflict may also involve litigation and legal manoeuvres over the disposition of will or property. In labour markets, conflict is associated with strikes, labour lockouts, and employee-employer remunerations and benefits. Conflicts also concerns terrorist campaigns designed to achieve political or cultural objectives, including resource transfers.

During 21st century, conflict will involve earth's natural assets, including its species, water, rivers, oceans, atmosphere, stone shield, and minerals. As populations grow and the Earth's carrying capacity is increasingly exceeded, more effort will be put into the appropriation of needed resources, resulting in conflict and defence growing in importance. Disputes over territories and resources already represent the leading cause of civil war and interstate conflicts.

NATURE OF CONFLICT

In everyday language conflict denotes overt, coercive interactions in which two, or more, contending parties seek to impose their will on one another. Fights, violence and hostility are the terms customarily employed to describe a conflict relationship. The range of conflict phenomena is, however, much wider than that implied by its physical connection, it is used to describe inconsistencies as well as the process of trying to solve them, it has physical and moral implications, it embraces opinions as well as situations and a wide range of behaviour. Conventional usage of the term is in consistent with the full range of conflict phenomena.

In attempting to analyse conflict phenomena, particular attention has to be paid to the term itself, to the explicit judgements that are made about it (*e.g.* is it 'good' or 'bad') and effort to distinguish it from related, if distinct, events (*e.g.* tension, war, hostility, etc.). Most perspectives on social conflict are etymological or they may be classified as 'actor-oriented' or 'system-oriented'. From an actor oriented perspective conflicts are necessary, indeed inevitable; from a system oriented perspective, conflicts may be undesirable because they may interfere with the goal of system maintenance.

Conflict refers to a situation in which a person is motivated to engage in two or more mutually exclusive activities. Motives are important in conflict and for this reason the term motivational conflict is often used. Conflict exists in every society. It may occur on many different levels:

(a) On the overt behavioural levels.
(b) On the verbal level.
(c) On the system level.

Conflict occurs only when the overt, verbal, symbolic or emotional responses required to fulfil one motive are incompatible with those required to fulfil another. Social existence involves a great many conflicts. The individual in society, subject to the pressure of the many groups to which he belongs and the demands of the many roles he must play, often experiences personal conflict. The entire process of socialization of the child has been viewed as a conflict between the individuals and society.[6]

Conflict is the fundamental form of opposition-oriented relationships and dissociative interaction. The process of conflict goes on in every society. Desire for social prestige, economic benefit, power and defeat or destruction of enemy result in conflict among individual and groups.

Jessie Bernard distinguishes between two kinds of conflicts, conflicts which are about something on the one hand which she calls issue conflicts and conflicts which are in some sense illusory, which are not really about anything, but which are simply developed out of dynamic reactions or misunderstandings. The fundamental characteristic of an issue conflict is that there should be scarcity of some desired resource or good. There are, however, two kinds of issue conflicts, those which arise out of the use of threats and those which arise out of exchange. When an armed robber accosts you with "your money or your life", though this may look superficially like an exchange, it is fundamentally very different system. It is certainly an issue conflict. If you give him money there a redistribution of economic goods, for he has more and you have less. This is, however, at best a zero-sum game (his gain equals your loss), Exchange is a positive-sum game in the sense that it will not take place unless both parties feel themselves to be better off.[7]

Conflict is more generic term than war—a perspective that is in back of the adage that war is just an extension of national policy in other forms. Wars and lesser struggles between nations are in their nature conflicts between organized structures.

George Simmel considers conflict as a separate subject, without references to any larger subject, like the historical dialectic or revolutionary survival. The Central idea in his essay 'The Functions of Social Conflict' is constructive. He gave a positive form of the concept of conflict. It is a kind of integration method: Conflict ends the opposition and equality prevalent in society.[8]

A.W. Green defined Conflict as the deliberate attempt to oppose, resist or coerce the will of another while Gillin says, Conflict is the social process in which individuals or groups seek their ends by directly challenging the antagonists by violence or threat of violence. As a process, it is the anti-thesis of cooperation.

According to Young and Meck, Conflict is the passionate and violent form of opposition in which the main concern is to achieve the goal by defeating the opponent.

Clinton F. Fink argues for a broad definition. Conflict is "any social situation of process in which two or more entities are linked by at least one form of antagonist psychology or at least one form of antagonistic interaction."[9] The concept at the psychological antagonism embraces such states as incompatible goals, mutually exclusive interests, traditional enmities and emotional hostility, and concept antagonism interaction ranges from the most direct violent and unregulated struggle to the most subtle, indirect and highly regulated forms of mutual interference.

Robin Williams, Jr. embraces diverse forms of conflict; although he is not always this explicit, he defines conflict in one essay as "interaction in which one party intends to deprive control, injure, or eliminate, another, against the will of that other. Pure conflict is a fight, its goal is to immobilize, neutralize, destroy or otherwise harm an opponent. In the impure world of actuality some overt struggles are conducted accordingly to roles and for limited goals, oppositional behaviour may then have the primary goal of winning rather than of injuring the opponent, we then usually call the encounter a game.

Some games merge into debates in which the primary aim is to convince or persuade opponents or others of the rightness or correctness or attractiveness of one's views or claims."[10]

Ralf Dahrendorf in his essay "Element entire Theorie des Soz Konflikte", in his Gesselleschaft und Freiheit[11] suggested that there are six basic needs for an adequate theory of social conflict. For him the most useful definition is one in terms of opposition between two, and only two parties, whether conscious or unconscious. He proceeds to offer a taxonomy that is here presented in tabular form adapted from Ralf Dahrendrof, Gesselleschaft Und Freiheit, p. 206.

Social Unit	*Equal Against Equal*	*Subordinate Against Part*	*Whole Against Subordinate*
A. Roles	Family role *vs.* occupational role	Occupational role *vs.* labour-union role	Social personality *vs.* family role
B. Groups	Boys *vs.* Girls (in school class)	Father *vs.* Children	Family *vs.* prodigal son
C. Sectors	Air Force *vs.* Army	Manufacturer's ssociation *vs.* labour unions	Episcopalian church *vs.* "high church"
D. Societies	Protestants *vs.* Catholics	Free Men *vs.* Slaves	The State *vs.* Criminal gang
E. Suprasocietal	Soviet bloc *vs.* Western bloc	Soviet Union *vs.* Hungary	Common Market *vs.* France Relations

For the purpose of analysis Dahrendorf reduces the fifteen cells of this table to six types as follows:

(1) Role Conflicts (A1, A2, A3)
(2) Competition (B1, C1)
(3) Class Conflicts (B2, C2, D2)
(4) Minority Conflict and Deviation (B3, C3, D3)
(5) "Proportion Struggle" (D1)
(6) International Relations (E1, E2, E3)

The most influential theory of social conflict has certainly been that of Karl Marx. Ever since the publication of 'The Communist Manifesto' in 1848, his ideas have been a force to be reckoned with. Since capitalist industrialism was spreading throughout the world and since his was a theory that promised a better life to those who felt exploited by that system, the wide acceptance of his theory is readily understandable.

Although Marx called his theory scientific and although he used historic material to buttress it, the part that most interested him—the conflict between the proletariat and the bourgeoisie was hypothetic rather than demonstrated theory because the industrial revolution had then not gone far enough to yield empirical data on its validity.

Marx concerned himself with only one type-class conflict, but he did look diligently for the structural causes of that type and did construct theory of how conflict evolves from those causes. He was little concerned with the interaction between the conflict and its context. He did not care about what effects it might have on society so long as the principal goal, the overthrow of the capitalist class, was achieved and he was likewise uninterested in external forces that might mollify it. There was only one logical termination, and that could be reached only in one way.

To Marx, social and political conflicts spring from an economic base. Prominent in his materialistic theory are the concepts of the relations of production, the dialectic process, surplus value (stemming from his labour theory of value), class interests, class consciousness, class struggle and the classless society. He finds the casual conditions of the conflict in the changing productive forces of the early industrial revolution which were inconsistent with the then existing relation of the production and their embodiment in principles of property. In his theory, the processes of the conflict itself are bitter and unconditional. The workers can expect no quarter from the capitalist for the political concessions are mere sops throughout to confuse and weaken the workers and the workers must press on with organization, general strikes, and preparations for violence. Finally, the day of violence must come, and out of it will emerge the dictatorship of the proletariat. The workers will then root out the last vestiges of capitalism, preside over the withering way of the state and usher in the classless society. Because Marx was both an analysist and reformer, his doctrine contains a curious mixture of inevitability and voluntarism. To him, the proletarian revolution is inevitable, but, at the same time, he wished to incite the workers to exert themselves—to hasten the day. The polemical aspect of his work has of course made many writers question whether he deserves to be called a social scientist at all. Can anyone who is so ardent a champion of a cause possibly explore the complexities of social organization objectively? We are so used these days to hearing his thought condemned without examination that it may be worthwhile to note the high praise bestowed upon his work by the first professor of sociology at the university of Chicago. Albion W. Small: "I confidently predict that in the ultimate judgment of history Marx will have a place in social science analogous with that of Galileo in physical science.[12]

Dahrendorf believes that the greatest contribution of Marx to sociology was realization that internal conflict derives from the existent social structure and that it produces changes in the structure. Thus, as against cumulative theories of progress, he saw the vital role of conflict in social change. As motive forces in the conflict, Dahrendorf also approves the Marxian concept of class interests. He does, however, quarrel with Marxian theory at a number of points.

First, he finds that Marx was wrong in his assumptions that all structural change is brought about by class conflict. He points out that external conflict may well produce change in social patterns and that in addition there are internal conflicts between religious and ethnic groups that do so.

A second point of differences is that Dahrendorf denies that all class conflicts must eventuate in revolution before they achieve structural change. He believes that the history of Western nations thoroughly refutes this. An allied criticism is that though it is true that classes have conflicting interests, Marx was wrong in holding that they are always in acute and violent conflict. Dahrendorf believes that conflict may remain latent during national emergencies or through negotiated "armistices" between workers and employers.

Of great interest for sociological theory is Dahrendorf's contention that instead of relations to the means of production being the crucial fact in class formation, it is relations of authority. Difference in structured power—such as in modern industrial governmental, religious, and educational bureaucracies are, he thinks, the determinants of interest.

Finally, Dahrendorf is critical of the identification, which Marx makes between the economy and the society. The notion that those who win the means of production therefore automatically control the destinies of the government and all other social institutions seems to him undemonstrated. He asks how Marx would explain the labour governments in England.[12]

What is the picture of Marx that emerges from Dahrendorf's critique? It is that of a great pioneer who got a firm grasp on an original idea—that internal conflict is a method of transition from one pattern of social structure to another. He gave this idea undue centrality in a general theory of change and embellished it unconvincingly in several directions. When, however, these mistakes are stripped away, there remains a solid contribution. According to him, "History of all hitherto existing society is the history of class struggle".

Lewis Coser has performed a notable service, therefore, in giving us a learned, critical restatement of Simmel's essay in his 'The Functions of Social Conflict'. He sorts out sixteen propositions, puts them in an analytic framework, and comments extensively on each.

If one can summarize so diffuse a piece of work, the central idea in Simmel's essay is that conflict is constructive. It is his belief not only that it gives rise to social change, as Marx would have it, but also that in many ways it is immediately integrative. This is of course obvious in the case of external conflict producing internal integration—to the spelling out of which three of Coser's propositions are devoted. But it is not at all obvious (and perhaps it is questionable) that internal conflict gives rise to internal integration or that external conflict unifies the antagonists.

Three of Coser's propositions in particular deal with the effect of internal conflict on integration. The most general one is represented by Simmel's words: "Conflict is designed to resolve divergent dualisms; it is a way of achieving some kind of unity... This is roughly parallel to the fact that it is the most violent symptom of a disease which represents the effort of the organism to free itself to resolve the tension between contrasts.[13]

Coser very well comments that these ideas of Simmel are valid only if one assumes that at the basis of the relations between parties there is strong consensus, so that the conflicts he speaks of concern less fundamental questions that do not bring that consensus into question. In that sense, Simmel is here stating at the most a half-truth. But, as Coser points out, there is perhaps implicit here another truth that Simmel did not clearly see: that open societies, which permit internal conflict on many fronts, by that very fact make it less likely that any conflict will endanger the basic consensus. The numerous conflicts will criss-cross each other in a confusing way that prevents their cumulation to form a basic line of cleavage.[14] He implies competition a basic feature of conflict, social conflict is "a struggle over values and claims to scarce status, power and resources in which the aims of the opponents are to neutralize injury or eliminate their rivals".[15]

Another of Simmel's ideas made into a proposition by Coser is that the more stable the relation between the parties, the more they will be willing to express hostilities through conflict. Thus, it is not sound to judge the instability of a relation by the amount of conflict expressed within it. Quite the contrary, much conflict can occur even in stable relation. People are willing to become embroiled in conflict if they have no doubt of their ultimate cohesion. In reality, then, we have a threshold phenomena. Below a certain integrative threshold, conflict betokens the possible breakup of the unity and is, therefore, negatively indicative of its stability. Above the threshold, the amount of conflict is positively related to the stability of the relationship. This is the most significant insight, which has no application to contemporary cold war conditions, since the relationship between the two sides is so fragile; but it is an insight that may become applicable to the common market, which may show its strength by the amount of internal conflict that develops.

The third of Coser's propositions derived from Simmel's thoughts on internal conflict is much more dubious. After indicating that internal conflict is a cause of integration, Simmel says: "Thus, the Hindu social system rests not only on the hierarchy, but also on the mutual repulsion, of the castes. Hostilities not only prevent boundaries within the ground from gradually disappearing... often they provide classes and individuals with reciprocal positions which they would not find if the causes of hostility were not accompanied by the feeling and the expressions of the hostility.[16]

What this proposition amounts to is saying that the expression of hostility in conflict clarifies the position of the contending parties and thus defines the situation more clearly. Once clearly defined, orderly processes of control and accommodation tend to set in. The lingering doubt about the validity of this proposition arises from two other possibilities: (a) that latent hostility will be gradually allayed from the very indefiniteness of an unstructured situation and (b) that the more structured situation, if it arises, will not necessarily give rise to the controlling mechanism, but rather tear a society apart.

To put the matter in contemporary terms, do we really believe that clear positions on either side of cold war are more conducive to peace than more elusive ones?

Three of the Coser's propositions deal with external conflict. These are the most relevant of Simmel's ideas to the present world situation. The first one states that if there is any limit at all to violence, conflict binds the antagonists. Simmel says: "One unites in order to fight, and one fights under the mutually recognized control of norms and rules".[17] Coser believes this to be true provided the conflict initiates another forms of interaction between the antagonists and specially if these other forms of interaction stimulate new rules, norms, and institutions.[18]

Even if true, the contribution of this proposition to human welfare is not great under modern conditions since the risk of conflict between nation going over into nuclear war is so great as to dwarf the chance benefits from the formation of the new normative controls. We had better aim to control directly rather than hoping that it will spring out conflict before millions are dead.

Another proposition suggests that in external conflict each side wants the other to be unified, because it is then easier to deal with it and its commitments can be trusted. This is no doubt true if each party is sure the other will survive the contest. But if one side thinks it can break down the resistance of its opponent and thus win a clear victory, it will surely prefer the opponent not to be well unified. Coser makes this point.

The third proposition in this field is one involving the balance of power. Simmel says, "The most effective prerequisite for preventing struggle, the exact knowledge of the comparative strength of the two parties, is very often attainable only by the actual fighting out of the conflict."[19] This principle too gives us scant consolation in the present world situation. If accommodation between the parties is only possible when relative strengths are known, and if these can be known only through conflict, World War III is a necessary prelude to accommodation—a dismal prospect.

Five of the other seven propositions drawn out by Coser are less relevant to our interest here. Four of them concern personal conflict in intimate or small-group relations. Though these may be suggestive for conflict among large aggregates, the parallels are not close enough to be very profitable. Another makes the obvious point that conflicts create associations and coalitions. Whether it is classes or other units within a society, or whether it is societies that are in conflict, the desire for allies is inevitable and understandable.

The other two propositions have to do with variables that affect the intensity of conflict. The first states that the closer the relationship of parties, the more intense the conflict if it breaks out. The more central in the lives of its members a collectivity is, the more bitter will be the conflict after schism.

The final proposition states that conflict is intense if it is ideological. Personal goals and ambitions are more easily compromised than impersonal causes. Coser suggests that an exception to this rule occurs when self-interest is given moral sanction, as in the Protestant Ethic. He concludes that the real principle at stake is not that ideological conflict is intense, but rather that conflict entered upon with a good conscience is so. This is a proposition that emphasizes the perilous nature of the cold war, since both sides are so sure of the justice of their respective causes.

One of Simmel's ideas which Coser does not propositionalise, but which has relevance to the contemporary international situation, is that slight dissonance will give rise to more intense conflict when the parties expect a high degree of consonance than when they do not.[20] The reconciliation of the two seems to be as follows: Strangeness makes us slow to anger because our expectations are not high, but once conflict has started, it will be more bitter since it is a conflict of conscience.

Park and Burgess have delt with the processes of competition, conflict and accommodation. According to them, competition can exist without any recognition of it on the part of the parties. Competition becomes conflict when the competitors identify each other and try to impair each other's efforts towards the common goal. Since means of communication make possible contact between distant parties, there is always the likelihood that competition will become conflict.

Kenneth Boulding considers conflict and competition to be basically interchangeable or treat conflict as representing an extreme form of competition. According to him, "conflict a situation of competition in which the parties are aware of the incompatibility of potential future positions and in which each party wishes to occupy a position that is incompatible with the wishes of the other." [21]

Park and Burgess point out that the competition is continuous and impersonal, whereas conflict is intermittent and personal. There is obviously an area of overlap—where competitors, in trying to reach the prize, become embroiled with each other. It is to keep conflict to a minimum and to retain the social value of competition that standards are set in morality and law to achieve fairness in the struggle. Wherever there is a force limiting the unscrupulousness and the violence of the conflict.[22] The authors believe that rivalry is best conceived as the struggle for public approval, status, or prestige. To the degree that the conflicting parties feel that appeal lies in the judgment of the public, they are rivals.

Conflict goes over into accommodation when a *modus vivendi* is worked out. Often frequent form of accommodation is superordination and subordination. Another is mutual adjustment through compromise. Since the equilibrium almost always involves a power differential, conflict remains and position of the parties shifts before the accommodation has become thoroughly embedded in the cultural tradition; the conflict may then be renewed.

CAUSES OF CONFLICT

Conflict is universal. It occurs in all times and places. There has never been a time or a society in which some individuals or groups did not come into conflict. According to Darwin the principle of struggle for existence and survival of the fittest are the main causes of conflict.

Conflict is ranked among the few basic forms of human interaction. Park felt: "Only where there is conflict, is behaviour conscious and self-conscious; only here are the conditions for rational conduct."[23] To Park, Conflict was not only the mechanism through which self-consciousness was achieved, it was in fact constitutive of any organized society: "Conflict," writes Park, "tends to bring about an integration and a superordination and sub-ordination of the conflict groups."[24]

According to Freud and some other psychologists, the innate instinct for aggression in man is the main cause of conflicts. It arises primarily from a clash of interests within groups and societies and between groups and societies. The moral norms that children should obey their parents has persisted in our country since times immemorial but now the younger generation wants to go its own way. In consequence, there is more parent-youth conflict than ever before. Present age is the age of competition.

Conflict occurs where there is a profound conflict of interests, "material or ideal, actual or traditional". The causes of conflict are deeply embedded in human society, institutions, and create a complex phenomenon. Sturzo stated "Conflict does not arise merely from differences of ideas nor from a clash of interests. Both these factors are overshadowed by a long range psychological preparation and conditioning".[25]

While there are some causes stemming from immediate needs, others get propped up as basic issues. Many confrontations are products of specific events or activities calling attention to deep seated passions and underlying ambitions. Each of these origins need careful study of trends necessitating the confrontations. The causes of conflict are embedded in national policy instrument, and in fulfilling national policy objectives. Recovery of lost territory, nationalism, investment interests, imperialism, national economic security, and preventive measures and seeking the preparation of another state are few of the many factors that become identifiable, driving national policy objectives and states to war.

Conflicts lead to tensions and tensions in their turn lead to violent conflicts. They are inter-related. One continually hears the words 'tensions' and 'aggression'. Both, until they are examined, may seem commonsense descriptions of facts. If a psychologist has to take the terms seriously, as he must, since they deal with the expression of human experience, he finds them far from unequivocal. Quincy Wright[26] has usefully examined the meaning of tensions, as the term has been applied in the physical sciences, and its derivations in sociological and psychological studies. In ordinary usage, tension means the act of stretching or the condition of being stretched, and in mechanics, stress caused by pulling, or the condition of a body when acted on by such stress. In physics, tension means the constrained condition in the particles of bodies arising from the action of antagonistic forces in which they tend to return to their former state (elastic force), or the condition producing an electric current of high electro-motive force (difference of potential). It also has the psychological and sociological significance of mental strain or any strained relation, as between governments.

Pierre Janet, early in last century, expounded his view of psychological tension[27] as being the force which synthesizes and integrates the personality, and which, when the tension is low, leads to neurasthenia or psychasthenia. This 'whole' tension is a normalizing factor; it is when tensions arise in and between particular fields of the personality that splits occur.

The tension concept, so far as it applies to individuals, was perhaps, one might say, reintroduced by Freud and popularized by Kurt Lewin.[28] In psychiatry, as Gardner Murphy,[29] observes, the concept of tensions is often used to describe a state of suspense, uneasiness or readiness for violent action. Quincy Wright[30] discusses whether tensions can be estimated or measured. His treatment involves an analogy with electricity. Robert W. Angell has criticized this, as leaning too hard upon an analogy. In reply, Wright takes the usual line, that new ideas seldom appear unless suggested by apparent similarities, and provided one discovers the point or points at which the analogy, on being stretched, snaps, its use is admissible.

There can obviously be conflict with little tension, *e.g.* when one is playing a competitive game for pure enjoyment with an opponent less skilled than oneself. There can also (especially today) be tension, deliberately caused and maintained by technical means, without actual conflict: one of the main aims of the 'cold war' is to exacerbate tension in as many directions as possible, without causing, for the time being at least, international conflict. But conflict may be intrapersonal, inter-personal, sectional, industrial, racial, international, or—to change the angle of approach slightly—almost purely legal.

Economic inequalities, insecurities, and frustrations are the main cause of tensions. Created group and national conflicts are an important source of tensions which have often led one group to see another group as a menace through the acceptance of false images and over-simplified solutions and by making people susceptible to the scapegoating appeals of demagogues."[31] "Tensions among nations," Krech and Crutchfield write, "take many forms—feelings of hatred and aggressiveness, attacks in the press and on the radio, diplomatic strife, persecution of other countries' citizens, economic conflict and sanctions, and ultimately, war. War, it should be emphasized, is only the last step in tensions."[32]

There is a conflict of civilizations today. A higher standard of living is preached for adoption all over the world. In under developed countries the propaganda for higher standard must follow a growth of economic prosperity. We have put the cart before the horse God created a craving for better life long before we could afford it. This leads to frustration and tension. This is the cause of strikes and demonstrations by public servants also starting from the NGOs including the professionals like doctors and engineers. There is constant tension in this regard and outbursts occur. Public servants must be satisfied with periodical revisions of scales of pay and grant of dearness allowances in the interim period to suit their growing needs. The masses are badly in need of better conditions of life. If the taxes collected and revenue raised are spent away for maintaining the services, nothing remains for social welfare of the people at large. We are not under a foreign rule. The services must realise the difficulties of the Government. Our culture is based on service and sacrifice but social values which depended on simple living and disinterested service, are fast being superseded by modern materialistic civilization whose one aim is greater happiness to mankind by catering to their senses. This leads to antagonism between the haves and havenots and tensions multiply. Tensions occur also on account of the practice of nepotism and corruption in public administration and exploitation of communal an other differences to get into power or for acquisition of office or of contracts. Just and impartial treatment alone can relieve this tension. The Public Service Commission has been appointed in, various States to decide upon the merits of candidates impartially and without any extraneous influences and to be beyond various pressures. Likewise the judiciary is kept independent of the control of the executive. This is to ensure fair dealing in justice. It may be considered whether the appointments of Chairman of the Public Service Commissions may not be vested in the hands of the President as in the case of Judges and it may be made a rule that the Chief Justice of one State shall belong to another State. To avoid strikes by labour and to bring about better relations, between labour and employment, it may be considered whether it may not be desirable to ban non-workers' participation in trade union activities and confine trade union membership and of their executive to genuine workmen belonging to the industry to which the trade union relates.

Man is born a wild animal, and civilized culture can only partially tame him. His instinctive urge to dominate others is coupled with a willingness to yield obedience to the strong when circumstances so require; not merely submission but also allegiance and support; when those divergent trends reach their peak, man may become the most cruel of tyrants or he may become the most long-suffering of beasts of burden... The strife that develops the strong leaders engenders in others the willingness to be led; it is perceived by them that fighting a common enemy is better than fighting each other.

On the basis of an immutable uniformity of human nature no speculations regarding conflict can be justified. Human behaviour differs from one civilization to another; and in modern times many men seem not to want wars. Hobbes conceived human nature as having inherent tendencies, which sought satisfaction, by seeking pleasure and avoiding pain. The main springs of human conduct, according to Hobbes, are: hunger, thirst, sex, fear and desire for honour. These forces, he believed, are not blind, but depend upon the perception of pain or pleasure which an object or person may give. If left to himself a man's self-interest to satisfy his own urges would put him into conflict with everyone else; social organisation, Hobbes thought, prevents the chaos, which would result if men were left on their own.

Religions are meant to create a heaven on earth so that man can live in peace. But they have often been used as instruments of conflicts and wars. Religious fanaticism is a major cause of tension the world over because it fails to see other religions as paths leading to the same destination. Racial superiority has also been a cause of tension. Hitler considered Aryans to be a superior race, policy of Aparthied was based on racial superiority.

A fanatic state would like to see the progress of only its own religion. Communal riots are very common for the beginning of the war. Fundamentalism blinds the vision of humans and does not recognise the unity of all races it tries to convert all the living beings as the follower of its own religion.

The skirmishes, conflicts, and wars wrought by religious misunderstanding throughout history are well-known. The Universal House of justice challenges followers of all religions to "face the basic questions, which this strife raises, and to arrive at clear answers."[33] It goes on to say that "The challenge facing the religious leaders of mankind is to contemplate, with hearts filled with the spirit of compassion and a desire for truth, the plight of humanity, and to ask themselves whether they cannot, in humility before their Almighty Creator, submerge their theological differences in a great spirit of mutual forbearance that will enable them to work together for the advancement of human understanding and peace."

There are, however, some parties' which have been formed on the basis of religion such as the Muslim League, the Hindu Mahasabha etc. There are also some parties really based on differences of religion but which put on the cloak of political parties. When they implement their policies and programmes they produced tension.

The existence of political parties is necessary for, and must be welcomed in a democratic State. Two parties are normal and at the most three. Any more parties lead to increase of conflicts and tensions. There is no place for independents as representatives in a Parliamentary democracy. A well-organised opposition is essential in Parliamentary democracy but their existence ought not lead to tensions, giving an opportunity to an enemy to exploit them nor should they work in such a manner as to weaken the State as a whole. They have a right to propagate their respective views and principles but they ought not to take the law into their own hands if they do not succeed in persuading the masses to adopt them. A single political party however good still it might be is opposed to democracy and will lead to dictatorship. This experiment is being tried in some parts of the world as in China, and North Korea. In countries like Pakistan theocratic states have been established. One language one religion and one State was attempted in Ceylon but conflicts have increased there. Even in the U.S.A. where there is linguistics unity, there is the problem of the Blacks based on racial differences. In South Africa also there is a racial conflict. Therefore, there cannot be a single solution for all these differences and for the removal of the tensions.

Further, there is no place in a secular democracy which we have adopted in India, for religious parties to take to politics because no amount of persuasion will effect a change in one's religion. A political party or a group or even an individual politician ought not identify itself or himself with a religion or community in any shape or form as far as public life is concerned.

Similarly, differences arising out of castes or sub-castes ought not be allowed to influence politics. Unfortunately such differences are exploited even by educated men in the matter of elections and even in public appointments and business transactions. These practices lead to discontent and conflicts.

Differences of language was the cause for a demand for a Punjabi Suba. The riots in Assam some years ago arose in connection with a scramble for employment in the public services between the Bengalis and the Assamese and linguistic differences and provincial feelings were fully exploited leading to tensions, and conflicts. It is the fanatics of religion, culture or sect that exploit social and religious differences and bring about tensions between Hindus, Muslims, Christians,

Scheduled castes, and Hill Tribes etc. Hindu-Muslim clashes on festive occasions have largely died down after Independence but they still flare up occasionally. In the case of minorities, indifferent treatment or illtreatment and denial of justice and legitimate opportunities, and discrimination are the causes of tension.

The general causes of conflicts and tensions are domination or attempts at domination for power and exploitation or attempts to grab wealth. It is natural for persons kept under domination as under the imperialist rule or those exploited by holders of monopoly to get rid of such domination and exploitation. Attempts to dominate or exploit cause fear of such domination or exploitation in the minds of the weaker section and generally bring tensions and conflicts in the social and religious field.

Interference with one another's freedom of action in matters of worship and religious conversions also causes conflicts. Let India, it is more so with regard to Adivasis and Tribals. The Nagas form part of India, now most of them have become Christians, and some leaders of the Nagas think that a foreign Christian Missionary is nearer to him than Indian leaders, and the former has to come to settle the differences between the Governmrnt and the Nagas.

Economic exploitation and consequent conflicts and tensions may arise between capital and labour, and strikes and lock outs may be the consequence leading to a great loss to the community. Other conflicts within industrial organisations are: between workers and managers, line and staff personnel, different departments (for example, marketing and production), different occupations or trades (such as carpenters and electricians). These conflicts occur within a single factory, a corporation with many plants, an industry, a society, and globally. The bases for social as well as economic conflicts exist in all these settings, but some are more likely than others to become manifest. The different occupations and positions within industrial organizations vary considerably in prestige as well as in power and income. Inequality in economic positions bring about such tensions. Conflicts arise in the agricultural field also between land owners and landless.

Unlike the consumers of industrial outputs, the primary consumers of college and university services are also organisational members. Divisions exist between many categories of members: faculty, staff, administrators, students, and trustees or other supervisory units.

Given the nature of students and administrators within colleges and universities, differences in prestige and money are generally not significant conditions underlying conflict. Their relative prestige and money is in great measure derived from their social and economic positions outside the colleges and universities. In societies where attendance at institutions of higher learning is restricted to children of the highest socio-economic stratum, the prestige of the students is high, and they may be able to maintain a high standard of living as well. In these cases, their prestige and income is not based on their position as students. In countries such as the United States, where attendance is widespread and the students are not drawn from homogeneously high stratum, the prestige of students has some independent value. Although the prestige of students and administrators has not been assessed in any systematic way, it is probably safe to infer that students have lower prestige within the university than faculty and administrators.

Power differences between students and administrators are clearly an inherent characteristic of colleges and universities as organizations. Students usually have relatively little individual power and often lack even collective power. The general difficulties in the assessment of power are compounded because power relations are always in flux, and they vary widely among organisations and in different spheres of organisational life. In curricular matters, students have little direct power, but they have influence through aggregate market conduct, namely, choice of college and the choice of courses and programs of study. They also have some control by their definitions of what is appropriate and necessary work, but this control is handled within powerful constraints which are essentially constructed by the faculty and administration.[34]

Although the physiological differences between males and females are usually unambiguous, the social differences between men and women are not. For some purposes it may be appropriate to consider the lines of cleavage for potential conflict to be those of males and females. But the social meaning of male and female is diverse, and, for purposes of studying social conflict, we have to recognize that a woman's position is dependent not only on her sex but also on the social role of women. That social role is partly defined in relation to male roles. Therefore, in noting possible lines of cleavage by gender, it may be appropriate to consider categories based on age, marital status, and employment in conjunction with sex.

One assumption should be made explicit: There are no innate

differences between men and women about what they would consider desirable. Males and females are presumed to be equally capable of valuing power, prestige, and material goods. Aside from differences directly and necessarily involved in human reproduction—conception and pregnancy—we can assume that whatever the differences, they are a matter of degree. Even if there were innate differences of the average between males and females in some human capacity, the overlap in that capacity between men and women is so great that the differences could be socially ignored. The differences that we observe between men and women in values and conduct are largely a product of the social structure that they have created and in which they live.[35]

As for other quasi-groups, we consider differential allocations of prestige, power, and economic resources. Measures of the relative prestige of men and women, aside from associated characteristics, is not obtainable. There is scattered evidence that men and women agree that men have higher status. One kind of evidence is the degree to which women talk less than men when in groups of men and women.[36] Furthermore, girls, asked if they wished they could have been boys, are ten times as likely as boys to say they wished they were of the other sex.[37]

The basic peculiarity of men and women as conflict groups is that they live more intimately with each other than among themselves. It is within the family as well as in their relations in the larger society that the objective conflict must be considered. In some states a wife did not have any legal claims over her husband's earnings or property while they are married, aside from that he supported her.[38] In other states a wife had an interest in the property that was commonly owned, but exclusive authority to manage and control that property generally belonged to the husband. In some states she was not an independent legal agent.[39]

The ideal of the nation-state is never fully achieved. In no historical case does one find all members of a particular 'nation' within one state's boundaries. Conversely, many states contain national minorities. This lack of full correlation has frequently given rise to dangerous tensions that can ultimately lead to conflict. A government inspired by nationalism may conduct a policy aiming at the assimilation of national minorities. There is no rational basis for deciding on the extent to which the self-determination principle should be applied in allowing national minorities to break away. As a rule, the majority group violently opposes the breakaway movement.

Violent conflicts can ensue and, through foreign involvement, turn into international wars. No suitable method has been found for divorcing nationalism from the state and for meeting national demands through adequate social and cultural provisions within a larger unit. Nationalism not only induces conflicts but, through the intensity of its influence, makes compromise and acceptance of defeat more difficult. It thus tends to prolong the duration and to increase the intensity of conflicts. Possibly, however, this is the characteristic, only of new, immature nationalism, for nationalism has ceased to be a major cause of conflict among the nations of Western Europe. Hitler is reported to have justified the invasion of other countries in following words: "It is a question of expanding our living space in the east, of securing our food supplies....Eighty million people must get what is their right. Their existence must be secured. Might is right."[40]

Nationalism according to Gandhi, "I cannot be internationalist without being a nationalist first." Believing in the universality of soul, Gandhi stands for cosmopolitanism. Nationalism is a stage to internationalism. As stated by Gandhi, "My nationalism is intense internationalism. The narrow definition of nationality has contributed in a big way to give a takeoff to any war. People think that they are citizens of the nation concerned and it becomes their duty to increase or protect the boundaries of their nation. The feeling of nationality gives rise to hatred towards other opponent nation and forms the basis of war.

Most of the states at present are sovereign, both internally and externally. But when a nation tries to interfere in other nations, the conflict ensues. Nobody wants the interference of any outsider in his domestic affairs and in the same way no nation wants the interference by other country in its internal affairs.

Many people believe that the growth of population and lack of living space are the causes of conflicts. The cases of Germany and Japan before the Second World War are cited as examples. This is the cause of war but it is not a main cause of conflict *e.g.* Great Britain solved the problem of over population by extension of industrialization, trade and colonization. And this is true even for extension of commerce.

Group competition is responsible for conflicts. There are different groups based on social, political, economic and ideological interests. The main things for which groups compete are the same for which individuals compete: acquisition of goods, propagation of their ideas and statuses. Groups fighting for status-focus on natural resources like land, soil, food, favourable climate, growth, raw material, petroleum, steel etc. They want to get more and more even in today's technology.

With the increase in nuclear arsenal and with the development of science and its use for destruction, the threat to the boundaries of every nation has increased. Every country in the world is apprehensive of attack leading to increase in its defence budget. A person kills the snake because he fears that the snake will bite him and the snake in return bites the man to save itself from being killed. Thus a nation tries to curb the neighbour's power to make its own boundaries safe.

"Racism has cost the world dearly. Even in India alleged differences of race and culture are the bases for the demand for a separate state by the Nagas as also for a separate Dravidasthan by the D.M.K. Certainly a divergence of views and values among the members of a society constitutes an actual or potential source of conflict and increases the difficulty of settling disputes peacefully. It is believed by some scholars that cultural differences among nations are supposed to be far greater than they actually are and this fact is more responsible for conflict than are the differences themselves. Systems of racial domination in the Americas, Asia, and Africa have left a trail of blood and anguish down through history, imposing upon the present generation a legacy of hatred and racial conflict. Centuries of racial dominance have created centuries of racial distrust among the oppressed. Centuries of distrust have festered into countless manifestations of racial disunity in multiracial societies around the world."[41] In the global community, the United Nations has recognized the connection between racial unity and justice on the one hand, and social progress on the other. Thomas reiterates the dynamics between racism and social progress by saying that citizens of multiracial societies "must be made to understand that there cannot be any lasting peace without genuine love and fellowship among racial groups. Then, it must be demonstrated to them that such love and fellowship among the various races of their societies will not only reduce and ultimately eliminate racism and racial conflicts but also elevate the entire society to new levels of material and spiritual development."

Remedies

The parties must observe certain fundamental principles in a democracy—to avoid political strifes. They should never resort to direct action. This depends also on the party in power, which must give an honoured place to the opposition political groups and take them into confidence and consult them on all matters, where the interests of the State as a whole are involved. The opposition parties must be made to feel that though on matters of basic policy they may not be able to change the party in power, on all legitimate issues affecting the welfare of the State, they have a guarantee that their voice will be heard and where their advice is proper it will be accepted. Otherwise it will lead to frustration on their part resulting in tensions and open conflicts outside the legislature. The Government must also feel that it ought not, to rule by a majority only but as far as possible carry the opposition with them. Democracy does not mean simple majority rule. Unanimity must he attempted wherever practicable and where it is not possible in spite of the best attempt, the majority views must be made to prevail.

Regarding communal parties and religious parties entering the legislature, the general opinion is in favour of not giving recognition to such parties. It is unfortunate that the canker of religious and communal differences as political parties does exist in our society. Educational institutions ought not to be run on communal or religious denominations. More than differences in politics, differences in religion bring about tensions when one religious group desires to dominate or exploit another or to convert them to their group.

Religious conflicts can be avoided by better understanding of one another's faith and view-points and for this purpose it may be considered whether the imparting of general knowledge in schools may not include a knowledge of the essentials of all religions and faiths and the greatness of their propounders. A clearer understanding of the essentials of Hinduism and Islam and the greatness of the prophets will remove much of the misunderstandings that occur during religious feasts and festivals. Greater attention may also be bestowed in schools even at early stages on corporate life and its benefits.

Education in higher principles of life may also bring about a feeling of brotherhood of man and a removal of tensions. This is a long range remedy but is a sure one.

Considerations of caste or religion ought not be imported into either election to the legislatures or appointment to public services either openly or covertly. A feeling of a just administration must be engendered amongst all sections of the community. Religious and other minorities must feel safe in the hands of the majority both in regard to their treatment by the administration. They are entitled to just and fair treatment and nothing more. They are no doubt not entitled to special treatment except in the case of poorer sections of the society. The administration must be scrupulously honest. A minister for minorities including the scheduled castes and tribes and linguistic minorities may be appointed both in the Centre and in the States. Tribunals may be established to watch an infringement to the minority rights and to take cognizance of infringement of minority rights.

The solution for conflicts arising out of access to natural resources undeveloping societies has been thought of as socialization of land or at any rate the adoption of the principle of land to the tillers as far as possible to remove this difficulty. Nationalization and socialization in the country will bring about democracy in economics as much as universal adult suffrage and absence of discrimination in politics. Scarcity of food and high prices are good causes of tension and conflicts.

Efforts to produce more food, and in the meanwhile to import more, can reduce the prices to some extent but hoarding and black-marketing ought to be penalised, otherwise the poorer section may take law into their own hands.

Above all, the spread of a spirit of co-existence born out of proper understanding of one another's faiths and viewpoints and proper education for citizenship, a growing love of the country and its culture, a desire to maintain freedom and democracy or, to inculcate both, amongst the children and amongst the adults, a sense of the danger arising to the country's freedom and its institutions by not resolving the conflicts, and working for national consolidation and economic prosperity where there will be equity amongst all sections and where liberty will be enjoyed by all citizens and a feeling of fraternity is established, are the real and enduring remedies for the removal of conflicts and tensions.

TYPOLOGIES OF CONFLICT

Although the origin and dynamics may be similar for many conflicts, for each party, its conflict is unique. In many important respects this is also the reality. There are no conflicts which are entirely similar, and special features always have to be kept in mind. Still, there are rules, norms and understandings which that try to equalize conflicts so that they can be treated in similar ways. This is true for violence in any society. One murder is not likely to be identical to another; there are still norms which treat them in similar ways. When society wants to contain violence and inflict punishment, it strives to do that in a fair way. Equal punishment for similar crime is a basic rule. These are general rules created for handling unique events. In the process, similarities are emphasized so as to make events comparable. The argument for dealing with conflicts in the global system is parallel. There are large-scale conflicts that are sufficiently similar to allow them to be handled in comparable fashions. Through international law, such a differentiation has already been introduced and has gained considerable acceptance in the international community.

Traditionally, a firm distinction has been drawn between international and internal conflicts. The first can be handled by, for instance, the international institutions, such as the UN, the International Court of Justice and regional organisations. Internal conflicts are, in this thinking, left to the domain of the states themselves, and placed outside the purview of the international bodies. Internal affairs may only become the affairs of the international community if the legitimate authority in the country, that is, its government, asks for such an intervention. This is a basic tenet of the UN Charter and was seen as an untouchable principle during the Cold War. It does not deny, however, the possibility of even making rules for internal conflicts. Indeed, otherwise, it would not be possible to draw a general distinction between internal and interstate conflicts. Furthermore, the political climate has changed the lively debate on humanitarian intervention since the Cold War has questioned the validity of the distinction, both normatively and in practice. By the end of 1990s humanitarian arguments resulted in large international support of NATO bombings of Yugoslavia during the Kosovo crisis in 1999 as well as for the international involvement in East Timor. Internal Conflicts have become central in the debate and policies on international peace.

The separation of interstate conflicts from other conflicts is, thus, well established. It will be maintained here because it is simple differentiation, which reflects realities of importance for conflict resolution. It needs to be seen, however, together with other conflicts, as well as within a larger framework to lead us to a complete picture.

Internal conflicts, argues Zartman, 'begin with the breakdown of normal politics'[42] Thus, there is a large number of issues that can be combined in such a way as to make conflict serious and escalatory. There are probably more such issues inside a particular country than between a given pair of states. Thus, it would be logical to expect more conflicts inside states than between them. These are matters that will be of concern to the ordinary citizen. To the citizenry, international affairs are often separate and distant. With increasing globalisation, their importance may become stronger and more obvious, particularly for small and dependent countries. However, to most inhabitants, what goes on in their own country is likely to be primary as it immediately affects income, well-being and freedom. It is noteworthy, that all countries seem to have an internal conflict, which at times is the dominant one. It is also readily identifiable by the citizens of that country. Conflict is a common experience in any society and not necessarily something that is outside 'normal' affairs. Almost to the contrary, as observed by Coser, conflict may contribute to keeping society together.[43] What is not 'normal' is the resort to arms. There is likely to be a universal preference for peaceful politics, within as well as between states.

Thus, for the population of this planet, internal conflict is as important a category as international conflict. It needs to get as much attention and to be treated in a similarly thorough way. It may be true that international law instruments have been restricted from dealing with internal issues, but legal rules are becoming more numerous and more intrusive. It is sufficient to remind the reader of the human rights issues, the convention on war crimes tribunals, the many democracy-promoting agencies, as well as the general integration through the global market. Internal affairs are a legitimate object of study and are amenable to conflict resolution also involving outside parties.

Let us now complement the dichotomy of interstate and intrastate conflicts. So far a dimension which deals with the actors in conflicts—whether they are states or other parties territorial conflicts have always been central in interstate conflicts. Military authorities are important for the control of territory. State security often depends on control over particular areas. Such areas are defined as strategic or vital and thus come to justify military action. The same, of course, is true for internal conflicts. If particular groups claim control over certain areas, and want to change their status, it affects the inhabitants of the state as a whole. It might mean drawing new borders and altering established rights of all citizens. It impacts on access to particular areas. It has implications for control over resources. The interest in maintaining the existing territorial arrangements is strong in interstate relations. International consensus is highly resistant to territorial changes which do not have the consent of the parties. The government in a state is likely to be equally conservative with respect to the territory it is set to administer. Challenges are likely to be taken very seriously. Thus, territorial issues also acquire a particular meaning in internal affairs. Recent studies point to the significance of territory in explanations of interstate war[44] and we suggest that same is true for internal conflict. The incompatibility over territory, in other words, cuts across the distinction between interstate and intrastate conflict.

The same is true for the second incompatibility, control over government. In this case, we refer to the command over the existing central government authority and the composition of the government. The most serious disputes in this category are those where an opposition challenges the existing authority and wants to have it removed, rather than just achieve a change in a particular policy. Repression by governments aims at keeping a particular group in power. Criticism of government policy may be interpreted as a challenge to its authority. Repression can set in at an early stage. In fact, a larger number of incumbent governments have come to power through non-democratic means. Coups, revolutions, civil wars and dynastic arrangements are still routes to power and they are as frequent as are democratic procedures. The struggle over governmental control is classic in politics and continues to be an important aspect of conflict. The state, as we have just seen, contains such attractive resources that many will find it worthwhile to fight to stay in power or take over power. Thus, it draws on a different dynamics from territorial issues, which focus on particular areas or regions, not the state as a whole. In internal affairs, this incompatibility makes sense.

Is this incompatibility also of value for the analysis of international conflicts? Yes, the Cold War demonstrated this very strongly. The interventions by the Soviet Union and the United States were not motivated in terms of territorial gains but with regard to government control. The ambition for both side was to promote particular types of regime, not change borders. The soviet interventions in Eastern and Central Europe—following the territorial realignments after the Second World War—concerned the installation of oriented governments. There were, no doubt, military and strategic considerations, but the conflicts placed local Communists loyal to the Soviet Union against non-Communist members of the same society. The USA and the West were supporting particular governments in Iran and other places in the Middle East, as well as in South America and Indochina, for instance, without the idea of changing their own borders.

The hot wars that were part of the Cold War focused on the control over government: which type of regime should there be in a particular country? Some countries may have had a more crucial, geographical position in these global strategies (for instance, Cuba and Turkey). Nevertheless, it was the allegiance of the country as such that was disputed, not the idea of breaking up existing units. The Cold War dualism is no longer present on the global level, but the issue of regime types remains important, both regionally (for instance, there are still Communist regimes in East Asia) and globally. The West remains committed to promoting democracy, even with military means, and other actors pledge to resist this, or argue for the right to make counter-actions (even justifying terrorism). Thus, we can observe that both internal and interstate conflicts have similar incompatibilities, when conflicts are armed and serious. It can be concluded that the distinction of territory and government as two separate incompatibilities is fruitful.

This gives us four categories of conflict to consider, but we will merge two into one, making three categories. This creates the trichotomy for conflict analysis. The first category consists of *the interstate conflicts around territory and government.* It is treated as one category, as this is an established group of conflicts, identified with criteria used in international law. Then there are *intrastate conflicts over government* and a third category containing the *intrastate conflict over territory.* It can be said that this trichotomy follows the distinction of international law, but develops it with respect to the intrastate conflicts. Interstate negotiations between sovereign states are similar no matter what the incompatibility concerns, but this, we will show, is not the case for intrastate conflicts. The trichotomy also makes sense as the number of interstate conflicts is limited, and much of today's conflict materials are of an intrastate nature. Furthermore, in the case of intrastate conflict resolution, there are likely to be different arrangements depending on the incompatibility.

It is interesting to note that this distinction for internal conflicts applied here is parallel to the one made by Zartman[45] between 'regional' and 'central' conflicts. However, there is no understanding here that conflict resolution, in Zartman's words, necessarily leads to the 'restoration of no politics'.[46] The political realities after a serious conflict are likely to be dramatically different, depending on the incompatibility. The solution to a conflict the government may aim at achieving is integration and thus some form of restoration and 'normalcy'. A negotiated settlement of a conflict over territory is not likely to have such an outcome. It is not going to be a return to the conditions that prevailed before 'the troubles', but rather involve different forms of separation, even to the point where new states are created. Relationships are changed in a fundamental way. There are, consequently, strong arguments for making the distinction between government and territory particularly important for internal conflicts.

It is not necessarily simple to separate one category from another. Thus, the following questions can help to sort out the categorization of the conflicts. For finding a conflict of the first type, it is helpful to ask the following: Does *a particular conflict have a significant interstate component?* This can be decided primarily by observing if there are troops from different states involved, meaning that the direct command goes to a particular decision-centre. If there are two regular armies fighting each other from two different states, the conflict is a classical interstate confrontation. Most important is if the troops of one or the other party are there as part of an alliance or have an internationally legitimate authorization (for instance, by the United Nations or an international regional organization). This shows an additional component of the interstate character of the conflict. The issue becomes more complicated if the 'foreign' troops are fighting on the territory of a country with the consent of the government. The problem is to decide whether this is a collective defence arrangement and, thus, a case of legitimate assistance, or whether it is a case of intervention, to which a particular government cannot but agree. An even more complex situation is if the external actor is supporting a non-state actor in the other country. Is this then to be regarded as intervention into an internal conflict between a non-state actor (the rebels) and the government? Or is this, in fact, an interstate conflict, where the external actor is only using the non-state actor as a Trojan horse, or an excuse for expansionism? Determining the true state of affairs is often easier than may first appear, if one applies strict criteria.

By observing where the non-state actors get training for their forces, how its finances are raised, how logistics are set up, how weapons reach the rebels and where political support is expressed, a picture emerges. Key questions are actually: who can stop the fighting, and who will sign an agreement that will be implemented? Two states in direct or indirect conflict are likely to prefer to settle the conflict between themselves and not allow space for others. Armed conflicts, which meet these criteria, are interstate conflicts.

The second type of conflict can be identified by asking: *Does a particular intrastate conflict have a significant component of being an incompatibility over government?* In this case we are considering a conflict between a government and a non-state actor, and the conclusion is based not only on the military actions of the parties, but on the stated purposes of the parties. If the goal is keeping or taking power within the same country to which both sides claim allegiance, it is clear that we are talking about a conflict, which traditionally has been identified as civil war. It is a struggle for power within a particular state, not only a fight for a change in the policies pursued by a government. This should be quite enough to delineate internal conflicts. Recent developments indicate that non-state actors may not be primarily interested in taking state power as such, but may settle for control over particular areas. For instance, the peace agreement in Sierra Leone in July 1999 gave the non-state actor, RUF/SL, access to the mining resources in the country. The war was, however, fought on more general grounds; furthermore, there were no stated intentions of breaking away a particular piece of territory from the country. On the contrary, the peace agreement reaffirmed the unity of the state. This conflict may indicate, however, that there is a set of new wars, where public welfare questions are no longer the primary driving forces. These are the 'warlord politics' and 'warlordism'.[47] In practice, they concern access to particular resources in a country, and aim at achieving this by forcibly removing the incumbent government from attractive areas. They challenge government control. Thus, they are also conflicts over government, even to the point that the warlord might take over the government entirely in order to secure access. In the case of Sierra Leone, the war was restarted, obviously with that ambition by the RUF leadership. It failed, however.

The third type of conflict can be found by asking: *Does a*

particular intrastate conflict have a significant territorial component? In this case the conflict posits a government versus a non-state actor, where the former demands the upholding of the integrity of the state. Its opponent, however, wants to break away a particular piece of territory from the existing state. This may come in different forms. It can include either demanding significant constitutional changes, achieving full sovereignty or attaining integration with the neighbouring state. These aspirations are here subsumed under one: the question of territorial control. More refined labels can be given, such as separatism, secessionism, liberation, irredentism, reunification, restoration, but all these labels have strong value connotations. Discussing them under the heading of territory as incompatibility makes possible a less charged analysis. These conflicts are labelled *conflicts over state formation.* From the government's point of view it is a matter of keeping the present state form intact. To the non-state actor, it is a question of changing this very setup in a profound way.

NOTES

1. George Simmel, *Conflict*, translated by Kurt H. Wolff, New York, Free Press to Glance, Inc., 1956, p. 109.
2. Alexis Tocquevile, De, *Democracy in America*, Volume I, 1954, pp. 9-11.
3. Max Weber, *The Methodology of the Social Sciences*, translated by Edward A. Shils and Henry A. Finch, 168, p. 26.
4. Jack Hirshleifer, *Theorizing Adult Conflict*, Amsterdam, North Holland, 1995, p. 167.
5. Avinash Dixit, Strategic Behaviour in Contests, *American Economic Review*, Volume 77, 1987, pp. 891-98.
6. Walter Enders, and Toda Sandler, Terrorism, *Theory and Applications*, Amsterdam, North Holland, 1996, pp. 213-49.
7. Jessie Bernard, "The Sociological Study of Conflict", in *International Sociological Association, The Nature of Conflict*, Paris, UNESCO, 1957.
8. George Simmel, *op. cit.*, p. 111.
9. Clinton F. Fink, "Some Conceptual Difficulties in the Theory of Social Conflicts", *Journal of Conflict Resolution*, Volume 12, December 1968, p. 456.
10. Robin M William, "Social Order and Social Conflict", *Proceedings of the American Philosophical Society*, Volume 114, June 170, pp. 217-25.
11. Ralf Dahrendorf, *Gesellеschaft and Freiheit Miinchen*, Verleg, R. Piper and Co., 1962.

12. Albion W. Small, "Socialism in the Light of Sociology", *American Journal of Sociology*, Volume XVII, 1972, p. 810.
13. Ralf Dahrendorf, *Class and Class Conflict in Industrial Society*, Stanford: Stanford University Press, 1959.
14. George Simmel, *Conflict, op. cit.*, p. 15.
15. Lewis Coser, *The Function of Social Conflict*, New York, Free Press of Glencoe, Inc., 1956, p. 80.
16. *Ibid.*, p. 8.
17. George Simmel, *op. cit.*, pp. 17-18.
18. *Ibid.*, p. 35.
19. George Simmel, "The Sociology of Conflict", *American Journal of Sociology*, Volume IX, 1904, p. 501.
20. Simmel, *op. cit.*, p. 44.
21. K.E. Boulding, *Conflict and Defense: A General Theory*, New York, Harper, 1962, p. 5.
22. Robert D. Park, and Ernest W. Burgese, *Introduction to the Science of Sociology*, Chicago, University of Chicago Press, 1921.
23. *Ibid.*, p. 578.
24. R.E. Park, "The Social Function of War", *American Journal of Sociology*, Vol. XLVI, 1941, pp. 551-70.
25. D.L. Sturzo, *Nationalism and Internationalism*, New York, Roy Publishers, 1946, p. 274.
26. Quincy Wright, *A Study of War*, Chicago, University of Chicago Press, 1942, Vol. 2, p. 1000.
27. G.W. Heath, *What People are: A Study of Normal Young Men*, Cambridge, Mass., Harvard University Press, 1946, p. 4.
28. M.R. Sapirstein, *Emotional Security*, London, Rider and Co., 1948, p. 291.
29. G. Murphy, *Human Nature and Enduring Peace*, New York, Reynal and Hitchcock, 1945, p. 475.
30. Quincy Wright, *A Study of War*, *op. cit.*
31. UNESCO, *Tensions That Cause Wars*, Chicago, University of Illinois Press, 1948, p. 18.
32. Krech and Crutchfield, *Theory and Problems of Social Psychology*, New York: McGraw Hill, 1948, p. 575.
33. Universal House of Justice, The Promise of the World Peace, National Spiritual Assembly of the Bahais of United States, 1985, p. 14.
34. Howard S. Becker, Blanche Geer, and Everelt, C. Hughes, *Making the Grade: The Academic Side of College Life*, New York, John Wiley, 1968.
35. Naomi Weisstan, "Kinder, Kuche, Kirche as Scientific Law: Psychology Constructs the Female," in Robin Morgan (ed.), *Sisterhood is Powerful*, New York, Vintage, 1970.
36. Fred Strodtbeck, Rita M. James and Charles Hawkins, "Social Status in Jury Deliberation", *American Sociological Review*, 22 (December) 1957, pp. 713-719.

37. Kate Millet, *Sexual Politics*, New York: Doubleday, 1970.
38. Mead, Margaret and Frances Bagley Kaplan, American Report, The Report of the President's Commission on the Status of Women and Other Publications of the Commission, New York, Scribner's, 1965.
39. Diane, B. Schulder, "Does the Law Oppress Women?" in Robin Morgan (ed.) *Sisterhood is Powerful*, New York, Vintage, 1970.
40. A. Hitler quoted in Huddleston, J., *Achieving Peace by the Year 2000: A Twelve-Point Proposal*, Oxford, One World Publications Ltd., 1992, p. 13.
41. R.W. Thomas, *Racial Unity: An Imperative for Social Progress*, Ottawa: Association for Bhai Studies, 1993, p. 1.
42. I. William Zartman, (ed.) *Elusive Peace. Negotiating an End to Civil Wars*, Washington, DC., Brookings, 1995, p. 5.
43. Lewis A. Coser, *The Functions of Social Conflict*, New York, Free Press, 1956.
44. John Vasquez, "Why Do Neighbours Fight? Proximity, Interaction and Territoriality," *Journal of Peace Research*, 32; pp. 277-93.
45. I. William Zartman, (ed.) *Elusive Peace. Negotiating an End to Civil Wars*, Washington, DC., Brookings, 1995, p. 5.
46. *Ibid.*
47. William Reno, *Warlord Politics and African Studies*, Boulder, Co. Lynne Rienner, 1998.

6

Conflict Resolution: General Strategies and Tactics

Conflicts are a complex human phenomena: they, are neither positive nor negative, neither inevitable nor necessarily disastrous in their consequences. They can be promoters of change and innovation as well as of disruption. The end result of a conflict is in a positive or in a negative direction for those involved in it (willingly or unwillingly), depends on the aims and the commitment to attain such aims regardless of the means employed, by those engaged in it.

Conflicts bring in its trail indiscriminate assassination and destruction, and an attempt is invariably made to settle disputes by means other than war before finally resorting to it. Therefore, throughout the course of history, all kinds of societal and international actors (from individuals to states) have striven to find a way to deal with their conflicts in order to effectively manage them and, whilst maximizing their gains, to contain their costs. The dispute may be political (non-justiciable) or legal (justiciable). There are, however, various modes of making up the political and legal differences between nations. Such differences may be resolved either by amicable means or by compulsive means, short of war.

Conflict resolution is concerned with processes of removing tensions between states or maintaining them at levels consistent with continued peaceful pursuit by states of their goals (individual or collective). A full description of the processes of conflict resolution within a community would entail a full description of the numerous and complex kinds and degrees of the divisive and common concerns among its members. This statement acknowledges, on the one hand, that conflict and even war are by no means an abnormal part of international life.[1]

The various amicable means of settling disputes may be enumerated as follows:

(1) Negotiations;
(2) Good Offices and Mediation;
(3) Conciliation;
(4) International Commission of Enquiry;
(5) Arbitration;
(6) Judicial Settlement through International Court of Justice and
(7) Machinery of the UNO.

Article 33, Paragraph 1, of the U.N. Charter also provides various means of settling disputes by amicable means. It reads:

> "The parties to any dispute, the continuance of which is likely to endanger the maintenance of international peace and security, shall, first of all, seek a solution by negotiation, enquiry, mediation, conciliation, arbitration, judicial settlement, resort to regional agencies or arrangements or other peaceful means of their choice."

The various methods of the settlement of disputes by amicable means as enumerated above are discussed below in seriatim.

NEGOTIATION

Negotiation is a form of interaction through which individuals, organizations, and governments explicitly try to arrange (or pretend to do so) a new combination of some of their common and conflicting interests. Two types of common interests can be distinguished: (i) an identical common interest in a single arrangement or object, which the parties can only bring about, or more easily, by joining together and (ii) a complementary interest in an exchange of different objects, which the parties cannot obtain by themselves but can only grant to each other. In other words, the term negotiation is used to denote intercourse between States for the purpose of arriving at a settlement of the dispute, or for relaxation of international tension.

To realize an identical common interest the parties must agree on the characteristics of the arrangement (concerning which they may have different preferences) and on the division of gains and costs (where their interests usually conflict). Two nations jointly constructing a dam and two corporations, merging into a single firm are examples of such arrangements. Complementary interests are realized through barters, sales, or agreements on mutual tariff concessions. Most international negotiations embrace a combination of common interests and complementary interest, whereas business negotiations are predominantly concerned with complementary interests.

The parties may relate their conflicts and common interests explicitly or tacitly. The term "negotiation" usually refers to the explicit process, with proposals and counterproposals. "Tacit bargaining occurs if the parties deliberately arrange a new combination of common and conflicting interests through hints and guesswork, without explicitly proposing terms for agreement. Tacit bargaining is of great importance in military confrontations, when negotiation may be difficult because of incompatible war aims, domestic opinion, or the lack of diplomatic relations. Tacit bargaining can help to keep the area of hostilities limited, restrain the use of force, and prepare the ground for negotiations to terminate hostilities. These functions of tacit bargaining received little detailed attention until the 1950s, when they were analyzed in connection with studies of limited war, arms control, and military deterrence[2]. Negotiation by contrast is necessary for more complicated forms of collaboration, for most exchanges, and for any arrangement where an explicit agreement is essential.

It was observed by J. Moore, that "in the international sphere and in the sense of International law, negotiation is the legal and orderly administrative process by which Governments, in the exercise of their unquestionable powers, conduct their relations with one another and discuss, adjust and settle their differences." Such negotiations are carried on either by the heads of the States or by their accredited agents. Often there is an exchange of correspondence for clearing up the controversy.

The process of negotiation can have side effects that do not concern the agreement that is ostensibly being negotiated. In international diplomacy these side effects are far more important than, say, in business or labour-management negotiations. Indeed, they are sometimes the principal or only reason why governments participate in an international conference. That is, governments may negotiate not so much to obtain favourable terms of agreement as to spread propaganda, to gather intelligence, to influence third parties, to divert the opponent from the use of force, to deceive him, or to maintain contact with him in order to communicate on the matters. (Hence the above definition of "negotiation" allows for the fact that parties may only pretend to seek an, agreement.) In areas such as disarmament, where public opinion generally favours negotiation, governments may attend conferences just to appear virtuous.[3] One advantage of private or secret diplomacy when agreement is desired is that it reduces the importance of some distracting side effects.

Negotiation can be analyzed in terms of (a) the interaction of some basic choices that the parties, must make and (b) certain basic moves through which each party can influence the opponents choice. Game theory provides the tools for simplified structure. Like other models in social science, they are, of course, of limited use in the study of negotiation, because they frequently do not represent enough of reality to be relevant and sometimes misrepresent even that part of reality which they address. What a model can easily, represent is the interaction between each party's choice of settling for the opponent's terms or not concluding an agreement, provided each party maintains unchanging evaluations of its gains and losses from each outcome (*i.e.*, provided the utilities of each outcome remain stable for each party).

Obviously, negotiation can result in agreement only if there exists at least one set of terms on which each party would prefer to having no agreement. Frequently, several sets of terms or a range of terms among which the parties have conflicting preferences meet this condition. The question arises, therefore, on which terms the parties will settle—who will get his way?

Commitments and threats are the two basic moves in negotiation, If you make a commitment, you try to alter the opponent's expectations about your future conduct by changing your own incentives; if you issue a threat, you try to alter your opponent's expectations about his payoffs that which results from his making certain choices. A commitment is a move to convince your opponent that will maintain your current position, or implement your prediction, by making it more difficult for yourself not to do so. A threat is a prediction addressed to your opponent (or to those who might influence him) that he will suffer a certain loss if he does not comply with your wishes.

Given a range of terms that both you and your opponent prefer to not having an agreement, you try to induce your opponent to accept those terms within this range which are most favourable to you by making it difficult, or virtually impossible for yourself to accept any other terms. In other words, you narrow the range within which you would prefer agreement so that it will include only your most favoured terms. If your opponent realizes this, he must then expect that you would reject an agreement unless he meets your favoured terms. Of course, the opponent might commit himself, too, and the terms of agreement will then depend, among other things, on the relative strength of these commitments. If the commitments are strong, no agreement might result even though both parties, initially, would have been better off with an agreement. The binding power of a commitment in interpersonal negotiations may stem, for example, from a wager, an oath or an accord with a third party not to settle for less than one's preferred terms. In international negotiations, governments can commit themselves by staking their prestige on a position or by the way in which they tie their military or economic resources to it.

The concept of a threat—more complicated than that of a commitment—has been analyzed more carefully in modern theories of military strategy than in studies on diplomacy (Military deterrence is based on a threat). The party that threatens, asserts it will make a special effort to cause the opponent a certain loss, should he fail to comply. But carrying out the threat (*i.e.*, inflicting this loss) may be costly for the threatener as well, perhaps even more costly than for his opponent. Hence, the question arises of the credibility of the threat, that is, whether it will be carried out when challenged or, whether, it will turn out to be a bluff. To make a threat more credible, it may be reinforced with a commitment.

In negotiations where a party wishes to change the *status quo* in its favour, at the expense of a party defending it, the offensive party always needs a threat to make the defensive party fear that it would lose more by not reaching an agreement than by agreeing to accept the detrimental change. The classic example of such negotiation is the Munich Conference of 1938.

In addition to this rudimentary structure of the negotiating process, a number of complications must be introduced into any theoretical scheme that is to explain or reflect reality. These additional features, are usually omitted in the formalized models and are difficult to simulate in laboratory experiments. Laboratory experiments have been developed to test models which include the more basic features of the negotiating process such as the combination of conflict and common interests, the choice between concluding an agreement and not concluding one, and the use of threats and commitments.[4]

An additional complication is the fact that the parties often are not unitary decision makers. This is of crucial importance in international negotiation and is often relevant in labour-management negotiation. These negotiators have to bargain not only with the opponent but also with members of the organisation that they represent. For example the union representative in labour-management negotiations must be mindful not to lose the support of the rank and file union members. A corporation executive engaged in negotiations for a merger must align other corporate officers and perhaps important stockholders. And diplomats, of course, have their domestic opinion, legislatures and, sometimes, even competing branches of the executive to worry about.

Secret diplomacy can keep some of these domestic groups ignorant of the day-to-day negotiating process. It often turns out to be advantageous, not just for the chief negotiator but also, for the organisation or the government as a whole, by helping it to defend a broader public interests that transcends parochial pressure groups. In the United States, the influence of domestic affairs on foreign policy is more apparent than in many other countries and has received considerable attention.[5] But domestic pressures can also help a negotiator to obtain better terms: they can serve as a commitment in that they may convince the opponent that he must yield because the first negotiator could not concede anything even if he wanted to.

A second complication in real-life negotiation is that, the parties are usually trying not only to get good terms for the agreement under negotiation, but also to protect and improve their future bargaining strength. This is particularly true in international negotiation. In the language of game theory: international negotiation is never a self-contained game but is a phase vaguely related to a never-ending "supergame." Although each negotiation yields its own payoffs, the tactics used in it affect the opponent's calculations in later negotiations and thereby influence subsequent payoffs. The reason for this continuity is that the opponent will impute to the government a certain diplomatic style, certain attitudes towards risk taking and the use of force, a degree of political will, a certain tendency to bluff or to hold fast to a position, and so forth. Of course, this reputation is not permanent, and it is often confined to a particular subject of negotiation. For example, a government may be known to haggle over a wide range in commercial negotiations but to modify its positions very little on political issues.

The third complicating feature in negotiation (as contrasted with more rudimentary bargaining situations) is due to the fluidity of the rules that regulate the way in which the partics conduct negotiations. This fluidity is particularly pronounced in international diplomacy in business, and labour-management negotiations where many rules are quite clear and firm, because they are enforced by higher authorities. For example, the use of force is prohibited or severely controlled, and an offer that has been accepted can usually no longer be withdrawn. According to the U.S. National Labour Relations Act of 1947, the parties must allow some rules even in the way in which they defend their positions.[6]

However, many rules in interpersonal negotiation and practically all the rules in intergovernmental negotiation are not enforceable. Here the concept "norms" may be more appropriate than "rules". Each party follows varying sets of norms, depending on the situation and on the type of opponent. Friendly parties share a far more extensive set of norms than do enemies. Indeed, the violation of certain norms is likely to terminate, or at least interrupt, a friendly relationship. For example, unambiguous lies and invective must be avoided, explicit threats must not be issued, and agreements in principle must not be deliberately misconstrued later on.

Since there is no enforcement, what keeps the parties from violating these norms when it would be to their advantage to do so? First, it must be observed that the norms frequently are violated. Even the most elementary norm of diplomacy, the rule that the opponent's negotiator should not be killed, has been violated not only in antiquity but also in modern times. The norms are usually observed for two principal reasons: (1) the parties want to induce the opponent to reciprocate and (2) they want to facilitate agreement, However, reciprocation is not always felt to be mandatory, nor do all the norms observed by diplomats facilitate agreement. In these cases, the norms are followed not because it is expedient but because they are felt to be in keeping with the proprieties.

Thus, the rules that are more or less observed in negotiation resemble the norms or mores studied by sociologists. They may be followed because (1) of expediency; (2) the negotiator does not want to shock others who feel the norms prescribe the proper behaviour; or (3) the negotiator himself considers it unseemly or immoral to violate these norms. Examples of such norms are that an agreed agenda ought to be adhered to, that partial agreements should not be reversed, that concessions should be reciprocated, and that emotional, outbursts and physical violence at the conference table are to be avoided.

A final complication of cardinal importance in negotiation must be added. The way in which the parties evaluate their own payoffs and those of the opponent is highly uncertain and keeps changing as a result of negotiation. This is true even in negotiations about simple, quantifiable issues, such as a purchase price, and it applies with particular force in diplomacy. In most negotiations, as is not the case in parlor games, there are no firm bench marks that divide gains from losses. To evaluate whether certain options would be advantageous or not, each negotiator must have a break-even point in mind that divides the plus side from the minus side. These points are subjective, ideas which keep shifting under the impact of negotiation. For instance, a party may initially feel that it breaks even as long as it preserves the status quo, whereas later on after having faced an aggressive opponent for some time—the preservation of the *status quo* may seem like a gain worth concessions on another issue.

Not only these break-even points keep shifting; the scales by which the parties evaluate the magnitude of their gains and losses show the same fluidity. If a large effort is being exerted to obtain a small improvement, this improvement may seem like a large gain in the end. And the reverse reaction is well known in everyday human affairs, characterized by the "sour grapes" story.

Important consequences follow from this instability of evaluations. First, the parties cannot know, before being faced with a specific choice, what their minimum terms are at which they would still accept an agreement. The notion of fixed minimum position for each party is realistic only for short time periods and simple issues, which are rarely found in diplomatic negotiation. Second, since the break-even point for each party keeps shifting as the negotiation proceeds, the point which equally divides the gains and loses between the opponents keep changing too. Concepts such as 'fairly distributed is in itself an outcome of the negotiating process. It is not an objective criterion by which one can evaluate negotiations. This is also true for mediators or arbitrators: their image or what is a "fair" division depends on how the parties succeed in presenting the issues to them.

Related to changing evaluations is the fact that the parties change their goals while they are engaged in negotiation. For example, when the goals become more modest, a settlement may turn out to be satisfactory that would have initially been found to be unacceptable. This relationship between one's goals and one's evaluation of the outcome achieved has been studied by psychologists using the concept "level of aspiration".[7]

Compromise is often considered essential for negotiation. And a settlement is often called "fair" just because it has been reached through compromise. However, there are several other ways of reaching agreement, and whether or not a particular compromise accords with given standards of fairness, must depend on the instinct merits of the positions. All that can be observed in a compromise is that the parties have revised their positions through concessions until they have met in an agreement. Yet one side may have retreated from an extravagant position while the other one has made sacrifices from a modest position.

Certain salient features in the area under dispute often provide a focal point where the expectations of the parties meet, regardless of whether their positions converge through a compromise or through some other manoeuver (such as one side catching up with rising demands by other side).

GOOD OFFICES AND MEDIATION

When the parties refuse to negotiate, a third State may come forward and tender its good offices for the purpose of conciliation. In making its good offices available, a third State or an international organisation acts as transmitting agency. The term "good offices" connotes the bringing about of the conflicting parties together and the counselling of advice or the suggesting of a settlement without participating in the negotiations. Such suggestions or advices may be disregarded by a party to a dispute without any compunction or breach of law.

The term "mediation" comes from the Latin *medius,*—middle, and refers to the process of stepping between disputing parties in order to settle their differences. It is one of a family of techniques for pacific third-party intervention in conflict. Mediation has existed in various forms throughout history and in most parts of the world, but in recent years its importance has increased substantially. Its traditional areas of application included disputes within families and between employees and management. Third party intervention as a response to conflict has been used everywhere and in a variety of contexts ranging from neighbourhood and personal conflicts, to group, organisational, environmental, and policy conflicts. In particular, elective mediation by a third party can help minimise the risks involved in establishing communication between opposing parties to a conflict. These have now been expanded to include community conflicts, ethnic group relations, confrontations between criminals and their victims, and many other areas. In international relations, mediation also has a long history, but it has been considerably less successful, and efforts are underway to improve its record. Traditionally, interstate mediation has been studied and practiced by political leaders, diplomats, and international lawyers; these have now been joined by peace researchers from a variety of disciplines. In the 1970s and 1980s, the surge of academic interest in both domestic and international mediation has produced a substantial body of scholarly literature, especially on the theoretical aspects of the subject. There appears be a growing belief in the peace research community that the problems of war and injustice in the world could be significantly ameliorated if ways are found to match, at the interstate level, the achievements of intermediaries at the interpersonal and intergroup levels.

The mediator either his own initiative or at the request of the disputing parties is entrusted with the duty of looking into the dispute and finding some method of peaceful settlement. He assumes the role of middleman and acts in a conciliatory way to reconcile the opposing claims and appease the feelings of resentment finding place between the States at variance. He deals with the substance of the dispute. The mediation presupposes the active participation of the third State in negotiations; but the mediator's suggestions have no binding force and the parties are free to accept, reject or modify them.

Mediators, as the word implies, are in the middle. They interpose between the conflicting parties in order to help them in their conflict management efforts. This usually occurs when (a) a conflict is long, drawn out and complex, (b) the parties have reached a deadlock with their own conflict management efforts,[8] (c) continuation of the conflict is seen as an exacerbating factor by all concerned (sometimes referred to as conflict fatigue), and (d) there exists some premise for communication or cooperation between the parties.[9]

What mediators try to do is to act as an instrument to establish or re-establish sufficiently good communications between conflicting parties, so that they can talk sensibly to each other without being biased by such emotions as anger, fear, and suspicion. This does not necessarily resolve the conflict. Mediation must be followed up by skilled negotiation, usually directly between two protagonists. Because mediators are expected to facilitate dialogue between conflicting parties, they should help the parties by providing reliable means of communication, by helping them to reformulate their ideas into clearer patterns and more precise terms (sometimes summarizing statements and asking direct or indirect questions), or by suggesting a non-threatening or neutral language. Most of all, they help the parties to listen to each other in order to unlock the issues at stake.[10]

Therefore, in traditional international negotiations, both sides to a dispute tend to think that their opponent is pursuing an interest. Traditional diplomatic methods adopted in response to this kind of perception are typical of a legal adjustment. These methods are: (a) good offices as discussed above is usually practiced by carrying out specific requests by the parties, for instance presenting one side's message, to the other; it is not rare that the third party acts merely as observer or point of reference for the parties; (b) facilitation, implies a more continued role in organising and sustaining a dialogue; (c) mediation: is the management of the dialogue through the power to influence the agenda and format for the talks and to formulate proposals for discussion as well as designing alternatives; (d) arbitration involves the parties' consensual delegation of power to a third party, which will design the dispute settlement. In this case the decision power is removed from the parties and transferred to an external authority but the parties themselves can be said to have had an active stand, in that it is still their decision, taken in the *ad hoc* situation, to hand over their decisional power that has to be taken into account by the third party who will have a mandate to respect; (e) adjudication, is, contrary to all the other methods, removed from the *ad hoc* dispute arising between the parties, in that the latter agree to authorize a third party to decide on the solution of a conflict between them in advance, that is, prior to the insurgence of the conflict itself, and even to enforce the chosen solution.[11]

Third party involvement usually starts out as good offices. In some processes, the mediator's intervention will not develop into different forms, but will just be carrying messages, or waiting outside the meeting room doors available at any request. In others, the third parties change their roles from mediators to arbitrators thus "escalating" the degree of their involvement in the dispute considered.

The Hague Convention for the Pacific Settlement of International Disputes laid emphasis on the need for frequent recourse to good offices and mediation by powers and laid down that a state not party to dispute had a right to offer mediation and good offices in a dispute which was advisory in character without any binding force and was not an unfriendly act.

Articles 34 and 35 of the Charter also provide for collective mediation on the part of the United Nations whenever there is a situation, which might lead to international friction.

The distinction between good offices and mediation is fine, being matter of degree only. In the former case the third State may make an inquiry into the dispute or offer suggestions, but it does not participate in the negotiations. The third State only brings the conflicting parties together in negotiation. In the latter case the State mediating takes active part in the deliberations conducted for a peaceful settlement of the dispute; in other words, here the third State conducts the negotiations between the parties. "Strictly a State is said to offer 'good offices' when it tries to induce the parties to negotiate between themselves, and to 'mediate' when it takes part in the negotiations itself but clearly the one process merges into the other." Mediation is a consequence of the tender of good offices and, in addition, a manifestation of their exercise."

A common feature of all kinds of third party intervention (not aimed at a direct involvement in the conflict in a belligerent capacity) is that "it must be seen as an extension of the negotiation process whereby an acceptable third party intervenes to change the course of action or outcome of a particular conflict."[12] What is relevant in the relationship that will grow among the parties is that, both the conflicting and the intervening parties will try to affect each other's behaviour, perception and alternatives of action in order to attain a defined outcome. Following this, it is very important to remove the misnomer that intermediaries of any kind act only for altruistic reasons and do not have any personal aim. Because by the very fact of intervening, third parties become parts to the conflict, they bring with them careful consideration of the costs, interests, and potential rewards to their involvement. Attempts by a third party to "unmake" a problem can at times complicate it by adding "third goals" which clash with the parties and therefore form a different issue.

As Christopher Mitchell explains: "The process of mediation is customarily carried out by individuals... at the level of the individual the nature of motivations involved can run from a genuinely altruistic desire to bring an end to some conflict regarded as tragic or misguided, to a wish for an increase in personal status and reputation, or for a desire for a place in history, rewards may be given by a sense of gratification... by a career advancement or by a sense of being in a position to affect important events."[13] Mitchell claims that at the individual level, underlying motivations can be conscious or unconscious. They can range from highly altruistic to those involving any form of personal advancement. Following this and moving to the organisational level, individuals representing or acting on behalf of organisations (be they voluntary, charitable, or state led ones) bring with them also the need to respond and foster the aims of the organisation they represent, thus following a more or less rigid definition of their mandate, and pursuing an interest of political and economic influence.

Mediation tends in practice to switch from one method to another when involved in a particular dispute. There is, however, general agreement that the various forms of pacific intervention may be arranged along a continuum, ranging from the weakest to the strongest methods of involvement. Mediation is in the center of the continuum, and is often described as a half-way house between conciliation and arbitration. But the term is sometimes used in a comprehensive sense, to describe the entire range of techniques of pacific intervention. In this usage, the "mediator" becomes a person or organization employing all relevant methods in an effort to resolve a conflict in a peaceable fashion.

The weakest form of pacific intervention consists of steps to restore and improve communication between parties whose conflict has caused the breakdown of their relationship. At the interpersonal and intergroup levels, there may be bitterness, estrangement, and hostility, at the higher levels of political relationships, normal communication channels may have been cut completely, so that the only contact between the parties may consist of actions designed to injure or destroy each other. In either situation, initial assistance can take the form of carrying messages back and forth—an activity typical of the "quiet diplomacy" practiced by private groups such as the

Quakers or undertaken in highly publicized fashion when a "special envoy" is dispatched to a region of conflict by the government of a state. Once indirect contact is achieved, the parties or their representatives can be helped to negotiate face-to-face. The extension of "good offices" to those in dispute can provide them with a neutral and safe location at which to meet and talk.

To be viewed as an impartial mediator he/she must not take sides but act as striving with the parties for them to find their own solutions to their shared problem represented by the conflicting situation. If any mediator's interest has to be one of aiming at a win-win solution and at maintaining the facilitation process he/she has established, this is the ideal image of the mediator; in reality things can be slightly different. It has been suggested that there might be two basic forms of bias in mediation: (a) one is called *bias of content,* which refers to the mediator's behaviour in favouring one side over the other in a settlement proposal; and (b) the other is the so-called *bias of source characteristic,* which pertains to the expectations that stem from the mediator's closer personal, political, or economic ties with one party.[14] Whilst the first kind of bias makes it difficult to mediate effectively with the non-featured side, it is sometimes possible to ignore the second kind of bias as convincingly illustrated by Paul Lederach in his study of the Esquipulas Agreements.[15] At times a perception of "fair decisions fairly arrived at" appears to be more important in the approval of the mediator than the attachment to a theoretical notion of bias and impartiality.

Mediation can be a low-cost and highly flexible approach to conflicts and may be adopted by private citizens, international organisations, and any actor whose behaviour can affect the dynamics of the conflicting parties' relations. In an environment lacking a centralised authority, the range of possible mediators is quite varied, but they can be categorized as: (a) Individuals; (b) States; and (c) Institutions and/or Organisations.[16]

Individuals

Although the individual mediator who engages in activities aimed at conflict settlement is usually an official representing his/her government in formal interactions with representatives of the disputing parties, less formal mediation efforts can be carried out by an altogether different type of "individual". This is exemplified by the image of unofficial, informal means made available to members of adversary groups or nations by the deeds of private citizens (church leaders and representatives, professors, members of parliaments, journalists, and businessmen[17]) that are willing to offer their expertise, personal contacts, and sensitivity in order to help them to resolve their conflict. Such individuals approach a dispute as private citizens only and by virtue of this can offer to the parties a very flexible arena in which to try out alternative solutions to a dispute. Nevertheless, this kind of individual, typically intervenes without any formal invitation by the disputants, as a result the mediator's legitimate power is likely to be relatively modest[18] as long as its acceptance is not formally sanctioned by the parties. Its acceptability, in spite of the mentioned shortcoming, depends on the fact that in this case he/she can be disowned easily without loss of face, he/she may be available at any time, and may allow the parties more control with their own conflict management efforts. This kind of mediation seems to be particularly sought when all else has failed and communications have severely deteriorated.

Despite the increase in number and relevance of this kind of activities in both intra- and inter-state conflicts, it is clear that private citizens alone do not have all the means, the status or the resources to warrant and guard an eventual peace agreement, thus, making official diplomacy's entry on the stage necessary anyway. Nevertheless this is better accomplished in the measure in which non-official contacts are successful in creating the setting and the conditions for formal contacts to prove fruitful.

States

It is undeniable that, although one cannot disregard the increasing number of non-state actors in the international arena, states are still widely regarded as the most significant actors in international policy and the world structure of relative power gives some governments a more or less appropriate status to provide mediation activities. The diplomatic system, as it has evolved nowadays, has been devised to deal with these kind of actors and the great majority of the rules shaping the international system are addressed to states. Even if it is true that the options available to states' representatives in a mediation context can be more limited than those available to informal mediators, the assertion, that officials can affect political outcomes more directly, is undeniable. Representatives of all states interact formally in various international forums. The strength of their stance and their bargaining position often depends on the power and economic resources available to the state they represent. In the same way, the relative political, economic, and military weight of a state in the international arena can determine the strategy it chooses to mediate a dispute. In fact, depending on the amount of its resources, a state can not only assist and suggest options for the resolution of a conflict, but also dictate and enforce the solution which is most functional to its own interests. The notion of the resources is relevant, in that it makes credible any "stick-and-carrot" policy a mediator-state might choose, thus letting the disputants realise that the mediator has the actual capacity (and the political will, one may add) to either reward or sanction them eventually even with military means. In doing so, a state can shift its mediating role from a less to a more intrusive one (*i.e.* from an "offer of good offices" to actual arbitration exemplified by pushing and rewarding actions), thus altering also the parties' perception of its impartiality.

For the sake of the conflict situation, if a third party such as a state, has got enough power as to apply sufficient leverage, then it may subdue or suppress the conflicting behaviour of the original parties, thus ending the violence. This way, the problem would be settled rather than resolved and in the long run, this kind of accommodation can prove both unable to secure stability and undesirable for those involved.[19]

Institutions and Organisations

What has been said with regard to the states can largely be understood also with regard to international and regional institutions and organisations. The difference being only that because their representatives act in representation of (ideally) concerted policies of the member states, their status is relatively higher than that of state's representatives, whilst they also enjoy a reputation of more impartiality. In reality, international organisations can be led by the strongest amongst their members (thus becoming a "directorium" of elite "states") as it has often been suggested in the case of the UN, or they can be paralyzed by inertia due to the need to come to an agreement with all their members. It is my opinion that, thanks to the great amount of resources available, international organisations can be tempted to assume a more direct role than individuals or states, thus becoming more intrusive. On the other side of the coin and for the same reason, their entry to the stage is most commendable in the final stage of a conflict resolution process and in the aftermath of it, in order to support its implementation.

The effectiveness of mediation actions is usually defined in terms of success or failure. The definition of success, though, remains difficult and can range from minimalist to maximalist. In the first case, success is seen as a situation in which both parties to the conflict formally or informally accept a mediator and a meditative attempt within five days after the first attempt.[20] On the other hand, a maximalist view maintains that successful outcomes can be said to be the production of a ceasefire, a partial settlement, or a full settlement.[21] Others focus on the equation between mediation success and effectiveness taking the mediator's (or the parties') objectives as their starting point.

The success of an attempt at mediation depends also on the proper timing of mediation initiatives.[22] According to one view, which supports late entry, mediation is most fruitful when failure to reach an agreement is precipitation of an emergency. On the contrary, some think that mediation needs to be initiated at an early stage, *i.e.* well before the adversaries cross a threshold of violence and begin to inflict heavy losses on each other, which makes them more and more inflexible.

Other analysts focus on the logic of the events in order to make an assessment of the right timing entry of the mediators. In this case what matters is the parties' perception of each other. Thus a conflict would be ripe for resolution when (a) a mutually hurting stalemate exists; (b) unilateral solutions proposed by the parties have failed and bilateral solutions can begin to be considered; (c) there is an ongoing shifting of power so that the party that had the upper hand at the beginning is now slipping and the underdog starts rising.[23]

It seems that some conflicts are inherently easier to resolve peacefully because the degree of the conflict of interest is less or the threats to the goals and values of the parties is minimal. Thus another characteristic thought to be important to the outcomes of mediation concerns the issues at stake. These can be listed as follows: (a) sovereignty issues involving adversaries with incompatible claims to a specific piece of a territory; (b) ideology issues, in which the parties disagree on the nature of a political system or/and on basic values and beliefs; (c) security issues concerning the stability of the system designed to embody and actuate the issues named in (b); (d) issues of self-determination and national selfhood. [24] It is possible to argue that some issues, such as those arising from deep-rooted values or ideologies, are basically zero-sum, leaving no room for assisted negotiation, while more interest related ones would be more easily manageable in a meditative attempt so that one strategy for seeking peaceful resolution should be to reformulate a conflict apparently over power or justice in terms of interests.[25] However, some authors think that it is possible to split the problem into different, more negotiable sub-units. Fisher states that where no permanent agreement is possible, perhaps a provisional one is. The parties can start on agreeing on what they disagree about (which is not always so obvious) making clearer the issues they are disputing on. They could later try a partial agreement, involving fewer parties, covering only selected subject matters, applying it only to some geographical areas, or testing it within a limited amount of time. This way the mediators can challenge the parties to devise new solutions and to explore those sub-issues where a cooperative behaviour is possible.[26] Indeed, the very fact of the parties choosing agreed procedures to deal with their conflicts (irrespective of the substance of the disagreement) signals the creation of momentum for settlement.

It is important to notice that in characterizing a particular outcome as either a success or a failure, the general background conditions to the conflict are of the utmost importance. In fact, it is possible that whilst the process of mediation in itself may have been excellent, the background circumstances might have prevented the conflict transformation towards a mutual accommodation; on the other hand, it is also possible that what is scholarly considered a clumsy mediation process turns out to be very successful in terms of conflict settlement because the time for resolution was "so ripe" that the conflict would have moved towards resolution anyway.[27] This could lead to the conclusion that it is not the mediators' efforts that can bring about a settlement but only and exclusively the parties' will and commitment and the set of circumstances characterizing the rising as well as the transformation of the conflict in terms of fighting actors, escalation and variation of issues at stake and destructiveness. In reality the success of a mediation initiative depends heavily on the capability of the mediator to understand those conditions and to construct a set of activities that will respond to them identifying possibilities for changes in roles and functions that result appropriately for them.[28] Following this, a mediator's effective entry on the stage should also consider (together with what is stated above): (1) the international context, (2) the support of the various constituencies for either escalation or de-escalation of the conflict, and (3) the relationship between the adversaries. In particular, the last aspect involves a careful consideration of the character of the conflicting parties: it does make a difference if the parties are (a) states *vs.* states, (b) non-state actors *vs.* non-state actors, (c) or states *vs.* non-state actors.

It, therefore, can be said that in the first case, power considerations[29] will be important in the definition of the dispute settlement, which will most likely "reward" the most powerful state, thus creating dissatisfaction to the opponent and bringing about an accommodation which could fall apart in the long run. On the other hand, if both actors in the conflict are states, the very difficult issue of the status of the parties and of the mutual recognition will not be a major concern of the mediator who will be engaged with either dissensual (when the parties differ on their values and thus may find it difficult to understand "where they disagree about") or consensual (where the parties value the same resources and agree on the issues at stake) matters.[30]

The status of the mediator will most likely not be less than that of the representatives of the states involved, thus identifying with a third-state's high representative or with envoys of international organisations which may act both at a formal or informal level, even if there are examples of non-governmental mediators involved in states disputes. The level of intrusion by the mediators will depend on their status and power in relation to the parties' and on the level of disruption that the dispute may cause to the power and alliance structures of the international system. In the case of state-representatives acting as mediators, the balance of impartiality and the level of the interests involved may create confrontational issues exogenous to the conflict. In the case of non-state actors involved in disputes against non-state actors, most of the considerations on status and mutual recognition in the case of states *vs.* states apply whilst the issue of power disparity is more difficult to measure than it is with regard to nations. In this case the mediator can be a government that is not regarded as a party to the conflict or a representative of an international organisation. Nevertheless the parties might feel "threatened" by the status and the resources of the intervener, which could be perceived as more likely to have the capacity for imposing rather than facilitating a solution, thus performing a more intrusive role. Non-governmental actors may be especially apt in dealing with disputes that involve the same kind of actors because they belong to the same category, they would more easily understand each other, and most of all the conflicting parties might feel that there are no exogenous interests brought into the conflict arena. Moreover, non-governmental mediators are sometimes able to remain engaged for a longer period of time than governments' subject to electoral change, and giving time to the parties to come to an agreed solution, they manage to reach more stable agreements.[31] A major feature of this sort of mediation is its long duration, often running on for several years, at times marking the substantive difference between regulating and terminating a conflict and reaching a real settlement of the *underlying* issues.[32] The case of disputes between intra-state groups can be particularly difficult to solve and to classify, as it often takes the tones of ethnic conflicts where in practice what matters is the groups' perception of their differences more than the scientific definition of who belongs to which genetic group. The issues at stake can be identity, territory, equal status with other groups, or the right to have equal access to decision-making. Polarization can be very strong, especially where there is the identification of the government with one ethnic group (like in the case of Sudan) or a struggle between ethnic groups for the control over a government.

Finally, in disputes involving governmental actors *vs*. non-governmental ones, both the issues of power and status can be more exacerbating to the conflict than in the cases analysed above due to the fact that the conflict seems to be between a legally recognised authority on one hand and a rather ill-defined and possibly illegal movement on the other. Parity of power is often assumed as a prerequisite for a mutually satisfactory accommodation but in this case it would be misleading to measure it purely in terms of material means as the motivation behind a non-governmental actor can be such as to compensate for the lack of resources and can keep a state seriously engaged for years (as in the case of Mozambique *vs*. Renamo). With regard to this third typology of conflict, a lot of the mediator's attention and efforts will be focused on the question of mutual recognition by the parties, factions, or movements that may not be easily identified. In fact, when adversaries do not recognise each other as legitimate, a negotiated end to any conflict between them is most difficult. The denial of legitimacy involved in this case means that not only the parties disagree on the issues at stake but they also deny the very existence of the counterpart as a political actor worth negotiating with. Like in the above mentioned case, this kind of disputes is more likely to be over values and relationship, thus more difficult to solve peacefully and more prone to an escalation of violence, than disputes involving only state actors.

The increasing popularity of third party intervention between conflicting parties at all levels demands that our understanding and skills be substantially increased. Making distinctions within the categories of mediation activities, actors and stages of conflict de-escalation is useful, as it offers a basis for understanding which kinds of actions contribute to mutual accommodation and which kinds do not. In particular, reference to past initiatives and both successful as well as unsuccessful experiences can suggest new or alternative ways to provide mediation services.

In the debate about the effectiveness of conflict resolution techniques, there are those who think that some types of conflict can never be resolved peacefully and therefore armed conflict is inevitable. There are others who believe that all kinds of conflicts can be resolved, given sufficient goodwill and skills. Various study cases have proved that: (a) conflicts involving issues of territory, resources, independence, post-independence, jurisdiction and ethnicity all include peacefully resolved cases; (b) conflicts involving ideological and minority issues include cases which were partially or peacefully resolved; and (c) conflicts involving secession, religious and struggles for control of government included no peacefully resolved cases.

The fact that conflicts over interests have proved easier to resolve than those over ideological issues seems to prove that the international dispute settlement system is better with coping with conflicts over interests between states, rather than with conflicts over values and relationships involving non-state actors. This is due to two reasons: first, governments and their representatives are accustomed to negotiating and bargaining over tangible assets and are less ready to deal with issues where fundamental clashes of values arise: if power and material benefits can be shared, a conflicting sense of identity seems more irreconcilable; furthermore, the international system seems to be ready to deal with international conflicts but was not designed, with the UN and the regional organisations at its core, to deal with non-international ones: the problem is that civil or intra-state conflicts are now the real majority. In particular, the UN has not seriously addressed the question of how it can effectively intervene at all levels (thus including the mediation one) in the intra-state conflicts.[33]

The theory of conflict resolution, as it has evolved until now, seems to privilege the assumption that the outcomes of the conflict should be of a "win-win" type. This view relies on the fact that decision-makers should want to reach a peaceful settlement. The reality is that often they do not want to and they might see a winning solution as their priority. Cases, where one side seeks a peaceful settlement but the other is determined to be coercive, are particularly difficult as it takes all those involved to resolve a conflict peacefully.

With the parties restored to direct contact, the task of the third party may be completed; negotiation may then enable the disputants to manage their own conflict without further assistance. But if the maligning characteristics of conflict dynamics are present, including polarization, stereotyping, rigidity, and the escalation of acts of violence, then negotiation alone may be unsuccessful. It may, therefore, be necessary and possible for the third party, to move to the next stage of pacific intervention.

CONCILIATION

Conciliation requires the third party to become involved in the substance of the dispute, although only to a limited degree. Conciliation is an eclectic process, consisting of whatever steps seem to be appropriate to enable the parties to reach a mutually acceptable settlement of their dispute by themselves.

According to Hudson, "Conciliation is a process of formulating proposals of settlement after an investigation of the facts and an effort to reconcile opposing contentions, the parties to the dispute being left free to accept or reject the proposals formulated." The term implies various methods adopted by a third party to amicably settle the dispute between two or more States. It involves the formulation of proposals of settlement after an investigation of the facts. The dispute may be referred to a commission for favour of proposals to the parties for settlement. Such proposals have no binding force on the parties to the dispute. The Hague Conventions of 1899 and 1907 provided for the pacific settlement of disputes by means of Conciliation Commissions. These Commissions were set up by agreement of the parties, which, after investigation of the dispute, made their report indicating the way to settle the dispute amicably.

The conciliator, therefore, always stops short of making substantive proposals, while, at the same time, assisting the negotiations between the parties in every possible way. The strategies of conciliation are to elucidate the nature of the conflict, which the parties may have difficulty in seeing clearly if they are angry and aggrieved; to clarify the attitudes of the parties to each other, ideally in each other presence; and to explore with the parties the possible range of options open to each of them.

The procedures of conciliation, therefore, are supportive, nondirective, and facilitative. The most important part of the task consists of listening to the parties' own accounts of their shared problem. But some more active tactics may also be employed. If the dispute is between individuals or small groups, conciliation may include personal and psychological counselling, as in marriage guidance and probation work. If the dispute is between occupational groups, organisations, or political groups, conciliation may extend to fact finding or "inquiry," together with authoritative interpretation and advice about legal arrangements which may apply to the matters under dispute. However, these more active steps continue, under conciliation, to serve the purpose of assisting the parties rather than directing them. The highest achievement of the technique is "reconciliation," whereby the conflict between the parties is completely resolved and their relationship is restored to normality.[34]

If conciliation is insufficient, then the third party's next step is mediation. A mediator employs all the basic techniques of conflict management, up to and including conciliation. But, in addition, the mediator goes beyond supportive activities into the formulation of constructive proposals to lay before the parties. Whereas a conciliator's work is restricted to clarifying the views of the parties and providing technical advice on attitudes or on the implications of a particular option, the mediator takes the further step of suggesting various ways around the obstacles to the path towards a settlement. As in all pacific party activities, the mediator seeks to maintain absolute neutrality in this delicate process, because rule of impartiality is easily violated when proposals about the outcome of a conflict are being laid on table. To be acceptable to the parties, the mediator's role must be perceived not only as disinterested but also as legitimate and expert. For this reason, there is now much emphasis in the United States where study and practice of mediation is most advanced, on the development of training schemes and codes of conduct. This has led in turn to the emergence of an independent profession of mediators, basing their work on the discovery that mediation "is ideally suited to polycentric disputes and conflicts those with a continuing relationship, since it minimizes intrusion, emphasizes cooperation, involves self-determined criteria of resolution, and provides a model of interaction for future disputes".[35]

However, if both conciliation and mediation fail, it may be possible for the management process to move, via mediation, to the strongest end of the spectrum of available methods: for legal settlement. This requires the parties to their dispute to abide by the decision of an impartial mediator, such as an arbitrator, a panel of judges, or an independent commission. At this end of the continuum, conflict management techniques merge into the executive process of government. Government consists of the authoritative allocation of values, which are in dispute between individuals or groups, and is made possible by a mixture of coercion, tradition, and the general consent of the governed. Both the political process (whereby issues are identified and personnel selected for government) and the mental process (making policies and laws, enforcing them, and adjudicating them) involve continual conflict management.[36] On the political or input government, the usual techniques are conciliation and mediation, as when a political party leader persuades an assortment of conflicting groups to consensus and merge into a broad coalition executive or output side of government, the usual techniques are coercive, carried out by agencies which are backed by the power to compliance.

Conciliation differs from mediation in as much as the former denotes references of a dispute to a body of persons for ascertaining the facts and suggesting terms of settlement, while the later denotes negotiations between the parties through the agency of a third party. Conciliation also differs from arbitration as in the former the parties to a dispute are free to disregard the result of the negotiations, but in the latter, there is a legal decision of the arbitrator in the form of an award binding on the parties.

INTERNATIONAL COMMISSIONS OF ENQUIRY

Although they are different from Conciliation Commissions indicated above, the Commissions of Enquiry serve the purpose of investigating disputes and suspending hostilities till they have made their report. The first Convention of the Hague Conference of 1899 suggested the establishment of International Commission of Enquiry for international disputes involving neither honour nor vital interests and relating to points of fact with a view to elucidating the facts and dispelling ignorance that ultimately lead to hostilities. The Conference provided that such Commissions might be constituted by special agreement between the parties, the members of such Commissions being appointed in accordance with the scheme laid down in Article 32 of the Convention for the appointment of the members of arbitral tribunals. The report of the Commissioners was limited to a statement of facts, and expressly divested of the character of an arbitral award. Considerable improvement was effected in the 1907 Convention by adding provisions for assessors, agents, counsel and advocates and for summoning of witnesses.

ARBITRATION, JUDICIAL SETTLEMENT AND GOOD OFFICES OF UN

Arbitration is the most important method of settling international differences between states by a judicial procedure based on respect for law, using judges, and on terms chosen by the parties to the dispute. It is a sophisticated process reflecting the wish of the parties to have their dispute settled by judicial rather than diplomatic processes. Modern international arbitration has developed from the practice of states and from the rules to be found in bilateral and multilateral treaties. In modern times international arbitration has not been chosen frequently, but it has played a role in the settlement of territorial and similar delimitation disputes between traditionally friendly states. Recourse to international arbitration may be the result of a general undertaking to refer future disputes to arbitration or of a specific agreement (*compromise*) relating to a specific dispute. In addition to choosing the judges and the procedures, the parties may specify the basis upon which the arbitration is to determine the dispute. This is often the rule of international law as encompassed in Article 38(l) of the Statute of the International Court of Justice, but may also include—either in the absence of any settled rules of international law or as an alternative to the settlement on an equitable basis as provided for under Article 38(2) of the Statute of the International Court of Justice.

Arbitral awards are binding on the parties, though they are not necessarily final. Either party may, if the compromise permits, take further proceedings to seek the interpretation, revision, or rectification of the award and in all cases may challenge the decision as a nullity if it is flawed by some failure to comply with the requirements of the compromise. Indeed there are many instances of lengthy legal disputes concerning the meaning or effect of awards. Yet there have been few outright repudiations of awards, the most famous recent example being the repudiation by Argentina of the award in the Beagle Channel Arbitration.[37]

The historical development of international arbitration refers to some modern examples of the process, and explains its place in the maintenance of international peace and security. Though there has been an increasing use of arbitration between large commercial concerns and states in recent years for the resolution of disputes concerning economic interests, this article is concerned only with arbitrations between states.

The First Hague Conference of 1899 established the Permanent Court of Arbitration, with an International Bureau at the Hague to serve as its secretariat and a permanent Administrative Council. Each signatory power was to select not more than four persons of known competency on questions of International Law and in the highest moral reputation to act as Judges on the Permanent Court of Arbitration. Out of the list of the possible Judges the parties were free to select the members of a tribunal. The Hague Conference of 1907 made some improvements in the scheme and provided for summary procedure in disputes about matters of secondary importance. Article 37 of the Hague Convention I of 1907, provided: "International arbitration for its object the settlement of disputes between States by Judges of their own choice and on the basis of respect of law. Recourse to arbitration implies an engagement to submit in good faith to the award." Strictly speaking, the Permanent Court of Arbitration was not a Court, but merely a panel of arbitrators from which Courts could be formed. As such it was not a Court in the real sense and had no permanency.

Modern international arbitration is often said to date back to the Jay Treaty of 1794 whereby the United States and the United

Kingdom established a number of mixed commissions consisting of commissioners from each state to resolve disputes between the two states which arose following the gaining of independence by the United States. These early commissions were a mixture of judicial and diplomatic processes aimed at providing a machinery for determining what was in effect a negotiated settlement. But the idea of mixed commissions took hold and the judicial aspects of the process soon came to predominate. In particular the success of the Alabama Claims in 1872, again between the United States and the United Kingdom, settled the model for future arbitrations. These claims related to allegations that the United Kingdom had not remained neutral during the American Civil War by allowing the South to have boats built and fitted out in British ship-building yards. These vessels, including the *Alabama* which gave its name to the arbitration, had caused much damage to the commerce of the North. Once the Civil War was over, the United States sought compensation from the United Kingdom for its failure to remain neutral. The arbitral tribunal consisted of representatives appointed by the heads of state of Italy, Brazil, and Switzerland sitting with a representative appointed by each of the disputing parties. The arbitration resulted in the award of US $15.5 million to the United States. Although the United Kingdom protested the legality of the award, it was nevertheless met. One commentator describes the Alabama Claims arbitration as "a turning point in the history of arbitration, marking its definitive breakthrough." Such successes led to the proposal that some permanent system of international arbitration should be established.[38]

The principal attempts to establish a permanent system were the Hague Conventions of 1899 and 1907 for the pacific settlement of international disputes. These treaties resulted from a conference called by Czar Nicholas II in an attempt to limit the armaments race of the day and to provide a viable alternative to "an appeal to arms." All the major powers of the day attended the conference. The two Conventions are still in force and have attracted widespread ratifications. Contracting states recognize the importance of international arbitration as a means of settling their disputes, but there is only a moral obligation to refer disputes to arbitration. The 1899 Convention describes international arbitration "as the most effective, and at the same time as the most equitable, means of setting disputes which diplomacy has failed to settle." The absence of any legal duty to refer disputes to arbitration is a defect of the Conventions, but it should be remembered that it was not until 1928 that the Kellogg Briand Pact sought to outlaw recourse to force in the settlement of disputes. The Conventions established the inappropriately named Permanent Court of Arbitration, which is neither permanent nor a court. Indeed there is only machinery in the form of a Permanent Administrative Council and the International Bureau, housed in the Peace Palace at The Hague, for establishing arbitral tribunals to hear specific cases. The Administrative Council consists of the diplomatic representatives of the contracting states and the International Bureau acts as a registry when states wish to set up an arbitral tribunal to settle a dispute. Contracting states nominate for terms of six years up to four persons "of known competence in questions of international law, of the highest moral reputation, and disposed to accept the duties of arbitrators" to a panel which is maintained by the International Bureau. If contracting states wish to use the machinery, each party to the dispute nominates two arbitrators from the panel, only one of who may be a national of the nominating state. The four arbitrators then nominate a fifth person to act as umpire. The 1907 Convention added a Summary Procedure involving only three arbitrators and a wholly written procedure. The Convention machinery has also produced a rudimentary system of procedural rules for submission of disputes to arbitration which are frequently adopted by states resorting to arbitration. Between 1900 and 1932 the Permanent Court of Arbitration dealt with 20 cases, but since then only three cases have involved use of the machinery. The decline in its use is partly accounted for by the establishment of the Permanent Court of International Justice, later to become the International Court of Justice.[39]

The major significance of the Hague Conventions is that they are the only treaties, which committed the then Soviet Union to any form of international adjudication, though it has to be noted that the Soviet Union did not take part in the running of the Permanent Court of Arbitration since the First World War. Today, the Permanent Court of Arbitration offers little advantage over a well-drafted *compromise* in an *ad hoc* arbitration, though the premises, staff, and facilities of the International Bureau at the Peace Palace at The Hague appear to be a resource often overlooked by states.

The creation of the Permanent Court of International Justice in 1920 and its replacement with the International Court of Justice in 1946 did not spell the death knell for international arbitration, though it has diminished its incidence. Attempts were made in the General

Act for the Pacific Settlement of International Disputes in 1928, and by its revision in 1949, to persuade states to accept compulsory reference of disputes to judicial settlement either by the Court, or, if the states agreed, by international arbitration. Neither attempt was successful. Today, the vast majority of states accept the international legal duty to resolve their disputes by peaceful means but assiduously reserve to themselves the choice of means, of which judicial settlement is but one.[40]

In 1949, the International Law Commission set about preparing a draft code of arbitral procedure. The result was that in 1953 the International Law Commission proposed a general multilateral convention on arbitral procedure based on its draft code.

This was designed to ensure the effectiveness of undertakings to refer disputes to arbitration. Under the proposed convention, once a binding undertaking to refer a dispute to arbitration was established, a party to the dispute could not frustrate the arbitration by refusing to agree on procedural matters. The convention would take over the establishment of arbitration, removing this aspect from the content of the parties in dispute. Such an approach was not acceptable to states and a watered-down form of the International Law Commission's proposals became draft articles which states could use as Model Rules on Arbitral Procedure in concluding bilateral and multilateral treaties or in, agreeing to the reference of a dispute to arbitration.[41] These draft articles were presented to the General Assembly in 1958. In the weak General Assembly Resolution 1262 of November 14, 1958, the General Assembly merely took note of the draft articles and drew the attention of member states to them. These draft articles have had less impact than the procedural rules of the earlier Hague Conventions.

The most cursory examination of modern instances of international arbitration shows that they are almost invariably the product of *ad hoc* arbitration agreements. Such agreements, not all of which are as full and complete as is necessary, commonly define the issues for arbitration, and the constitution, powers, and procedures of the tribunal. Such special agreements are of great significance, because the arbitrators only have authority to deal with the issues referred to them under the agreement on the basis set out in the agreement. Any failure to respect the terms of the agreement can result in any award being challenged as a nullity. Arbitrations between states resulting from *ad hoc* arbitration agreements have not been numerous, possibly because in the era of the United Nations Charter, most states choose to implement the obligation to settle their disputes by peaceful means by using the private diplomatic processes of negotiation, conciliation, inquiry, and good offices rather than judicial processes.

A number of regional treaties recognize the value of international arbitration as a method of settling disputes, but few go beyond the obligations set out in Article 2(3) and Chapter VI of the United Nations Charter, which stress that states have an unfettered freedom to choose any peaceful means to settle their disputes. This principle of freedom of choice is also enshrined in bilateral treaties between states which contain obligations to settle disputes by peaceful means. Consequently few examples can be found of international arbitrations being based on obligations in such treaties. But the figure may be artificially low because the obligation in the bilateral treaty may have been the catalyst which led to the special agreement to refer the dispute to international arbitration. Finally, a preference for arbitration for disputes concerning the law of the sea is reflected in the Law of the Sea Convention 1982 which establishes International Tribunal for the Law of the Sea.[42]

Some examples of international arbitration will add substance to this description and willingness of states, if the circumstances are right, to illustrate the new variety of issues affecting vital national interests to arbitration.

The Island of Palmas Arbitration of 1928 concerned a dispute between the United States and the Netherlands about the ownership of the Island of Palmas. The United States claimed title on the basis of the Treaty of Paris under which Spain had ceded all its territory in the region to the United States. The crucial question therefore became the nature of Spain's rights over the territory in 1898 when the Treaty of Paris came into force. The sole arbitrator was the Swiss Professor Max Huber, whose decision is still today a leading authority on principles of international law relating to title to territory. The arbitrator held that it was vital to look not just at claims to title but to the actual display of peaceful and continuous sovereignty over the territory. His extensive consideration of the relative claims of Spain and the United States as its successor, and of the Netherlands, established that there had been unchallenged acts of peaceful display of sovereignty by the Netherlands from 1700 to 1906 (the date the dispute between the United States and the Netherlands arose) and this was sufficient to establish the title of the Netherlands to the island.

The Trail Smelter arbitration of 1941 between the United States and Canada is another landmark arbitration, because it established a principle of good neighbourliness concerning air pollution at a time when there was no international law concerning protection of the environment. The dispute concerned air pollution from a lead and zinc smelter operated by a Canadian company which caused damage in the United States. The arbitration agreement enabled the Tribunal to consider the liability of Canada and to establish and monitor emissions from the smelter for the future. No other form of adjudication could have established the obligations of Canada towards the United States.

The Rann of Kutch arbitration of 1968 is a good example of the use of arbitration to resolve a dispute which had already resulted in hostilities between the parties. For centuries there had been boundary disputes concerning 3,500 square miles of territory known as the Rann of Kutch. This dispute was inherited by India and Pakistan when they attained statehood. The territory is salt desert for part of the year and flooded territory for the remainder of the year. In April 1965 India and Pakistan had engaged in hostilities over the territory and in the ceasefire agreement of June 1965 agreed to international arbitration. Each side chose an arbitrator: India chose a Yugoslavian judge, and Pakistan chose the Iranian former President of the General Assembly. The Secretary General of the United Nations chose Judge Lagergren of Sweden as the President of the Tribunal. The arbitrators went to great pains to assemble the facts supporting each side's claims to the territory and the arbitration took the familiar form of adjudicating between the competing claims. On some issues the evidence was finely balanced. The award of the Tribunal gave some territory to each side, and enabled the parties to the dispute to fix a boundary by the erection of 847 pillars and the execution of final maps. It is especially significant that the decision to award certain territory to Pakistan was based on the consideration that it would "promote peace and stability in the region." The arbitration provides a modern illustration of the use of the process to resolve a dispute which has been the cause of the use of force between large states, though it should be noted that the character of the territory made its loss to either side not particularly significant.[43]

The Beagle Channel arbitration (1977) between Chile and

Argentina is a rare example of an arbitration resulting from a long-standing treaty obligation to refer disputes to arbitration by the British Government. The Queen as Head of State appointed five members of the International Court of Justice to act as her advisers and to produce a report on the disputed title to certain islands in the Beagle Channel. The Tribunal reported substantially in favour of Chile. The Queen adopted the report and declared it as her award under the terms of the treaty. But the award was not acceptable to Argentina which comprehensively repudiated it for reasons which had little merit. The repudiation very nearly led to hostilities between Chile and Argentina which were only averted by the skilful diplomacy of the papal envoy Cardinal Samore. The whole unedifying episode illustrates the weakness of long-term treaty commitments to refer disputes to arbitration and the wisdom of the modern approach of preferring *ad hoc* references to arbitration.

The final happier example is of the 1977 arbitration between the United Kingdom and France for the delimitation of the continental shelf boundary in the English Channel and in the Western Approaches. The arbitrators were charged with the actual delimitation of the boundary on a chart. The successful outcome has been important not only for the parties but also for the contribution it has made to international law on the delimitation of maritime zones.

What then is the contribution of international arbitration to the maintenance of international peace and security? It provides a valuable, though frequently used, process for the resolution of disputes. It is but one method for settling dispute peacefully and seems to have a special role to play where the dispute involves technical issues. Hence its frequent use in territorial disputes where there is a degree of mutual trust between the states in dispute. It is clearly not a process to be thrust upon the parties as the unfortunate Beagle Channel case illustrates. Ultimately its effectiveness rests on the political will of states both to refer the dispute to arbitration and to honour the award resulting from the arbitration.

Arbitration and judicial settlement closely resemble each other. The parties decide, perhaps with the assistance of a mediator, to grant their consent in advance to a judgment to be made by an outside body. The process falls short of in that the consent granted by the parties is limited to the matter under dispute, and also because compliance cannot be guaranteed in the absence of a coercive authority. It follows that legal settlement is most likely to be effective when the parties are easily identified, and when the issues are clear-cut or concern the interpretation of an agreement. It is widely practiced in disputes over property, in conflicts over pay or conditions of work, and generally where problems arise within a well-defined hierarchy. It works least effectively in situations where the parties are dispersed or poorly led, where issues of principle arise, where attitudes are inflamed, and where the stakes have been raised by acts of violence.

In many sectors of domestic society, legal settlement has been successfully institutionalized. More generally, conflict management using all the forms of pacific intervention is widely practiced in many countries of the world. In consequence, academic interest has in the past generation shifted away from its traditional concern with the laws and forms of government as a means of managing the simpler types of disputes, and towards the most intractable kinds of conflicts—those for which conciliation and mediation are the most appropriate methods.[44]

CONCLUDING REMARKS

In the world society as a whole, the picture is very different. Extensive machinery for most forms of pacific intervention in conflict does exist in international relations, notably direct negotiation through diplomacy, along with a considerable array of procedures and institutions for legal settlement.[45] However, it is traditional in both the theory and practice of international relations to lay the greatest weight on the procedures available at the extreme ends of the spectrum: negotiation (bilateral or multilateral) on the one hand, and legal settlement on the other. The assumption, traditionally, has been that where good offices and negotiations fail, arbitration and other quasi-governmental processes are the next significant step. The success rate of legal settlement, however, is extremely poor[46]; if negotiations cannot solve a problem, then it is common practice in world affairs either for the problem to remain unsolved, or to be dealt with by force. It is, of course, the case that the intermediate stages of peaceful conflict management, conciliation, and mediation, are provided for in the institutions and practices of international relations. But they are frequently used by comparison with their rate of employment in domestic society; they have been little studied until recently, and they have rarely been successful.[47] As Burton[48] and other scholars have pointed out, this gap in international relations theory and practice contrasts sharply with domestic theory and practice where conciliation and mediation are now the main focus of attention. Filling the gap in international relations provides a major opportunity for peace research activity, and may be the basis for the most significant reform that is possible in international relations.

There has been extensive discussion, among scholars and practitioners, of the reasons for the almost routine failure of the mechanisms for the legal settlement of international problems. Three distinct views have emerged. First, the traditional analysis, advanced by diplomats, international lawyers, and some political scientists of a "realist" persuasion, has identified the international "anarchy" (that is, the absence of world government) as the major obstacle. In the absence of coercive authority, it is argued, many of the worst disputes in international relations are inherently resistant to conciliation or mediation still less to arbitration and judicial settlement. International disputes are often said to be "non-justiciable" (that is, political rather than legal in character). It is noticeable that states lack both the willingness to yield control of their most serious disputes to an external authority, and to accept (or impose) sanctions which could enforce compliance with its decisions. The conclusion of the traditional analysis is that no progress is possible.

A second group of scholars, however, note that a great deal of mediation is actually conducted, although it takes place within the diplomatic framework, rather than the legal one. They suggest that the study and practical development of this activity could bring many of the benefits of legal settlement techniques to world affairs. The international system does possess some characteristics of order and stability which are quasi-governmental in character; they are created by the vast discrepancies in power and resources between the strongest states and the weakest states. Leaders of major states often regard themselves as holding responsibility for the management of conflicts within and between weaker states, and can draw upon the whole range of foreign policy instruments, including military means, to do so. In this context, the use by diplomatic officials of good offices, negotiation, and mediation is relatively commonplace, and the settlements that they bring about sometimes have the binding character of international law.

As Touval and Zartman report, this "mediation as power politics"[49] has a significant record of success. Prominent cases include the Camp David Accords of 1978, the Zimbabwe Settlement of 1979, and the ending of the United States Hostage Crisis in Iran in 1980. The success is based largely upon the superior resources or bargaining position of the mediating state, which can provide "leverage" enabling it to offer inducements and threaten penalties in order to impose a settlement. Mediation of this type should be regarded as a branch of foreign policy, rather than as an autonomous technique of pacific third-party intervention, because there is no question of the mediator being impartial. The mediator's political interest in the dispute is well-understood by all parties, and the diplomat who intervenes becomes in effect a participating party in relation to the issues under dispute.

A third group of scholars has emerged in recent years, arguing that neither the means of legal settlement as studied by the lawyers, nor the negotiation activities of the diplomats, are adequate approaches to the problems of world politics under contemporary conditions. They justify their position by reference both to the dismal record of conflict management in world affairs (with particular reference to the prospect of nuclear war and the high incidence of terrorism, local war, and guerrilla warfare), and also to the underdeveloped condition of the techniques of conciliation and mediation at the international level. They stress that the conflicts which are characteristic of world society as a whole, cannot be treated only as static disputes between states, but must instead be seen as dynamic social processes. International conflicts, within this view, have roots which run much deeper than clashes of interest between governments. These roots include ideology, clashes between ethnic groups, rigidities and misperceptions. In decision making, the spillover of domestic difficulties into foreign policy, and profound structural problems caused by economic and political injustice. Before conflicts of this extremely complex type can be resolved or even settled by a compromise agreement, they must be fully understood by those involved in them. Once analysis has been carried out and understanding achieved, the knowledge gained enables the parties to make adjustments which can mitigate the worst aspects of their relationship. A highly analytic form of conciliation and mediation, therefore, is seen as the appropriate means for dealing with international disputes.

The terminology employed to describe this new approach has been evolving rapidly in recent years. Early work by Burton, Doob, Kelman, and others during the 1960s and 1970s described the technique as "controlled communication," the "casework method," or "the therapeutic workshop," all of which reflected its origin in the methods of mediation developed in the handling of domestic disputes. Later publications have referred to "pre-negotiation" to "problem-solving workshops"[50] and to "third-party consultancy."[51] It seems likely that "the problem-solving approach" will become the standard term. All the scholars working in this area lay heavy stress on the importance of non-directive techniques, so that the method is much closer to conciliation than to mediation. Where the third party makes suggestions, it is argued, they should never include matters of substance in relation to the dispute, but instead focus "academic" points drawn from conflict theory to the procedures of communication. Of all the work in this area, de Bono[52] comes closest in advocating a strongly directive role for the mediator.

NOTES

1. Boasson, Chables, *Societal and Aspects of Law and International Adjustment* (Amsterdam: Holland Publishing), 1950.
2. Thomas C. Schelling, *The Strategy of Conflict*, Cambridge, Mass.: Harvard Univ. Press, 1960.
3. John W. Spainer and Nogee Joseph, *Two Politics of Disarmament: A Study in Soviet-American Gamesmanship*, New York, Praeger, 1962.
4. Anatol Rapopart and Orwant Carol, Experimental Games: A Review, *Behavioural Science*, 1962, 7:1-37.
5. Bradford Westerfield II, *Foreign Policy and Party Politics: Pearl Harbor to Korea*, New Haven, Yale University Press, 1955.
6. Archibald Cox, The Duty to Bargain in Good Faith, *Harvard Law Review*, 1858, 71:1401-1433.
7. Sidney Siegel and Fouraker, Lawrence E., *Bargaining and Group Decision Making: Experiments in Bilateral Monopoly*, New York, McGraw-Hill, 1960.
8. In this case the disputants may want to choose a face-saving way out of the conflict. In such situations, negotiation through an intermediary may help protect a party's prestige. Because the desire for a settlement implies the need to make concessions, the parts could feel that conceding by means of a third party is less harmful to their reputation and their future bargaining positions than conceding to the adversary in direct negotiations. S. Touval and I.W. Zartman, eds., *International Mediation in Theory and Practice*, Boulder, Colorado, Westview Press, 1985, p. 255.
9. Jacob Bercovitch, *Social Conflicts and Third Parties: Strategies of Conflict Resolution*, Boulder, Colorado, Westview Press, 1984, p. 13.

10. C. Hume, *Ending Mozambique's War.' The Role of Mediation and Good Offices*, Washington, US Institute of Peace, p. 73.
11. This behaviour has been observed in the case of the Oslo Channel, where the Norwegians were never present at the meetings between the parties but kept (handy) in order to grant any kind of needed assistance.
12. J. Bercovitch and A. Houston, The Study of International Mediation: Theoretical Issues and Empirical Evidence in J. Bercovitch, *Resolving International Conflicts: The Theory and Practice of Mediation,* Boulder, Lynne Rienner, 1996, p. 12.
13. C.R. Mitchell, "The Motives for Mediation," in C.R. Mitchell and K. Webb, (eds.), *New Approaches to International Mediation*, London, Greenwood Press, 1998, p. 31.
14. F.J. Carnevale and S. Arad, "Bias and Impartiality in International Mediation" in Bercovitch, (ed.), *Resolving International Conflicts*, p. 45.
15. This is the analysis of a regional process of conflict resolution as it has evolved in Nicaragua within the Esquipulas II Agreement of 1987 where Lederach has developed his concept of the "insider partial" as opposed to the "outsider neutral." He suggests that a an intermediation from a mediator whose acceptability is based in connectedness and trusted relationship with the conflicting parties rather than in his/her distance from them, might prove significantly effective.
16. J. Bercovitch, "The Structure and Diversity of Mediation in International Relations", in Jacob Bercovitch and Jeffrey Z. Rubin (eds.), *Mediation in International Relations: Multiple Approaches to Conflict Management*, London, Macmillan, 1992, p. 10.
17. A good example of a businessman entering in a process of conflict resolution is given by Tiny Rowland. A man with enormous economic interests threatened by the war in Mozambique, he decided to help the peace process providing flights and accommodation for many RENAMO representatives. Conversely, his presence seems to be exacerbating the ongoing conflict in Sudan.
18. J. Bercovitch and Jeffrey Z. Rubin (eds.), *Mediation in International Relations: Multiple Approaches to Conflict Management*, p. 257.
19. Christopher R. Mitchell, *Handbook of Conflict Resolution: An Analytical Problem Solving Approach*, London, 1996, p. 3.
20. Marieke Kleiboer, "Understanding Success and Failure of International Mediation," *Journal of Conflict Resolution*, Vol. 40, No. 2, June 1996, p. 361.
21. *Ibid.*
22. This factor has repeatedly been stressed by Cameron Hume in his description of the mediation performed by the Community of Sant Egidio in the war in Mozambique. See C. Hume, Ending Mozambique's War, *The Role of Mediation and Good Offices*, Washington, U.S. Institute of Peace, 1994.
23. Marieke Kleiboer, "Understanding Success and Failure of International Mediation", p. 363.

24. *Ibid*, p. 364.
25. Hugh Miall, *The Peacemakers: Peaceful Settlement of Disputes Since 1945*, Oxford: Macmillan, 1992, p. 110.
26. Roger Fisher and William Ury, *Getting to Yes: Negotiating Agreement without Giving in*, London, Hutchinson Business, 1981, pp. 72-73.
27. Louis Kriegsberg; "Varieties of Mediation Activities and Mediators in International Relations", in J. Bercovitch (ed.), *Resolving International Conflicts*, p. 220.
28. *Ibid.*
29. The definition of power here must be considered in connection with the goals for which it is being exercised and must comprehend military, geopolitical, economic, ideological, social, and cultural resources. *Ibid., p.* 222.
30. *Ibid.*
31. In all cases conflicts involving a higher degree violence have a proportionally higher mediation duration than those involving minor violence. See Hugh Miall, *The Peacemakers: Peaceful Settlement of Disputes since 1945*, p. 125.
32. See Oran R. Young, *The Intermediaries. Third Parties in International Crises*, Princeton, Princeton University Press, 1967, p. 35.
33. R. Cooper and M. Berdal, "Outside Intervention in. Ethnic Conflicts," in Michael E. Brown, (ed.), *Ethnic Conflict in International Security*, Princeton; N.J., Princeton University Press, 1993, pp. 199-201.
34. Bercovitch J., Social Conflicts and Third Parties: Strategies of Conflict Resolution, Colorado, *Westview*, 1984.
35. Boulder, J. Folberg, Taylor A., *Mediation: A Comprehensive Resolving Conflicts Without Litigation*, Jossey Francisco, California, 1984.
36. Marshall T.F., *Reparation, Conciliation and Mediation*, London, Home Office Research and Planning Unit Paper Office, 1984.
37. H. Fox, *Arbitration, International Disputes—The Legal Aspects*, London, Europa Publications, 1972.
38. D.H.N. Johnson, International Arbitration—Back in favour? *Yearbook of World Affairs, 1980*, pp. 305-28.
39. J.G. Merrills, *International Dispute Settlement, op. cit.*
40. P. Sanders, *International Arbitration*, The Hague, Martinus Nijhoff, 1967.
41. J.L. Simpson, Fox H., *International Arbitration*, London, Stevens, 1959.
42. L.B. Sohn, *The Function of International Arbitration Today*, Hague Receuil, 1963, 108(l): 1-113.
43. J.G. Wetter, *The International Arbitral Process: Public and Private*, New York, Oceana, 1979.
44. D.M. Kolb, *The Mediators,* Cambridge Massachusetts, MIT Press, 1983.
45. J.G. Merrills, International Dispute Settlement, London, Sweet and Maxwell, 1984.
46. *Ibid.*, pp. 184-87.

47. C. Berman M.R., Johnson J.E. (eds.), *Unofficial Diplomats*, New York, Columbia University Press, 1977.
48. E.E. Azar, Burton J.W. (eds.), *International Conflict Resolution: Theory and Practice*, Brighton, Wheatsheaf, 1986.
49. Touval S, Zartman I.W. (eds.), International Mediation in Theory and Practice, *Westview*, Boulder, Colorado, 1985.
50. M. Banks (ed.), *Conflict in World Society: A New Perspective on International Relations*, Brighton, Wheatsheaf, 1984.
51. C.R. Mitchell, *Peacekeeping and the Consultant's Role*, Gower, Farnborough, 1981.
52. de Bono E., *Conflicts: A Better Way to Resolve Them*, London, 1985.

7

Gandhian Approach

There is a political maxim, almost an axiom, that you cannot permanently govern large numbers of people merely by violence or deceit or both. Despite the events of the last century this maxim stands. Part of the converse of this maxim is a proposition whose truth is much less generally recognized, namely that in nonviolence and truth there is power.

The struggle in India during the freedom movement proves that the method of non-violent resistance, which Gandhi advocated and used is a potent method . If, then, this method of dealing with conflicts has elements of practical validity, the vastly increasing perils of war and class conflict make it imperative for us to use it both as a preventive and curative measure to establish peace and harmony.

Is nonviolent resistance intellectually and morally acceptable? to what extent, it is at all practical, and why? Is it applicable in the West, or not? The issue of pacificism, in both individual and collective sense, should be removed from emotional adjectives and vague mysticism, futile protests and sentimentalism combined with confused thinking. Both the advocates and opponents of nonviolent resistance need to understand it much more clearly and fully.

It is difficult for one trained in modern Western modes of thought and action to understand this idea or to believe that its practice can be cogent. Even Gandhi's explanations of it fail to carry weight with most of scholars and statesmen. His explanations come out of a background of thought, feeling, and attitude to life very different from the West.

Nonviolent action "works" in very special ways which must be grasped if the technique is to be understood, evaluated intelligently and applied most effectively. These ways diverge significantly from popular assumptions about conflict and struggle in particular the assumption that violence can be effectively met only with violence.

Nonviolent action is designed to operate against opponents who resort to violent sanctions. There is no assumption in technique that such opponents will, when faced with nonviolent action, suddenly renounce their violence, or even that they will consistently restrict their use of violent repression.

However, the use of nonviolent means against violent repression creates a special, asymmetrical, conflict situation, in which the two groups rely on contrasting techniques of struggle, or "weapons systems—one on violent action, the other on nonviolent action. To have the best chance of success, the nonviolent actionists must stick with their chosen technique. An extensive, determined and skilful application of nonviolent action will cause the opponent very special problems, which will disturb or frustrate the effective utilization of his own forces.

MORAL JIU-JITSU[1]

If one man attacks another with physical violence, the victim hits back, the violent response gives the attacker a certain reassurance and moral support. It shows that the victim's scale of moral values in regard to violence as a mode of settling disputes is the same as that of the attacker. A mere display of either fear or anger by the victim is sufficient to have this effect. It makes the attacker sure of his own *savoir faire*, of his choice of methods, of his knowledge of human nature and hence of his opponent. He can rely on the victim's reaction in a definite way. The attacker's morale is sustained, his sense of values is vindicated. His confidence in his general method of dealing with his opponent is reassured. But suppose the assailant attacks with physical violence a different sort of person. The attitude of this new opponent is fearless, calm, steady, and because of a different belief, training or experience, he has much self-control. He does not respond to the attacker's violence with counter-violence. Instead, he accepts the blows with good-tempered reasoning, stating his belief as to the truth of the matter in dispute, asking for an examination of both sides of the dispute, and stating his readiness to abide by the truth. He offers resistance, but only in moral terms. He states his readiness to prove his sincerity by his own suffering rather than by imposing suffering on the assailant, through violence. He accepts blow after blow, showing no signs of fear or shrinking or resentment, keeping steadily good humoured and kindly in look of eye, tone of voice, and posture of body and arms. To violence he responds nonviolently.

The assailant's first thought may be that the opponent is afraid of him, is a coward, ready to give way and acknowledge defeat. But the opponent's look and posture show not fear, but courage. His steady resistance of will reveals no subservience. His unflinching endurance of pain is startling. All observers agree that it is easier and require less courage to attack than to withstand fire without retaliation.[2]

At such an unusual and unexpected reaction, the assailant will be surprised. If at first he was inclined to be scornful or contemptuous of the victim as a coward, those feelings are rapidly displaced by curiosity and wonder. As the psychologist Shand points out, "Wonder tends to exclude Repugnance, Disgust and Contempt in relation to its object."[3]

Thus nonviolent resistance acts as a sort of moral jiu-jitsu. The nonviolence and good will of the victim act like the lack of physical opposition by the user of physical jiu-jitsu, to cause the attacker to lose his moral balance. He suddenly and unexpectedly loses the moral support, which the usual violent resistance of most victims would render him. He plunges forward, as it were, into a new world of values. He feels insecure because of the novelty of the situation and his ignorance of how to handle it. He loses his poise and self-confidence. The victim not only lets the attacker come, but, as it were, pulls him forward by kindness, generosity and voluntary suffering, so that the attacker loses his moral balance. The user of nonviolent resistance, knowing what he is doing and having a more creative purpose and perhaps a clearer sense of ultimate values than the other, retains his moral balance. He uses the leverage of a superior wisdom to subdue the rough direct force or physical strength of his opponent.

Another way to state it is that between two persons in physically violent combat, there may appear to be complete disagreement, but in reality they conduct their fight on the basis of a strong fundamental agreement that violence is a sound mode of procedure. Hence, if one of the parties eliminates that basic agreement and announces by his actions that he has abandoned the method used generally by his forefathers back, almost to the beginning of animal life, no wonder that the other is startled and uncertain. His animal instincts no longer tell him instantly what to do. He-feels that he has plunged into a new world. Here is something as new, apparently, as an airplane to an tribal in a jungle.

Just as in the case of wrestling jiu-jitsu, the violence itself helps to overthrow its user. There are several reasons for this, in addition to the element of surprise.

The first is that prolonged anger is very exhausting. Undoubtedly anger at first gives an eccess of muscular and sometimes mental energy. But it also consumes energy very rapidly, and if long sustained it may completely exhaust the person feeling it.

Secondly, part of the energy of the violent assailant is reverted and used up against himself. The steadfast appeals of an individual nonviolent resister work on the personality of the violent attacker, arousing the latter's more decent and kindly motives and putting them in conflict with his fighting, aggressive instincts. Thus the attacker's personality is divided. The appeals, like commercial advertising, may require considerable repetition before they are effective, but the result is pretty sure. They act on the psychological principle of "summation of stimuli."[4]

The violent assailant realizes that he made a mistake at first in thinking that his opponent was a coward. He is bothered by the thought that he may have made or might in the future make another mistake about this unusual opponent, and that another mistake might be more embarrassing. He, therefore, becomes more cautious.

If there are onlookers, the assailant soon loses still more poise. Instinctively, he dramatizes himself before them and becomes more aware of his position. With the audience as a sort of mirror, he realizes the contrast between his own conduct and that of the victim. In relation to the onlookers, the attacker with his violence perhaps begins to feel a little excessive and undignified, even a little ineffective; and by contrast with the victim, less generous and in fact brutal. He realizes that the onlookers noted his mistake in regard to the nature of his adversary. He senses a lessening of respect from the crowd. He realizes he has lost prestige. He somewhat loses his inner self-respect, has a sense of inferiority. He, of course, does not want to acknowledge it, but his feelings betray themselves in hesitance or decreasing firmness of manner, speech or glance. The onlookers perceive it, and he himself senses a loss of public support.

If anyone feels inclined to doubt such a reaction of the outsiders against the assailant's violence, let him recall what happens in time of a labour strike if any striker loses his temper and destroys property or attacks any person. Immediately the employers blazon the news in the press and try to make it appear that all the strikers are men of violence and that public safety is threatened. They play on the fears of the public and then persuade the administration to call out extra police or soldiers. Public opinion, swayed by the press, reacts strongly against the strikers and their cause is lost. Violence opposed not by violence but by courageous nonviolence, if it is in the open, is sure sooner or later to react against the attacker. The burden of justification rests heavily on the violent one and the presumption is against him.

The disadvantage of the attacker increases by reason of a further loss of inner assurance. He becomes increasingly aware that the victim's scale of values is strangely different from his own and from most people's. He dimly realizes that the courage of the nonviolent opponent is higher than mere physical bravery or recklessness; that it is somehow a clearer and stronger realization of human nature or perhaps of some ultimate powers or realities in the background of life. He is surprised into an uncertainty of his own valuations and methods.

A final disadvantage and continuing causes of relative weakness in the attacker is that he is in a very suggestible and receptive state of mind and emotion, more so than the nonviolent resister. The reasons for this are several. The emotion of the struggle of course tends to make both parties suggestible. But the surprising conduct and attitude of the victim presents suddenly a new idea to the attacker. "The effect of surprise is to make us attend to the event that surprises us. Wonder tends to arrest and detain the attention on the thing which excites it."[5] The struggle is a process of mutual interacting influence. As this process proceeds there is a cumulative effect of the several disabilities of the violent assailant as above described, together with advantages of the nonviolent opponent, which we are about to set forth. This cumulative effect acts upon the sub-consciousness and imagination of the attacker to keep him more suggestible than the nonviolent resister. Thus the violent assailant has less chance of influencing the opponent than the opponent has of influencing him.

So much for the factors that tend to upset the moral balance of the violent assailant and keep him off-balance and at a disadvantage.

What are the advantages of the non-violent resister?

In this moral Jiu-jitsu the nonviolent person has position, poise and power for many reasons. Firstly, he has taken the moral initiative. His conduct is new and unexpected and unpredictable by the conservatively acting user of violence. Secondly, he is not surprised. He knows, by reasoning or by intuition and faith, what is really taking place in such a struggle, and how to control the process. Thirdly, his self-control and lack of anger conserves his energy. Moreover, he is not in as suggestible a condition as the violent assailant.

He has still another element of superior power; his proved sincerity and conviction. Deep conviction is a great power. One writer has said, "To be willing to suffer and die for a cause is an incontestible proof of sincere belief, and perhaps in most cases the only incontestible proof."[6] Nonviolence coupled with such suffering is still further proof of sincerity. Voluntary suffering is probably also a sure sign that the whole being of the sufferer, body, mind, will and spirit, is integrated and at work with single purpose. This means that immense and unpredictable resources of energy are in action and ready to endure. The sight and realization of this is profoundly impressive and moving.

Again, the refusal of the victim to use violence is a strong indication of his respect for the personality and moral integrity of the assailant. From childhood, we all tend to like people who show respect for our personality. This tendency operates even between the parties to a conflict. Such respect for the personality of the opponent was one of the important elements in the practice of mediaeval European chivalry, and, added much to the charm and power of that code. Respect for personality is a prerequisite for real freedom and fine human association. It is proof of unselfishness and of moral poise and understanding. The self-regarding sentiment is the foundation of all the higher morality, a demonstration of respect for personality exercises a much deeper and more far-reaching influence than is generally realized. This respect gradually tends to put the violent attacker to shame and to enhance the respect of any onlookers towards the gentle resister.

Both opponents feel a desire and need for the approbation of others. Social approval and opprobrium are very strong forces. They act through and are a part of the herd or gregarious instinct, which is so powerful in mankind. The tremendous pressure of social approval or dislike is well known. Competent observers have stated that fear of social disapproval was the strongest of all the motives to enlistment in the armies in the World Wars. The desire for outside approval was strikingly shown by the great efforts devoted to propaganda by all the parties of the World War. Again, it is demonstrated in labour strikes and lockouts, in which both parties are at great pains to win public support and sympathy. All politicians recognize the force of public opinion.

For these reasons, in a struggle between a violent person and a nonviolent resister, if there are any onlookers or a public who hear of the conflict, the nonviolent resister gains a very strong advantage from their reaction. When the public see the gentle person's courage and fortitude, note his generosity and good will towards the attacker, and hear his repeated offers to settle the matter fairly and peaceably and in the open, they are filled with surprise, curiosity and wonder. If they have been hostile to the victim before, they at least pause to think. His good humour, fairness and kindness arouse confidence. Sooner or later his conduct wins public sympathy, admiration, and support, and also the respect of the violent opponent himself. Gandhi's chivalrous and generous conduct towards the South African Government when it was threatened by a railway strike is an instance of this sort. Once the respect of the opponent has been secured, a long step has been taken towards a satisfactory solution of the controversy, no matter whether it be public or private.

But what is the psychology of the affair if the assailant is filled with the sort of cruelty or greed, pride, bigotry, or hardness that seems to grow on what it feeds on?

Cruelty is a complex of fear, anger and pride. Greed is really a desire for security and completion, though badly mistaken as to method, means and material. In a sense it is a fear of lack. Pride is another mistaken sense of divisiveness. Bigotry is an obstinate narrow religious pride.

In all such instances, the tendency of nonviolent resistance is to remove fear, anger, and any foreboding of death or loss or sense of separateness, and to give instead a feeling of security, unity, sympathy, and goodwill. Inasmuch as fear and anger are elements of cruelty, the removal of fear and anger will tend to reduce cruelty. Shand tells us that "wonder tends to exclude Repugnance, Disgust and Contempt in relation to its object."[7] In so far as these may be elements involved in pride, the wonder evoked by the conduct of the nonviolent person also tends to reduce pride and hence to reduce cruelty. In so far as cruelty is due to a desire for power or for feeling superior, the ability of nonviolent resistance to win for its user the support of the outside public presently makes the cruel person realize that that sort of power is disadvantageous and that perhaps he is not so superior as he had previously supposed. Even aside from its effect on the spectators, nonviolent resistance gradually creates even in the violent opponent, a partial realization of human unity and a different idea of what kind of power is desirable. To the extent that cruelty may be due to a defect in the cruel person's intelligence or imagination or to dullness of observation, the dramatic scenes of prolonged nonviolent resistance act to stimulate his intelligence and powers of observation, and hence to reduce his cruelty. If avarice, ambition, or desire for revenge are factors in a particular case of cruelty, these also are reduced by prolonged nonviolent resistance. The removal of fear or of sense of separateness tends to reduce greed and hardness.

The attacker gradually loses divisive emotions or sentiments in relation to the victim, fear, anger, hatred, indignation, pride, vanity, scorn, contempt, disdain, disgust, anxiety, worry, apprehension. It is not that such feelings are balked or suppressed; they merely no longer have a cause or basis.

The art of jiu-jitsu is based on a knowledge of balance and how to disturb it. In a struggle of moral jiu-jitsu, the retention of moral balance seems to depend upon the qualities of one's relationship to moral truth. Hence, part of the superior power of the nonviolent resister seems to lie in the nature of his character. He must have primarily that disposition best known as love ; an interest in people so deep, and determined, and lasting as to be creative; a profound knowledge of or faith in the ultimate possibilities of human nature ; a courage based upon a conscious or subconscious realization of the underlying unity of all life and eternal values or eternal life of the human spirit; a strong and deep desire for and love of truth; and a humility which is not cringing or self-deprecatory or timid but rather a true sense of proportion in regard to people, things, qualities and ultimate values. These human traits of love, faith, courage, honesty and humility exist in greater or less strength in every person. By self-training and discipline they can be developed sufficiently to make a good nonviolent "soldier" out of average human material. Of course, leaders of a nonviolent movement require these qualities to an unusual degree, just as generals of armies require qualities developed to a higher degree than those of the common soldier.

Not only is love the most important of all these qualities of the nonviolent person; it may almost be considered the origin of all the others. If the name "love" in such a context seems too impossible or sentimental, call it a sort of intelligence or knowledge. This love must be strong and clear-sighted, not hawkish or sentimental. It does not state or hint that it is going to "do good to" the other person, nor does it make a parade of itself. It must be patient and full of insight and understanding and imagination. It must be enduring, kind and unselfish. It is wonderful but it is not superhuman or exceedingly rare. We have all seen such love in many mothers of all classes, nations and races, also in the best teachers. Its creativeness in these instances is well known.[8]

If through love for your enemy you can create in him respect or admiration for you, this provides the best possible means by which your new ideà or suggestion to him will become an auto-suggestion within him, and it will also help nourish that auto-suggestion.[9]

Anger, as well as love, can be creative, for both are expressions or modes of energy. But love contains more energy and endurance than anger. Love involves the very principle and essence of continuity of life itself. If considered as an instrument, it can be more efficiently and effectively wielded, has better aim, and has a better fulcrum or point of vantage, than anger. Love gains a stronger and more lasting approval from the rest of mankind. The probabilities in favour of its winning over anger in the long run are strong.

But if one party to a contest cannot develop towards the conflict or towards his opponent an attitude that is creative or akin to love, he should certainly be honest and true to himself. As long as men have uncontrollable anger or enmity in their feelings, it is better to express it honestly and courageously than to be hypocritical and refuse to fight out of cowardice. Christ, searching for a change in men more profound and important than immediate external acts, told them to get rid of anger and greed, knowing that if this took place, war would disappear.

Courageous violence, to prevent or stop a wrong, is better than cowardly acquiescence. Cowardice is more harmful morally than violence. The inner attitude is more important than the outer act, though it is vitally important always to be true to oneself, to make one's outer conduct a true reflection and expression of one's inner state. Fear develops out of an assumption of relative weakness. Since all men have the innate possibility of moral strength, to be afraid is really a denial of one's moral potential powers and is therefore very harmful. Violence and anger at least show faith in one's own moral powers and thus provide at least a basis for further growth. He who refrains from fighting because he is afraid, really hates his opponent in his heart and wishes that circumstances would change so that he could hurt or destroy his opponent. The energy of his hate is present but suppressed. If one has not the special courage or discipline or conviction to resist wrong or violence without counter violence, then it is better to be violent than to be cowardly. But he who has the courage to fight and yet refrains, is the true nonviolent resister. Because the coward fears, he cannot love, and if he cannot love he cannot be wholly successful in nonviolent resistance. He cannot use this moral jiu-jitsu completely, effectively. Refraining from outward violent act through fearless self-control of anger is better than acting violently; but getting rid of anger is best of all, and the only sure way. True nonviolent resistance, where the outer act is an expression of inner attitude, gradually creates among all beholders an awareness of essential human unity. But if the inner condition is one of anger or hate, cowardly nonviolence of deed is inconsistent with the inner condition, and this cowardly inconsistency or insincerity is soon detected by others and perhaps openly called hypocrisy; and this inconsistency makes impossible any considerable increase in the awareness of essential unity.

As to the outcome of a struggle waged by nonviolence, we must understand one point thoroughly. The aim of the nonviolent resister is not to injure, or crush and humiliate his opponent, or to "break his will," as in a violent, fight.[10] The aim is to convert the opponent, to change his understanding and his sense of values, so that he will join wholeheartedly with the resister in seeking a settlement truly amicable and truly satisfying to both sides. The nonviolent resister seeks a solution under which both parties can have complete self-respect and mutual respect; a settlement that will implement the new desires and full energies of both parties. The nonviolent resister seeks to help the violent attacker re-establish his moral balance on a level higher and more secure than that from which he first launched his violent attack. The method withdraws a mistaken support not in order to harm the opponent but to help both parties into a more secure, creative, happy, and truthful relationship.

In his interesting attempt to apply game theory to human conflicts, Anatol Rapaport[11] divides conflicts into three varieties: fights, in which opponents try to destroy each other; games, in which they attempt to outwit each other; and debates, in which they strive to convert each other. The last variety is the only kind which could be productive, and our best hope of survival is to convert fights into games, and games into debates. Under Gandhi's conception of *ahimsa* its votary pits his refusal to hurt or injure his opponent—despite the inconveniences of such an attitude to himself—against those who desire to fight or outwit him; and he seeks to convert them to the use of noncoercive methods to gain their ends by finding an area of common interest, based upon common humanity, which would put the conflict of aims into a proper perspective.[12] In the arena of power politics, power experts meet power experts and the struggle continues to be cast in power-play manoeuvers if not in terms of outright or subtle coercion. The framework of assumptions which underlies the strategy of power conflicts may make it impossible for rivals or antagonists to choose the mutually advantageous course because there is nothing in their experience which allows them to make the assumption of similarity in regard to their relative positions. If they could do this, they might solve the dilemma to the advantage of both. Indulgence in *himsa* is the result of short sightedness, lack of vision, arising out of the inability to put oneself in the position of an antagonist and to disarm or convert him so that he ceases to regard himself as an irreconcilable enemy. Far from denying the existence or reality of conflicts of interest in human society, Gandhi admitted their existence in every walk of life and sought to make *ahimsa* the basis of a method of action which could cope nonviolently with such conflicts by limiting if not wholly removing the *himsa* involved.[13]

Violence and nonviolence, like war and peace, are the obverse and reverse sides of a coin and hence should not be treated as conflicting, exclusive or antithetical terms. The two terms are relative and coexist simultaneously. Reason, culture, emotion, economic activity and force are the five common elements, that are present, when nations are plunged in mass scale violence and when nations are at peace with one another. The difference between the two states (violent and nonviolent) is noticeable whenever there is shift of emphasis among the five elements.

There is no such thing as absolute violence or absolute peace. When certain quarters engage themselves in violence, peace reigns in others. For instance, when one nation pitches itself in war against another, the members of each nation maintain peaceful relations with each other. Similarly when one class, group or community having social, political or religious moorings, sets out against another, the relations within the members of each group become more friendly and cooperative.

Durbin, Bowley and others hold that fighting and peaceful cooperation are natural forms of behaviour. They say that in spite of the peaceful co-operation, transition from peace to war is effected when the balance between the desire for cooperation and the conflicting desire to obtain self-regarding ends by force, is disturbed by the circumstances of the group.

For decades, there have been sincere efforts by prophets and religious saints to restrain people from drifting to the side of war and taking recourse to the technique of violence to settle the issues responsible for it. So much so that in 1928 a world Conference for International Peace through Religion took place in Geneva. The representatives of all great religions unanimously voted for certain principles of life, viz. human solidarity, unity of life, interests, destiny, cooperation instead of competition, help of the weak and the backward. These principles, it was hoped, would provide all nation, with freedom and security.

Instead of concord, coordination and harmony, however, we find today rampant discord, competition and conflict. The world seems to be well in the grip of materialists and power seekers. Conflict is all pervasive and the method sought to resolve this conflict is not cooperation and love but war and hatred. As a matter of fact, for a time, the peoples of the world did not know the practical use of any other method than 'that of war. It is only in the 20th century that a nonviolent technique better known as *Satyagraha* was introduced and demonstrated in a masterly way to resolve social conflicts.

The history of the world has never been free from some sort of conflicts—social or otherwise. The *Zend Avesta* states that conflict existed due to the contending forces of good and evil. The theory of inevitability of conflict remained unchanged until the 19th century when it underwent modifications first at the hands of Darwin, and then subsequently at the hands of Spencer, J. Novicow and G. Tarde who, while furthering the conflict theory contended that there exist conflicted among different elements of nature, nay even among the stars, planets and molecules, thereby implying that conflict among human beings was natural because of the varied ideals and interests of the people.[14]

Gandhi, the author of the new technique, did not agree with the foregoing theorists of conflict to whom struggle and disunity was the law of the universe. Instead he believed that unity, love and cooperation were the fundamental laws of life, hence of the universe. He agreed with Prince Kropotkin, the Russian biologist, who arrived at the 'mutual aid' doctrine after years of observation of the lives of insects and animals.

Nevertheless, Gandhi paid due cognition to repulsion in nature and apprehended factors that caused discord and repugnance in the minds of men leading them to bellicose and warlike designs. Gandhi points to self-interest as the cause of all social conflicts. To fight this, he felt the necessity of a permanent institution or instrument, which he lately evolved in the form of *Satyagraha* or nonviolent resistance.

Non-violent resistance, in other words, nonviolent direct action is a principle to resolve social conflicts. It has greatly affected the trend of thinking of the oriental people and the occidental people. It seeks to resolve different kinds' of conflicts. The dynamism inherent in the very technique had made its wider application possible. K. Shridharani has classified these conflicts into three categories: (1) An individual versus another individual; or an individual pitted against a group; or (2) A group pitted against another one; or (3) A community versus a state.[15]

INDIVIDUAL *VERSUS* AN INDIVIDUAL

Satyagraha has been applied to all the three categories of conflicts. It has been used against one's own and dear ones, viz. mother, father, brother, sister, wife, friends and neighbours, as well as against stray individuals and groups within the orbit of one's social and political operations. Gandhi's own life is sprinkled with its instances. He adhered to the method of *Satyagraha* in dealing with his teacher, father, bad characters, caste, mob and followers. He applied it in his professional life of a lawyer.

INDIVIDUAL *VERSUS* A GROUP

The first instance of this kind of *Satyagraha* occurred when Gandhi returned from London after completing his law course. He was excommunicated and all privileges of caste were denied to him. Gandhi, instead of insisting upon admission to the caste, respected caste regulations about ex-communication. The scrupulous conduct shown evoked affection and generosity of the caste-people. This was the result of *Satyagraha* of an individual against a group—"It is my conviction that all these good things are due to my nonresistance".[16]

Through another example Gandhi demonstrated that the greater and purer the suffering, the better are the chances for victory. Gandhi undertook fasts for the moral lapses of the ashramites; this technique widened in its scope after Independence. The first fast Gandhi undertook at the Phoenix Settlement in South Africa to improve the conduct of a young man and woman of the ashram.

GROUP PITTED AGAINST ANOTHER GROUP

Group conflicts occur due to difference in values—interests and goals of different groups, viz. between a minority and a majority or between labour and management or between some social group and the government. A *Satyagrahi* who seeks to resolve these conflicts takes up *Satyagraha* or non-resistance as an individual obligation and a social duty to defend the right of self-determination and it is his moral duty not to submit to the swaggering and rollicking authority whether of the family, society, superior economic group or of the government that he is faced with.

The first application of *Satyagraha* of group conflicts was made outside India. On September 11, 1906 Gandhi called a meeting at Empire Theatre, Johannesburg, protesting against draft ordinance against Indian Immigrants in Transvaal in South Africa. Indians as a group decided not to submit to the new ordinance but to suffer all penalties, if it became law. This was a *Satyagraha* by a group of Indians constituting a minority, against Europeans who were in majority and formed the Government.

In India the first significant group conflict in which Gandhi used the *Satyagraha* method, took place in Champaran. The Champaran *Satyagraha* sought to resolve the dispute between the agriculturists and the Government. The 'Kheda' and the 'Bardoli' *Satyagrahas* which took place in subsequent years also aimed at reconciling grievances of the peasants against the Government.

The success of *Satyagraha* in a 'class war' in Champaran cast a fascinating influence on the workers of the country. The Ahmedabad workers were first to derive lesson from it. Their grievances were low pay, and overwork. When they approached Gandhi, he advised them to take to nonviolent strike, a byproduct of the nonviolent direct action. The *Satyagrahic* strike succeeded in changing the hearts of the managements and their demands were fulfilled. Thus the conflict between the two economic classes was resolved.

COMMUNITY *VERSUS* THE STATE

The third kind of conflict, that *Satyagraha* or nonviolent direct action handles arises out of discontent among the in-group members of a community against the ruling power of the state. Its potentiality was manifested in 1920 and again in 1930.

The non-cooperation movement of 1920-22 marks the culmination of a number of conflicts. The first of these conflicts, between the people and the Government began in 1857. It was followed by a number of conflicts, viz. the partition of Bengal in 1905, Rowlatt Act in 1919, and the Punjab atrocities the same year. The 1921 movement would have been bloody, had Gandhi not canalised the sentiments and emotions of the people on nonviolent lines.

This experiment with nonviolence on such a wide scale, being the first of its kind, could not obtain the immediate objective, yet the experience achieved and the consciousness it aroused in the masses served as an asset for the 1930 movement.

ORGANIZATION AND DISCIPLINE OF SATYAGRAHA

The success of any method or technique on a group scale very much depends upon the organisation and discipline of its proponents and followers. *Satyagraha* or nonviolence as a technique has been used both for individual and corporate action. Gandhi once said that nonviolence was not an individual virtue but a course of spiritual and political conduct both for the individual and the community. It was a force that may be used by individuals as well as by communities. It might be used as well in political as in domestic affairs. Its universal applicability was a demonstration of its permanence and invincibility. It could be used alike by men, women and children.

Satyagraha's wide application and its hope and promise for being an equivalent to war suggested among other problems, the problem of organisation, discipline and training. As an equivalent of war *Satyagraha* became a virtue for the individual and a rule of conduct for society to be practised for peace and a force against force. Its success both during peaceful periods as well as during periods of individual and group conflicts was made possible because of a mighty organisation at its back. This organisation, namely the Indian National Congress, was modelled and repatterned according to the needs of *Satyagraha* by the *Satyagraha* innovator and leader.

In 1919 Congress accepted nonviolence as its policy to win freedom. Gandhi in one of his earlier speeches explained *ahimsa* as love. "I must love my enemy.., as I would do to my wrong doing father or son.... Gift of love is the greatest of all gifts".[17] He described "love as the strongest force, the world possessed and yet it is humblest imaginable".[18] Such statements of Gandhi mitigated caste, colour and creed distinctions and brought the drifting masses under one camp holding nonviolence as their policy and looking forward to Swaraj as their goal.

Slowly, but surely, Congress became the strongest and the best organised party. Millions joined it and regarded it as their representative body. Sir Samuel Hoare declared in the House of Commons during the hectic days of 1930, that only one village out of ten had taken to civil disobedience. Even at that, Sir Samuel's "official version" concedes the Congress some 50,000 villages and over five million rural Indians. Gandhi placed a formula, which he practised and mastered in South Africa before the Congress and the latter accepted it with great confidence in its workability. Henceforth Congress became the platform and the via media of all Gandhi's nonviolent and *Satyagraha* movements. Every social, political or economic movement launched by Gandhi received the full support of the masses.

To consolidate the Congress organisation, and thereby strengthen the *Satyagraha* movement, committees were founded, Congress offices were established and ashrams started. No province, district, city was left where Congress strong hand had not reached. In quite a large number of villages Congress had its office.

"It would be difficult to estimate the exact number of villages that have a Congress office today, but the wholehearted response which Gandhi's call in 1930 received from these areas, indicates that one hamlet out of three is thoroughly indoctrinated in the creed of *Satyagraha* and has a Congress office of its own".[19]

During peace times all the units, in village or city, kept themselves busy in constructive programmes, spinning, weaving, studying *Satyagraha* literature, delivering lectures on *Satyagraha*, manual labour, social reconstruction schemes and training the people through political education. In times of group conflict or corporate action against the government, when the clarion call was given by the Congress for *Satyagraha*, non-cooperation, or civil disobedience, the units propagated the charted programme among the community members who in turn refused payment of taxes, defied unjust laws or boycotted the whole system of government. Expressing satisfaction over Congress adoption of nonviolence as a policy and over the power it brought to congress, Gandhi said:

> "God has blessed me with the mission to place nonviolence before the nation for adoption for better or for worse. The Congress has adopted it, and for the past nineteen years the Congress, admittedly the most popular, and powerful organisation, has consistently and to the best of its ability tried to act up to it".[20]

The volunteer organisation (corps of Servants of India), or the permanent corps of Swayam Sevakas served to reinforce the Congress and to augment the power of the organisation. Also known as the Hindustani Sevadal, its members were experts in *Satyagrahic* strategy and discipline and worked as commissioned officers for recruiting and training in nonviolent technique. Provincial and village units were financed and controlled by the central office of the congress. During long vacations camps were organised and each village unit was represented in the camp by one of its few best volunteers who upon demand could take up the responsibilities of a leader. Thus, the summer camps became leadership training camps.

The Congress organisation and the *Satyagraha* movement were further strengthened by the Ashramas, which were the training centres of "Gandhi workers" who after completing the requisite period could be sent out in villages to acquaint the masses with the fundamental tenets of *Satyagraha* and to develop the village community economically as well as politically. Even today the sphere of their activities consists of the following with slight variation from place to place:

(i) They supplemented the work of the All India Spinners' Association by popularizing hand spinning and weaving; they also teach other cottage industries and eulogize hand-made goods. (ii) Ashrama physicians give medical relief. (iii) Ashrama instructors conduct night schools for the poor of all ages struggling for a living by day. (iv) Ashrama workers organize and advise cooperative societies. (v) They spread hygienic and health propaganda among the people; they even go so far as to clean the village streets, and wells and ponds. (vi) The ashrama's book collectors give their books as the foundations of free libraries. (vii) Workers with law degrees help farmers with their own panchayats (village five) to settle disputes and to direct civic organisation of the community; in this way poor litigants are spared the draining off of their resources, which a hearing in a government court entails. (viii) Once a year the ashramas organise educational and agricultural exhibits for those who can not read. (ix) They spread scientific knowledge regarding dairy farming. (x) Every man and woman in the ashrama is given strong and forceful arguments against child marriage and untouchability, and day in and day out Gandhi workers urge villagers to give up child marriage and untouchability, as well as to forgo the tradition of spending lavishly over marriage and death rites.[21]

The ashramas, which had aimed at multi-dimensional development of villagers, succeeded in winning their faith and confidence in the Congress and in its policies. Giving their full loyalty to Gandhi, to Congress and to its policies the ashramas turned into *Satyagrahi* camps at the time of the national movement.

Howsoever well organized an institution may be, it cannot lead to defined goals unless its constituent elements are well-disciplined. It becomes truer still in the case of nonviolence where the contending parties are represented by physical and moral forces; where the participants of the latter are not disqualified because of their age, blindness or any other physical defect. The only thing required is courage and discipline. 'If I have to win swaraj nonviolently, I must discipline my people,'[22] said Gandhi. Discipline has not to be imposed by any authority like the one in military. The virtue of iron discipline has to be developed from within, without which non-violence can only be a veneer.

To have a disciplined *Satyagraha* army, the spirit of service, sacrifice and renunciation has to be cultivated in its members, who should be guided by justice, truth and love, the essential factors of peace. The traditional training in the art of killing has to give way to the training that would teach the art of dying for nonviolence. In order to make this training in discipline effective, its sphere should be extended from nonviolent overt behaviour to nonviolence in thought, speech and action. The perfect state of disciplined nonviolence would be, as Gandhi said, 'when mind and body and speech are in proper coordination'.[23]

The best means to effect such a coordinated discipline among the rank and file of the *Satyagrahi*s was the constructive work. Manual work was one of the important terms in Gandhiji's scheme of constructive work. It was destined to provide the worker with self-respect, self-reliance and self-control. It developed in the worker a sense of order and cooperation and made him feel that he was the protector of the community because he was consciously making an economic contribution to the country's wealth. Other qualities that automatically developed in a manual worker were equanimity, poise, patience, humility, and love of truth.

The other activities of the constructive programme, viz. singing, dancing, prayers and other social services besides disciplining people created in them a sense of unity, brought the divergent groups closer and bound them in one unit of the *Satyagraha* force.

To develop and maintain discipline in every soldier of the *Satyagraha* force, Gandhi as early as 1921 asked each one of them to take a pledge. In 1930 he laid nineteen rules for them. In 1938 be laid down the basic assumptions for a successful *Satyagraha*. To implement *Satyagraha*, Gandhi, shortly after a period of five months, brought forth the qualifications of a *Satyagrahi*. He said that the success of an organised and disciplined *Satyagraha* was due to two things put together, the organised institution of the Congress and a disciplined body of volunteers.

NONVIOLENT RESISTANCE

Satyagraha may aptly be described as nonviolent *Satyagraha*, in its essentials, is active and dynamic resistance to evil. As Romain Rolland had put it: "No one has a greater horror of passivity than this tireless fighter, who is one of the most heroic incarnations of a man who resists. The soul of his movement is active resistance—which finds outlet, not in violence, but in the active force of love, faith, and sacrifice. This threefold energy is expressed in the word *Satyagraha*."[24] Gandhi himself stressed upon the active aspect of his non-violent weapon. "Yours should not merely be a passive spirituality that spends itself in idle meditation, but it should be an active thing which will carry war into the enemy's camp."[25]

The western pacifists, because of their absolutistic concept could not appreciate the dynamic and militant character of Gandhi's non-violence. In the words of H. Runham Brown, a well-known pacifist of Britain: "Gandhiji was unlike other saints. He was a practical statesman of the world. Ideals in the clouds never appealed to him. He must make them work, and he did. I had the great privilege of receiving and passing on a long correspondence between Gandhiji and Vladimir Tchertkoff, Leo Tolstoy's great Secretary, and Russia's greatest pacifist and anarchist, there being no direct post between Russia and India. I was invited to read that correspondence, and I did. Tchertkoff was telling Gandhiji that he was not really a pacifist at all. I think the mistaken idea of the Russian was not so much due to the fact that Gandhiji had come more slowly to his pacifist convictions than the great anarchist had, but because of certain things that the Mahatma had said or written. He had declared that it was better to fight even with carnal weapons than to cravenly submit to injustice. Sayings like this were quite incomprehensible to Vladimir Tchertkoff. To him pacifism was a great religious faith; nothing could shift him."[26]

To Gandhi, resistance to evil was the supreme duty. He always emphasised upon direct action and he declared that "Never has anything been done on this earth without direct action."[27] To resist nonviolently was the most manly course. But he did not make a fetish of nonviolence. He was not a literalist in his conception of *ahimsa*. To him the test of *ahimsa* is a violent intention behind a thought, word or deed, *i.e.* an intention to harm.[28]

Gandhi's theory of nonviolence is no cover for cowardice. As he himself wrote, "My creed of nonviolence is an extremely active force. It has no room for cowardice or even weakness. There is hope for a violent man to be some day nonviolent, but there is none for a coward. I have therefore said more than once that if we do not know how to defend ourselves, our women and our places of worship by the force of suffering, *i.e.* nonviolence, we must, if we are men, be at least able to defend all these by fighting."[29] "Nonviolence and cowardice go ill together. I can imagine a fully armed man to be at heart a coward. Possession of arms implies an element of fear, if not cowardice. But true nonviolence is an impossibility without the possession of unadulterated fearlessness."[30]

He would rather prefer violence to cowardice. "I would risk violence a thousand times than the emasculation of the whole race."[31]

"I do believe that, where there is only a choice between cowardice and violence, I would advise violence. I would rather have India resort to arms in order to defend her honour than that she should, in a cowardly manner, become or remain a helpless witness to her own dishonour."[32]

It was not the outer manifestation of violence that he despised so much as he did cowardice. He wrote: "Cowardice is perhaps the greater vice from which we suffer and is also possibly the greatest violence, certainly far greater than bloodshed and the like that generally go under the name of violence."[33]

Refuting the charge that his weapon was a weapon merely of the weak, he wrote as early as 1909: "Believe me that a man devoid of courage and manhood can never be a passive resister."[34]

RESISTANCE 'ALMOST NON-VIOLENT'

An analysis of Gandhi's attitude towards war shows that he did not share the absolutistic notion of non-violence of the western pacifists. For the present, we would like to point out that on two occasions he characterized resistance of the people, in two different situational contexts, as 'almost nonviolent'.

Gandhi appreciated the resistance of Poland, albeit violent, against Nazi aggression and went the whole length to write: "If Poland has that measure of uttermost bravery and an equal measure of selflessness, history will forget that she defended herself with violence. Her violence will be counted almost as nonviolence."[35] Later he explained it more precisely. He said: "If a man fights with his sword single handed against a horde of dacoits armed to the teeth, I should say he is fighting almost nónviolently. Haven't I said to our women that, if in defence of their honour they used their nails and teeth and even a dagger, I should regard their conduct nonviolent? She does not know' the distinction between *Himsa* and *Ahimsa*. She acts spontaneously. Supposing a mouse in fighting a cat tried to resist the cat with his sharp beak, would you call that mouse violent? In the same way, for the Poles to stand valiantly against the German hordes vastly superior in numbers, military equipment and strength, was almost nonviolence."[36]

This epithet he used on a second occasion, with respect to the violent outbursts manifest during the Quit India movement of 1942 in some parts of the country against the brutal repression by the government which Gandhi described as 'leonine violence'. He gave voice to his thoughts on this subject more than once during his twenty one-day fast in the Aga Khan Palace in February, 1943. He unequivocally expressed his emphatic disapproval of the sabotage, secrecy and violence resorted to by the people in the country. He said that his name must not be used in support of these activities, and that he still swore by nonviolence to the same extent as he did before, and that, again, he still wished people to fight in a purely nonviolent manner. "Let me warn you", said he "that India will never succeed in attaining her freedom through violence. If a vast country like ours, with a population of four hundred millions, takes to the path of violence, the world cannot escape destruction. If, on the contrary, we keep on the straight path, we may be able to show the same to the war-weary world." On the next day he dwelt further on the same theme: "Though I do not at all like what is going on outside, I am not prepared to criticise and condemn that violence while I am in jail; because I have got to criticise the Government's policy much more severely. If the Government are bent on goading people to violence, they can succeed in their design. The masses are not angels, and are likely to be misled in the absence of leaders capable of advising them to adhere to nonviolence. Nevertheless, Governmental violence has been many times greater than popular violence. It would not be right for me to criticise from here the people alone. My own faith in nonviolence has grown stronger, and there has been no change in my views on the subject except in one respect. I do not now say that nonviolence can work only if there is a non-violent atmosphere in the country; for I have now come to believe that the power of non-violence lies in its ability to work even in the midst of a conflagration."

"Had you been out, what would you have said about the violence of the people?" Gandhi was asked the next day. "I would have had to say much more against the Government's violence than against that of the people. I can do so as a free man, but not while I am in prison. You should also know that I cannot express any opinion about events without a full inquiry. It is one thing to discuss whether a particular act can be considered non-violent and whether it is likely to help in the attainment of Swaraj. It is another thing to condemn the same act publicly. There ought to be a thorough inquiry prior to that. Had I been free, I would not only have criticised or condemned several things that have happened but would not have allowed them to happen and would have shown to the people a more effective method. It would have produced greater effect because it would have been purely nonviolent. My conception of a struggle was different from what is taking place in the country today. But it is insufferable that those people who have tried for years past to tread the path of non-violence should be sought to be suppressed through the fiercest violence. If the Government grow mad out of anger and perpetrate unprecedented frightfulness against weak, unarmed men and women, and if in consequence, the people out of sheer desperation, are seized with frenzy and thoughtlessly commit untoward sots, history will pronounce their violence to be nonviolent in comparison with the violence of the Government, just as I wrote in *Harijan* (in 1939) that the violent resistance of Poland against the German aggression was almost nonviolent."[37]

This shows that Gandhi was not a stickler for the form of *ahimsa*; he prized bravery and fearlessness as manly virtues and adhered to nonviolence for it symbolized, according to him, the noblest expression of the greatest courage.

MORAL EQUIVALENT OF WAR

The Catholic philosopher, Jacques Maritain, writes: "...there are two different orders of means of warfare (taken in the widest sense of the word), as there are two kinds of fortitude and courage, the courage that attacks and the courage that endures, the force of coercion or aggression and the force of patience, the force that inflicts suffering on others and the force that endures suffering inflicted on oneself. There you have two different keyboards that stretch along the two sides of our human nature, though the sounds they give are constantly intermingled; opposing evil through attack and coercion—a way, which at the last extremity, leads to the shedding, if need be, of the blood of others; and opposing evil through suffering and enduring—a way which, at the last extremity, leads to the sacrifice of one's own life. To the second keyboard the means of spiritual warfare belong."[38] He would like to call *Satyagraha* a "means of spiritual warfare."[39] According to Maritain, Gandhi's theory and technique of *Satyagraha* should be related to the Thomistic notion of courage in enduring. While he rightly stresses upon one essential element of *Satyagraha* and notes a fundamental similarity between war and *Satyagraha*, namely self-suffering "the strongest of the strong" as Gandhi would call it, he does not take into account the direct action or the 'aggressive' aspect of this technique. This element of direct action, with the stipulation of nonviolence, however, is shared by *Satyagraha* in common with war. It is this similarity between Gandhi's nonviolent resistance and the institution of war that demands close attention.

The great American psychologist, William James, wrote: "So far war has been the only force that can discipline a whole community and until an equivalent discipline is organised, I believe that war must have its way. But I have no serious doubt that the ordinary prides and shames of social man, once developed to a certain intensity, are capable of organizing such a moral equivalent as I have sketched, or some such other just as effective or skilful propagandism, and of opinion-making men seizing historic opportunities."[40]

So far as is known, Gandhi was acquainted neither with William James' essay on *The Moral Equivalent of War* (1910) nor with his *Varieties of Religious Experience* (1902). But he actually evolved what William James demanded but failed to offer.

Gandhi in an article outlining the origin and development of *Satyagraha* termed it as 'the moral equivalent of war'. "The term war is generally applied to armed conflict between population groups conceived of as organic unities..."[41] It is the symbolic expression for the 'violent' method of adjusting disputes, while *Satyagraha* is based on non-violence. The essential difference between war and *Satyagraha*, according to Professor Nirmal Kumar Bose, amounts to this: while the former aims at coercion, the latter aims at conversion. In war one inflicts punishment upon the adversary, in *Satyagraha* one draws the maximum suffering on oneself, without a trace of bitterness against the opponent as a human being.[42] But it is war nevertheless. As the same learned authority says: "*Satyagraha* is not a substitute for war, it is war itself shorn of many of its ugly features and guided by a purpose nobler than we associate with destruction. It is an intensely heroic and chivalrous form of war."[43]

Dr. K.L. Shridharani has broadly outlined the common features between the war-process and the *Satyagraha* as follows:

First, both are modes of social action aiming at the resolution of social conflict. *Secondly*, both come into being when and where negotiation and arbitration fall short of solving disputes.

Underlying these two characteristics common to both violence and nonviolence, is the basic assumption that certain radical social changes cannot be brought about, save by mass action capable of precipitating an emotional crisis, and that the humdrum of everyday existence of human life needs shaking up in order that men may arrive at fateful decisions. Constant habitual action that flows undisturbed under a tranquil social milieu blurs the vision of the people when it comes to novel social forces and their potential gravity. Consequently, the issue "Must be successfully and sufficiently dramatized in order to arouse mass enthusiasm and mass enthusiasm preparatory to reaching a crucial decision". This requires not merely an intense consciousness of the issues involved, but also an emotional crisis in the life of the community. With respect to this particular reading of social psychology, there is no disagreement at all between the exponents of violent warfare and Gandhi. In a statement given to the press on December 4, 1932, on the eve of his famous fast unto death, Gandhi said:

"Those who have to bring about radical changes in human conditions and surroundings, cannot do it except by raising a ferment in society. There are only two methods of doing this, violent and non-violent. Violent pressure is felt on the physical being and it degrades him who uses it as it depresses the victim, but non-violent pressure exerted through self-suffering, as by fasting, works in an entirely different way. It touches not the physical body, but it touches and strengthens the moral fibre of those against whom it is directed."[44]

The occasion, which inspired this statement contained many factors of the war-process. Surrounding Gandhi's "Epic Fast" were action, drama, elan, and imaginative appeal. The cause for which Gandhi staked his life was also enriched by the halo of sacredness. What is more important, there was no trace of bitterness on either side involved in the crisis, nor was there any of the objectionable qualities entailed in the violent procedure of war. There appears to be an amazing agreement between Gandhi's analysis of his *Satyagrah* process and the, formulation of the war-process in the *Encyclopaedia of the Social Sciences.* Sidney Hook writes in his article on violence:

"It is not hard to understand why violence seems to be an invariable concomitant of all mass movements of social reform. First of all, it symbolizes in dramatic fashion the issues involved and forces upon them the attention of those elements in the community which cannot be stirred into activity by rational appeal. There always seem to be more individuals susceptible to the emotionalism bound up with the immediacies of action—Its thrill, its imaginative appeal and the ultimate sacrifices which make the cause sacred—Some theorists, such as Sorel, offer as the only practical justification of the poetic cult of violence its usefulness in dramatizing the conflict of ethical values."[45]

Nonviolent direct action, then, bases itself on the same principles of mass appeal and the effectiveness of the resultant mass action as the tested ideology of war does.

Thirdly Satyagraha as An Instrument of Aggression: It was this "appeal to direct action," analogous to the military "appeal to arms," that captured the imagination of an inactive and stagnant Indian people, both in India and in South Africa.[46] The result was the cavalcade of mass movements, some comprising small interest-groups or big regional units and others embracing the whole populace, under the leadership of Mahatma Gandhi. The "incidents" that took place in South Africa between 1906 and 1914 and the continuous struggle in India since 1914, which culminated in national freedom in 1947, have left no sceptics as to the mass appeal of *Satyagraha* and its pliability as a device for huge populations. This factor naturally leads us to a consideration of the third characteristic that *Satyagraha* and war have in common. A mass movement employing direct action, *Satyagraha* lends itself to the training, of soldiers and generals (*Swayamsevakas*), to organization, discipline and strategy. One significant aspect of *Satyagrahic* strategy is that, like war activity, it has both defensive and offensive sides. There is an inexhaustible store of material to illustrate these various subdivisions of *Satyagraha*, especially in the Indian vernaculars.

However, we should make an exception for the "offensive" or "aggressive" phase of *Satyagraha*. This is made necessary mainly because of the inept use of words in describing *Satyagraha* in English. Besides, the average Westerner's conception of Gandhi's movement as "merely a passive refusal to do things" requires 'a thorough overhauling'. *Satyagraha* compels the opponent to do things or to stop doing them. But this phase of' nonviolent direct action is generally missed, and part of the blame should fall on the poor translations of the word. In order to distinguish Gandhi's practice from war, the former has usually been symbolized by some sort of resistance, ranging from nonresistance (Christian doctrine), passive resistance (Tolstoyan variety), to non-violent resistance (Gandhism). The last of these three expressions, no doubt, conveys the essence of *Satyagraha*. But the very inference of "responsiveness" implied in the word "resistance" creates an impression that *Satyagraha* can never be an instrument of aggression or of the offensive. It also reads as if *Satyagraha* is always a "reaction" but never "action." Looking at *Satyagraha* in the light of events in India, this impression seems to be misleading. Although always conscious of the magnitude of gravity involved in "Assertive Civil Disobedience," Gandhi himself has declared in favour of offensive non-violent direct action under certain conditions.

In answer to a letter from one of his lieutenants who was seeking instructions, he wrote in *Young India* of 9th of February, 1922;

"aggressive Civil Disobedience is a right to be exercised when necessary and when we are thoroughly ready, and is also a duty we must discharge, if we are ready and circumstances require the performance of it. But aggressive Civil Disobedience, whether mass or individual, is a most dangerous weapon though also the most effective among all the peaceful weapons at our disposal. Assertive Civil Disobedience is a right that accrues to us only after severe *tapasya* (disciplinary rigours) through which we have not yet gone. The least, therefore, that we must do is to await the result of the experiment I personally wish to conduct."[47]

That was written in, 1922, and even then Gandhi was contemplating making "the only exception" in the case, "of a group of 100 villages in Andhradesha" who were exceptionally well prepared under the leadership of one of Gandhi's chosen and trusted followers. The 1930 movement, however, was rich in instances of "aggressive *Satyagraha*." of carrying the fight to the opponent's camp without any immediate provocation.

The fourth fundamental similarity between war and *Satyagraha* lies in their identical conception of the source of power, to wit, suffering. A close scrutiny of the doctrine of violence will invariably show that war practically stakes its existence on the dynamic concept of suffering as the generator of power. By inflicting suffering on the enemy, the warriors seek to break the former's will, to make him surrender, to annihilate him, to destroy him, and with him all opposition. Suffering thus becomes a source of social power which compels and coerces. What is more important from a practical viewpoint, the "law of suffering" has worked in the history of the human race, and worked with more inexorable effectiveness than perhaps any other law. Practically all the effectiveness as well as the usefulness of war, consequently, depends on this human reality and social dynamic. It is at this crucial point, it is worth noting, that *Satyagraha* resembles war *par excellence*.

Gandhi's whole theory is based on the concept of suffering as a source of human as well as social force. However, there is a paradoxical twist in the *Satyagrahic* method of generating power from suffering. In *Satyagraha*, it is by inviting suffering from the opponent and not after inflicting suffering upon him that the resultant power is produced. The basic formula is the same, but its application is about-face. It almost amounts to putting the energy in reverse gear. This novel method of generating social power from suffering produced the desired results in India during freedom's battle. It is enough to say here that since the effectiveness of suffering has been tested for centuries through violence and war, it is hard to challenge the effectiveness of the doctrine of *Satyagraha*, the core of which is conscious suffering and not mere moral persuasion. "I have therefore," wrote Gandhi, "ventured to place before India the ancient law of self-sacrifice. For *Satyagraha* and its off-shoots, Non-co-operation and Civil Resistance are nothing but new names for the law of suffering."[48] And again: "No country has ever risen without being purified through the fires of suffering. The condition of wheat-growing is that the seed grain should perish. Life comes out of death. Will India rise out of her slavery without fulfilling this eternal law of purification through suffering?"[49] It is interesting to note in this connection that the following lines from Shelley are quoted in the pages of Gandhi's Young India:

> "To suffer woes which hope thinks fit;
> To forgive wrongs darker than death or night,
> To love, to bear, to hope till Hope creates
> From its own wreck the thing it contemplates;
> Neither to change, to falter, nor repent;
> This like the glorious Titan is to be
> Great, good and joyous, beautiful and free;
> *This is alone* life, joy, Empire and Victory."[50]

Fifthly the Romance of *Satyagraha*: Since *Satyagraha* is based on self-imposed and openly courted suffering, it demands from its adherents the willingness and the ability to endure hardships for their cause, sense of self-sacrifice and courage, of control over anger and fear. *Satyagraha* requires a sense of chivalry and a spirit of adventure. This announces *the fifth* characteristic common to both war and *Satyagraha*. There is romance in non-violent direct action, as there is in war. It also offers an opportunity to display heroism and to earn glory and fame. The glow of self-gratification that follows the feeling that one has done his bit for the Cause is also a significant reward of *Satyagraha*.

An opportunity to endure for one's cause, to display heroism and courage, to engage in adventures and to "do or die" is indisputably one of the premiums of war. As William James once said it, "Militarism is the great preserver of our ideals of hardihood, and human life: with no use for hardihood would be contemptible."[51] Similar reasons led Ruskin to remark that "War is the foundation of all high virtues and faculties of men."[52] In our over-zealousness for peace, we cannot and should not dispense with opportunities for adventure and human endurance, self-sacrifice and the "do or die" spirit. In evolving, therefore, an effective substitute for war, we should look for one which would also offer its participants the supreme dilemma of "to be or not to be."

Satyagraha campaigns in India and elsewhere have shown that there is plenty of drama in non-violent resistance. Since the opponent does not give way easily and is apt to inflict injuries and violence upon the non-violent resisters, the latter is often given the alternative of "life or death." In fact these are the necessary conditions for *Satyagraha* to succeed. In 1930, about 100,000 persons were imprisoned in India, 30,000 of whom were women. The number stopped at that, not because there were no more Indians to solicit arrest but because all the jails were filled to capacity. Consequently, the sight of "lathi-charges," resisters being dragged through the streets, and shot, became more frequent than before. The confiscation of property and bank-accounts, seizure of farm and cattle, exile for life, and death by shooting were the common fate of *Satyagrahis* in those days. But the suffering, instead of cowing the masses, provided opportunities for the Indian people to "do or die." And there was also the satisfaction of doing one's little bit for the freedom of one's country. The toll taken by the Quit India struggle was far greater.

The sixth and final fundamental likeness of *Satyagraha* to war lies in the former's capacity to be an organized institution even in the time of peace. Armed forces are the peacetime institutional and associational form of war. They insure "preparedness" to meet any eventuality. They also help maintain the morale of the people. No substitute for war can be effective until it has troops in reserve. For it also has to be an instrument of protection for the people against attacks from the outside. William James, therefore, proposed an "army against nature." Similar was Gandhi's suggestion, to wit, a permanent corps of volunteers to replace the "standing army." Scores of training centres, where "village workers" and "social servants" carried on even during the period when Indians were not engaged in direct action was a significant feature of an India trying to win her freedom. There was also the "*Hindustani Sevadal*," an all-India organization for training and maintaining *Satyagrahis*.

Of greater significance from the standpoint of the study of *Satyagraha*, as distinct from the study of the Swaraj movement, were efforts at forming what Gandhi designated as the Indian Peace Brigade. This Brigade was conceived of as a permanent corps of non-violent resisters which might be used, in part or as a whole, for all tranquillizing and peace-restoring purposes at all times. As Gandhi suggested in the last months of 1938, its members could be called upon to quell, of course nonviolently, a communal riot in Bombay, or they could be commissioned to the tribal Nagaland to be the out-posts of civil authority.

Gandhi's suggestion was vigorously taken up by the *Gandhi Seva Sangha,* an organization composed of celebrities more famous for their Gandhism than for their nationalism, and devoted solely to the development and the continuation of *Satyagraha* as a technique and as a social philosophy. In the northern hills of the frontier, Gandhi's call received its lusty echo from the activities of Khan Abdul Ghaffar Khan and his *Khudai Khidimatgars*. The Khan claimed at that time that he had already under him such 100,000 non-violent resisters ready to work among the unruly tribes.

Under ideal conditions, that is, when *Satyagraha* becomes the doctrine of a State, this system can be evolved as elaborately as the present-day department of war. Volunteers trained in the technique of *Satyagraha* can; overnight, be posted by the government at strategic points. This system also has the potentiality of being worked out along the lines of the system of compulsory military training in order to train the whole populace in the use of the various forms of *Satyagraha* against aggression from outside or against a warring state.

The idea of a permanent army of non-violent resisters is not as new as it sounds. The Brahmin *gurus* of ancient India, the Buddhist monks from 400 B.C. to the early part of the Christian era, the medieval Christian monks in Europe and the Near East, served similar, if not the same, purposes in a limited scope. In Burma, even today, it is compulsory to send every child to a monastery for a few years with a view towards preparing him for the service of society afterwards when he becomes the head of a family. In modern India there are such organizations as the "Servants of the People Society," "Servants of India Society," "Ramakrishna Mission," "Aryasamaj, and various "Ashramas". In the United States the CCC was perhaps the best example of what William James envisaged. These organisations, however, are not the ideal types that Gandhi's doctrine of *Satyagraha* implies. But the ideal type of *Satyagraha* corps, thoroughly indoctrinated in nonviolence and trained in the techniques of *Satyagraha*, cannot possibly be evolved until the State takes over the job, as there surely cannot be a "standing army" without the patronage of the government. *Satyagraha* has not yet been so fortunate. India became free largely through it, but it was discarded with the British Raj. Vinoba Bhave had revived the Gandhian idea of a *Shanti Sena,* or a Peace Brigade, but only at a non-official and, therefore, limited level.

COERCION AND COMPULSION

Satyagraha, then, has these six effective and practicable attributes of war. It is unnecessary to add that there are equally fundamental differences between the two methods for solving social conflicts. The greatest of the difference lies in the diverse methods of generating social power through suffering. In *Satyagraha*, unlike war, suffering is utilized, as it were, through reverse gear. Consequently, non-violent direct action operates to compel riot through inflicting horrors and destruction as war does, but by disrupting the morale of the opponent by various psychological suggestions. As Gandhi sees it, "it touches not the physical body, but it touches and strengthens the moral fibre of those against whom it is directed."[53] In other words, *Satyagraha*, unlike war, is a process of conversion in a special sense of the term; special because there is always present in it what for the lack of a better term we will call the compelling element. Non-violent direct action, by compelling the opponent to realize the error of his ways, prepares a mental plateau where both parties can resume negotiations, the initial failure of which had necessitated the engagement, on the terms of equality and with a view to a just settlement of the dispute. This is a process entirely different from that of war, which, when successful, destroys the very existence of opposing claims.

The crucial point involved here is the question of whether *Satyagraha*; like war, is also a *coercive force.* Gandhi himself has time and again refused to see any element of coercion in non-violent, direct action. In the light of events in India as well as in the light of certain of Gandhi's own activities, however, it becomes apparent, that *Satyagraha* does contain an aspect of coercion, if in a somewhat modified form. The word "coercion" has numerous connotations, and there is also, in it, a trace of punishment, the self purifying and self-suffering phase of *Satyagraha*, on the other hand, to be a part of the compulsion of nonviolent direct action. The *Satyagrahi*, as Gandhi puts it, "knowing that the remedy lies with himself, ceases to harbour the spirit of revenge and learns to be satisfied with a redress of the wrong he is seeking to remedy." Herein perhaps is founded Gandhi's refusal to acknowledge the element of coercion as a part of his ideology of non-violence. It is misleading, therefore, to describe *Satyagraha* as a form of non-violent coercion as C. M. Case has done in his book bearing that title.[54] But it is equally misleading, on the other hand, to call *Satyagraha* a pure and simple process of conversion as Gandhi and some of his followers would have it. There is an element of what, for want of a better, term, we shall call *compulsion* in it, if not of coercion, since the latter implies revenge and punishment.[55] As a matter of fact, Gandhi himself once used the very word compel in connection with his ideology. Criticizing Lord Chelmsford's speech in 1920 which upheld the Punjab Martial Law and justified, subtly, the Jallianwalla Bagh Massacre, Gandhi said in a statement to the press:

> "The remarks on the Punjab mean a flat refusal to grant redress. He would have us to concentrate on the problems of the immediate future! The immediate future is to compel repentance on the part of the Government on the Punjab matter."[56]

Nevertheless, there being no spirit of punishment or revenge, compulsion does not achieve the extent of coercion. It stops with effecting what Gandhi calls "a change of heart," and the consequent "redress of the wrong." As a result, the opponent is not vanquished, but victory comes to both sides. *Satyagraha*, therefore, does not entail the vicious circle of defeat and revenge and settles the question once and for all by an amicable agreement.

In spite of it all, it is well to remember that there is an element of compulsion in *Satyagraha* as it is worked out in India. From careful study, as well as from personal experience, it appears that *Satyagraha* would not be so satisfactory a substitute for war, had it not this element of compulsion. The adjustment of the line of demarcation between *Satyagrahic* compulsion and the coercion employed by war, between non-violent direct action and violence, will always remain a moot question unless the distinction is made on the broad basis of the non-physical and the physical. Compulsion, in this special sense, must and does exclude injury to the physical being of the opponent. It also must and does leave unscathed the primary necessities of the opponent's life. This distinction is, no doubt, crude, as every distinction which is not merely theoretic, but also has a bearing on the behaviour of millions of men, should be.

CAN SATYAGRAHA OPERATE IN A TOTALITARIAN STATE ?

Gandhi believed that *Satyagraha*, if properly applied, would always meet with a high degree of success. He appears to have believed, too, that it could have been used in such concrete cases as the oppression of the Jews in Germany. His faith in *Satyagraha* was unshakable since he believed that the stoniest heart could be melted if the method was applied in a genuine spirit of love. The theory of *Satyagraha* posits some humaneness in the opponent. The question of the success of operation of *Satyagraha* in a totalitarian regime is as speculative as controversial. We do not have any direct empirical evidence on which to base an answer to this hypothetical question. Varying opinions have been given on this question. We shall attempt a brief survey of opinions which may help in stimulating fresh thinking on the subject.

Jacques Maritain says: "Gandhi's successes were possible only against the background of the relative freedom granted to colonials by the British administration, both by virtue of an old liberal aristocratic tradition and a mistaken cynical belief as has been rightly remarked—in a possible utilization of Gandhi. The fate to which the inner logics of a totalitarian State tend, is not a revolution which finally gives control to the people, but an ultimate disintegration by a slow rotting of human conscience within it.[57]

Karl Jaspers points out: "His example, however great in its suprapolitical seriousness, is impossible as a signpost for our political action. We cannot follow the concrete method of a kind of politics that could succeed only in the atmosphere of British rule and for the limited purpose of Indian liberation. For the extremity of present world-wide realities Gandhi gives us no answer.

"In the struggles against totalitarianism, Gandhi's procedure would not be a political way but a way to certain doom. Every sacrifice would be secret, rendered without publicity, untouchable in its metaphysical substance to be sure, but unknown to men. Because no echoes would reach the public, no political consequences would result. Against a terror that knows no restriction by legal or conscientious qualms, sacrifice is futile in so far as it remains outside the communication of human activities.

"Against total violence there is no help in less violence, nor in non-violence. Only one limit is conceivable: the destructive engine would cease to obey if the human being in it were touched by the power of conscience. This is a hope and not an impossibility, but it is contingent upon the unfolding of suprapolitical reasons in every individual. Gandhi demonstrated the power of the suprapolitical in the situation in which he was active, but the contents and methods are neither transferable nor exemplary."[58]

P. Spratt comments: "Though India is a political autocracy, it has hitherto been an autocracy leavened by nineteenth century liberalism. *Satyagraha* could develop only in such conditions."[59]

Professor Hancock in his study lays emphasis on the constitutional aspect of the regime in which the non-violent method is applied and on the personal aspect of the combatants involved in struggle. He refers to "something within Smuts himself which made him receptive of this public opinion and sympathetic towards the man who was inciting it." He says that both in South Africa and India, even the most troublesome individuals enjoyed the fundamental liberties of speaking, writing, publishing, petitioning, and propagandizing. "There were open skies for Gandhi's propaganda not only in South Africa, but also in India, Great Britain and the whole British Empire."[60] The implication that *Satyagraha* could only operate in a constitutional democratic set-up is obvious.

In a recent study on nonviolence, Professor Rajkrishna remarks: "The victory of Gandhian non-violent resistance against British imperialism in India, which is rightly cited as proof of the power of such resistance, must be attributed—apart from the dynamics of the political events leading up to it—to the fact that the crucial condition required for the success of such resistance was satisfied. We and the

British shared the same norms of ethical judgment, and spoke the same ethical language. And so we succeeded in persuading the British that the course of imperialist rule was evil.

"But it is foolish and potentially suicidal to rush, from our unique experience, to the sweeping generalisation that any people anywhere can similarly convert any unjust adversary. Where the contestants in a dispute do not share the same conscience, non-violence on the part of the oppressed may only lead to the indefinite prolongation and aggravation of their misery or to their glorious suicide."[61]

That the *Satyagraha* campaign in India owed its success largely to the British attitude has been acknowledged even by an orthodox Gandhite like Dr. Rajendra Prasad. Speaking about the British rulers in January 1953, he said: "...he [Gandhi] found suitable ground in this country and he found also—I must confess–noble adversaries who were capable of yielding to the appeal which non-violence makes. They had set a limit to their own action below which the British could not and did not go and we must admit, we must confess, that Gandhiji's success was due very largely to himself and his people but also to the British."[62]

A serious academic approach to this question has been made by Dr. Bondurant who contends the view that there is no chance of a successful operation of *Satyagraha* in a totalitarian country. She concedes that some of the steps required in an ideal *Satyagraha* campaign would be impossible under circumstances obtaining in monolithic authoritarian states. Such, for instance, is the step of widespread publicity and propaganda conducted without secrecy. Yet, she argues, certain points may be reasonably supposed with regard to the success of *Satyagraha* even under totalitarian conditions. According to Dr. Bondurant: "... it appears that this may depend to a substantial extent upon the prior knowledge and/or experience of members of that society with *Satyagraha*. It is doubtful that any totalitarian system, however effective in its policing, could prevent word-of-mouth propagation of an idea, or even of an understanding of a technique, if there had been some previous understanding of its meaning and its effectiveness. For example, had the Jews of Germany been schooled in the art of *Satyagraha*, an organized effort of *Satyagraha* might have got under way. The chances for success are certainly as great as are the chances for violent revolution under the modern police state system. *Satyagraha* may, in fact, be the only possibility open to an oppressed people in this age of highly technical means of oppression. Reflection upon this likelihood suggests the utility of developing techniques akin to *Satyagraha*, as well as education in their use.

"There is no longer validity to the proposition that *Satyagraha* can be successful only in the Indian milieu which supported and gave rise to it. Doubtless, the technique would necessarily undergo modifications and development in its adaptation to other social circumstances and cultural experiences."[63]

Gandhi himself said that "*Satyagraha*...is a science in the making",[64] and true to that spirit, experiments may be made to see whether *Satyagraha* can operate in such a conflict-situation. Success on a practical scale alone can dispel doubts as to the efficacy of this method in a totalitarian country. The test of any theory lies in action.

A universal panacea or not, *Satyagraha* served some positive function in a particular historical context of India. Jawaharlal Nehru rightly said that the "dynamic of *Satyagraha* largely justified itself in India."[65] Gandhi met the needs of the hour with his practical programme of *Satyagraha*. The novelty of this weapon lay in harnessing the moral strength of the people and at the same time it acted as a good political tactic. The combination of moral force with political realism distinguished *Satyagraha* from other conventional methods. Ostensibly Pacific, it was in essence a revolt against weakness. *Satyagraha* launched a battle against the age-old weaknesses of the people. It roused the masses from their torpor and made them conscious; it stirred them and steeled their will, made them fearless and threw them into unarmed but heroic battles. Therein lay the superiority of this method.

Whether *Satyagraha* would operate equally well and with equal success in the struggle against the rule of capital and for the establishment of a new social order, is a matter of opinion. The basic assumptions underlying this technique may be subject to question from quarters which are committed otherwise. But even then there are elements in *Satyagraha* technique that compel admiration even from non-believers and deserve emulation. A social actionist, of any persuasion, must forge methods to develop mass consciousness, mass initiative, discipline, a spirit of fearlessness, courage and self-suffering and must put unhesitating reliance on the creative political role of the masses, the absence of which renders ineffective any mass resistance action. Accept it or not, *Satyagraha* is a none-too-blunt weapon of resistance. *Satyagraha* shall remain 'eternal' until the message of resistance is lost upon mankind

NOTES

1. The Traditional Japanese System of Unarmed Self-defence perfected by the Samurai.
2. F.C. Barlett. *Psychology and the Soldier*, Cambridge, Cambridge University Press, 1927, p. 175.
3. A.T. Shand, *The Foundation of Character*, London, Macmillan, 1914, p. 448.
4. T. Burrow, *The Social Basis of Consciousness*, London, Kegan Paul, 1927.
5. A.T. Shand, *op. cit.*, p. 430.
6. Richard Gregg, *op. cit.*, p. 26.
7. A.T. Shand, *op. cit.*, p. 448.
8. Richard Gregg, *op. cit.*, p. 30.
9. *Ibid.*
10. *Ibid.*, p. 31.
11. Anatal Rapaport, *Fights Games and Debates*, Ann Arbor, University of Michigan Press, 1960.
12. Jai Narain Sharma, *Gandhi's View of Political Power*, *op. cit.*, p. 103.
13. Raghvan Iyer, *The Moral and Political Thought of Mahatma Gandhi*, *op. cit.*, p. 188.
14. Anthony Obserschall, *Social Conflict and Social Movements*, New Jersey, Prentice Hall, Inc., 1973, pp. 12-13.
15. K.L. Shridharni, *op. cit.*
16. M.K. Gandhi, *An Autobiography*, *op. cit.*, p. 116.
17. Mahatma Gandhi, *His Writings and Speeches*, *op. cit.*, p. 346
18. *Young India*, 6-8-1925, p. 272.
19. K.L. Shridharni, *op. cit.*, p. 139.
20. *Harijan*, 2-12-1939, p. 359.
21. G.D. Rastogi, *Psychological Approach to Gandhi's Leadership*, Gorakhpur, Gorakhpur University, 1969, p. 150.
22. M.K. Gandhi, *Non-violence in Peace and War*, *op. cit.*, p. 130.
23. *Young India*, 1-10-1931, pp. 277-78.
24. Romain Rolland, *op. cit.*, p. 46.
25. Nirmal Kumar Bose, *Selections from Gandhi*, Ahmedabad, Navajivan Publishing House, 1957, p. 460.
26. Quoted in Chandrashanker Shukla, *Reminiscences of Gandhiji*, Bombay, Vora and Company, 1951, pp. 52-53.
27. *Young India*, 12-5-1920, p. 569.

28. *Harijan*, 19-12-1936, p. 362.
29. *Young India*, 16-6-1927, p. 196.
30. *Harijan*, 15-7-1939, p. 201.
31. *Young India*, 4-8-1920, p. 246.
32. *Ibid.*, 11-8-1920, p. 260.
33. *Ibid.*, 20-12-1928, p. 420.
34. M.K. Gandhi, *Hind Swaraj or Indian Home Rule*, Ahmedabad, Navajivan Publishing House, 1975, p. 60.
35. *Harijan*, 23-9-1939, p. 281.
36. *Ibid.*, 25-8-1940, p. 261.
37. *CWMG*, Vol. LXXVII, pp. 71-84.
38. Jacques Maritain, *Man and the State*, Chicago, The University of Chicago Press, 1961, p. 69.
39. *Ibid.*, p. 68.
40. William James, *The Moral Equivalent of War*, New York, American Association for International Conciliation, 1910, pp. 17-18.
41. Alvin Johnson, '*War' in Encyclopaedia of the Social Sciences*, *op. cit.* Vol. XV, p. 331.
42. Nirmal Kumar Bose, *Studies in Gandhism*, *op. cit.*, p. 123.
43. *Ibid.*, p. 120.
44. *CWMG*, Vol. LXI, pp. 113-14.
45. Sidney Hook, "*Violence" Encyclopaedia of the Social Sciences*, Vol. XV, pp. 265-67.
46. K.L. Shridharni, *op. cit.*, p. 256.
47. *Young India*, 9-2-1922, p. 85.
48. *Ibid.*, 11-8-1920, p. 3.
49. *Ibid.*, 16-6-1920, p. 3.
50. K.L. Shridharni, *op. cit.*, p. 259.
51. William James, *op. cit.*
52. K.L. Shridharni, *op. cit.*, p. 259.
53. *Speeches and Writings of Gandhi*, *op. cit.*, p. 165.
54. C.M. Case, *Non-Violence Coercion*, London, George Allen and Unwin, 1923.
55. K.L. Shridharni, *op. cit.*, p. 260.
56. *CWMG*, Vol. XVII, pp. 288-89.
57. Jacques Martin, *op. cit.*, p. 71.
58. Karl Jesper, *The Future of Mankind*, (translated by E.B. Ashton), Chicago, The University of Chicago Press, 1961, pp. 39-40.
59. P. Spratt, *Gandhism: An Analysis*, Madras, The Huxley Press, 1939, p. 514.
60. W.K. Hancock, *Four Studies of War and Peace in this Century*, Cambridge, Cambridge University Press, 1961, pp. 81-82.
61. Raj Krishna, "Non-Violence, War and Peace", *Quest* 42, July, September 1964, p. 16.

62. *Gandhian Outlook and Techniques*, New Delhi, Ministry of Education, Government of India, 1953, p. 338.
63. Joan Bondurant, *op. cit.*, pp. 225-27.
64. *Harijan*, 24-9-1938, p. 266.
65. Quoted in Joan Bondurant, *op. cit.*, p. x.

Bibliography

Alexis Tocquevile, De, *Democracy in America*, Volume I, 1954.

Ambedkar, B.R., *What Gandhi and Congress Has Done to the Untouchables*, Bombay, Thacker and Co. Ltd., 1946.

Arthur Moore, "The evolution of Mr. Gandhi", in S. Radhakrishnan (ed.) *Mahatma Gandhi: Essays and Reflections*, Allahabad, Kitabistan, 1944.

Azar, E.E., Burton J.W. (eds.), *International Conflict Resolution: Theory and Practice*, Brighton, Wheatsheaf, 1986.

Bandyopadhyaya, Jayanti, *Social and Political Thought of Mahatma Gandhi*, Bombay, Allied Publishers, 1969.

Banks, M. (ed.), *Conflict in World Society: A New Perspective on International Relations*, Brighton, Wheatsheaf,1984.

Barlett, F.C., *Psychology and the Soldier*, Cambridge, Cambridge University Press, 1927.

Becker, Howard S., Blanche Geer, and Everelt, C. Hughes, *Making the Grade: The Academic Side of College Life*, New York, John Wiley, 1968.

Berman, M.R.C., Johnson, J.E. (eds.), *Unofficial Diplomats*, New York, Columbia University Press, 1977.

Bernard, Jessie, "The Sociological Study of Conflict", International Sociological Association, The Nature of Conflict (Paris: UNESCO), 1957.

Bernard, Jessie, "Parties and Issues in Conflict", *Journal of Conflict Resolution*, June 1957.

Bercovitch, J., *Resolving International Conflicts: The Theory and Practice of Mediation,* Boulder, Lynne Rienner, 1996.

Bercovitch, J., *Social Conflicts and Third Parties: Strategies of Conflict Resolution*, Colorado, Westview, 1984.

Bercovitch, Jacob and Jeffrey, Z. Rubin (eds.), *Mediation in International Relations: Multiple Approaches to Conflict Management*, London, Macmillan, 1992.

Bloch, Ivan, *The Future War in Seven Volumes* (Boston: Boston Press), 1914.

Boasson, Chables, *Societal and Aspects of Law and International Adjustment* (Amsterdam: Holland Publishing), 1950.

Bondurant, Joan, *Conquest of Violenzce: The Gandhian Philosophy of Conflict*, Bombay, Oxford University Press, 1959.

Bose, N.K., *Studies in Gandhism*, Ahmedabad, Navajivan Publishing House, 1962.

Bose, Nirmal Kumar, *Selections from Gandhi*, Ahmedabad, Navajivan Publishing House, 1957.

Boulding, K.E., *Conflict and Defence: A General Theory*, New York: Harper Bros., 1962.

Boulding, K.E., *Stable Peace,* Austin: Texas University Press, 1978.

Brailsford, Henry, *Rebel India*, London, Leonard Stein, 1931.

Bryson, L., Finkelstein, I., Maciver, R.M. (ed.), *Conflicts of Power in Modern Culture,* New York: Harper and Bros., 1947.

Burrow, T., *The Social Basis of Consciousness*, London, Kegan Paul, 1927.

Cantril, H., *Tensions that Cause Wars,* Urbane: University Illinois Press, 1951.

Case, C.M., *Non-Violent Coercion*, London, George Allen and Unwin, 1923.

Coser, Lewis, *Continuities in the Study of Social Conflicts,* New York: Free Press, 1967.

Coser, Lewis, *The Functions of Social Conflict,* New York: Free Press of Glencoe, Inc., 1956.

Clark, Evans, *Boycotts and Peace,* New York: New York Press, 1932.

Cooper, R. and M. Berdal, "Outside Intervention in Ethnic Conflicts," in Michael E. Brown, (ed.), *Ethnic Conflict in International Security*, Princeton: N.J., Princeton University Press, 1993.

Cox, Archibald, *The Duty to Bargain in Good Faith*, Harvard Law Review, 1858.

Dahrendorf, Ralf, *Class and Class Conflict in Industrial Society,* Stanford: Stanford University Press, 1959.

Dahrendorf, Ralf, *Gesselleschaft and Freiheit Miinchen,* Verleg: R. Piper and Co., 1962.

Diehl, Paul F. and Gary Goertz, "Territorial Changes and Militarized Conflict", *Journal of Conflict Resolution*, 32, 1, March 1988.

Diwakar, R.K., *Saga of Satyagraha*, New Delhi, Gandhi Peace Foundation, 1969.

Dixit, Avinash, "Strategic Behaviour in Contests", *American Economic Review*, Volume 77, 1987.

Doke, Joseph, J., *M.K. Gandhi*, Varanasi, Akhil Sarva Sewa Sangh Prakashan, 1959.

Duffield, Mark, "Post-Modern Conflicts: Warlords, Post Adjustment States and Private Protection", *Civil Wars*, 1998, 1: 65-102.

Ellis, Havelock, *The Philosophy of Conflict*, New York: New York Press, 1919.

Elton McNeil (ed.), *The Nature of Human Conflict*, Englewood Cliffs, N.J.: Prentice Hall, 1965.

Enders, Walter and Toda Sandler, *Terrorism, Theory and Applications*, Amsterdam: North Holland, 1996.

Falk, Richard A., Samuel S. Kim, and Saul H. Mendlovitz, (eds.), *United Nations and a Just World Order*, Boulder, CO: Westview Press, 1991.

Falk, Richard A., Robert, C. Johansen, and Samuel, S. Kim, (eds.), *Constitutional Foundations of World Peace*, Albany, NY: State University New York Press, 1993.

Fenivick, C.G., "The Legal Aspects of Neutralism", *American Journal of International Law* (Lancaster, Pa.), 51 (January 1957).

Feuerbach, *Ludwig The Essence of Christianity* (translated by Marion Evons), London, John Chapman, 1954.

Fink, Clinton, F., "Some Conceptual Difficulties in the Theory of Social Conflicts", *Journal of Conflict Resolution*, Volume 12, December 1968.

Folberg, Boulder, J. Taylor A., *Mediation: A Comprehensive Resolving Conflicts Without Litigation*, Jossey Francisco, California, 1984.

Fox, H., *Arbitration, International Disputes—The Legal Aspects*, London, Europa Publications, 1972.

Fromm, Eric, *Escape From Freedom*, New York, Rinehart, 1941.

Galtung, Johan, *Peace by Peaceful Means, Peace and Conflict, Development and Civilization* (London: Sage), 1996.

Gandhi, M.K., *An Autobiography or the Story of My Experiments With Truth*, Ahmedabad, Navajivan Publishing House, 1988.

Gandhi, M.K., *Constructive Programme: Its Meaning and Place*, Ahmedabad, Navajivan Publishing House, 1975.

Gandhi, M.K., *Non-Violence in Peace and War*, Ahmedabad, Navajivan Publishing House, 1944.

Gandhi, M.K., *Satyagraha in South Africa*, Ahmedabad, Navajivan, Publishing House, 1975.

Gandhi, M.K., *Hind Swaraj or Indian Home Rule*, Ahmedabad, Navajivan Publishing House, 1975.

Gandhian Outlook and Techniques, New Delhi, Ministry of Education, Government of India, 1953.

Geoffery, K. Roberts, *A Dictionary of Political Analysis*, London, Longman, 1971.

Gregg, Richard B., *The Power of Non-Violence*, Ahmedabad, Navajivan Publishing House, 1960.

Guyde, Mallac, *Seven Steps to Global Changes: Gandhi's Message for Today,* Santa Fe, New Mexico, Ocean Tree Book, 1987.

Hancock, W.K., *Four Studies of War and Peace in this Century*, Cambridge: Cambridge University Press, 1961.

Hancock, W.K., *Studies in War and Peace*, London, Cambridge University Press, 1961.

Heath, G.W., *What People are: A Study of Normal Young Men*, Cambridge, Mass., Harvard University Press, 1946.

Hirshleifer, Jack, *Theorizing Adult Conflict*, Amsterdam, North Holland, 1995.

Hirst, M.E., *The Quakers in Peace and War,* London: London Press, 1923.

Holisti, Kalevi, J., *Peace and War: Armed Conflict and International Order, 1648-1989,* Cambridge: Cambridge University Press, 1991.

Hook, Sidney, *From Hegel to Marx: Studies in Intellectual Development of Karl Marx*, London, Victor Gallancy Ltd., 1936.

Huddleston, J., *Achieving Peace by the Year 2000: A Twelve-Point Proposal*, Oxford, One World Publications Ltd., 1992.

Hume, C., 'Ending Mozambique's War.' The Role of Mediation and Good Offices, Washington, US Institute of Peace.

Inozemtsev, N.N. (ed.), *Global Problems of Our Age,* Moscow: Progress, 1984.

Iyer, Raghvan, *The Moral and Political Thought of Mahatma Gandhi*, Delhi, Oxford University Press, 1973.

Jacques, Maritain, *Man and the State*, Chicago, The University of Chicago Press, 1961.

James, William, *The Moral Equivalent of War*, New York, American Association for International Conciliation, 1910.

Jawaharlal Nehru, *An Autobiography*, London, The Bodley Head, 1958.

Jesper, Karl, *The Future of Mankind*, (translated by E. B. Ashton), Chicago, The University of Chicago Press, 1961.

John Lewis, *The Case Against Pacifism*, London, George Allen and Unwin, 1939.

Johnson, D.H.N., *International Arbitration-Back in favour?* Yearbook of World Affairs, 1980.

Johnson, L. Gunnar, *Conflicting Concepts of Peace in Contemporary Peace Studies*, Beverly Hills: Sage Publications, 1976.

Jones, J.H., *The Economics of War and Conquest.* London: London Press, 1915.

Kalelkar, K. (ed.), *To a Gandhian Capitalist*, Wardha, Jamnalal Seva Trust, 1951.

Kallen, Horace M., "Coercion" in R.A. Edwin (ed.) *Encyclopaedia of Social Sciences*, Vols. 3 & 4, New York, Macmillan, 1956, pp. 617-19.

Kleiboer, Marieke "Understanding Success and Failure of International Mediation," *Journal of Conflict Resolution*, Vol. 40, No. 2, June 1996.

Klineberg, O., *Tensions: Affecting International Understanding*, New York: Roultedge, 1964.

Kolb, D.M., *The Mediators*, Cambridge Massachusetts, MIT Press, 1983.

Komarnicki, T., "The Race of Neutrality in the Modern System of International Law", *Recueil des Cours*, 1952.

Krech and Crutchfield, *Theory and Problems of Social Psychology*, New York: McGraw Hill, 1948.

Kriesberg, Lowis, *International Conflict Resolution*, New Haven, CT: Yale University Press, 1992.

Kripalani, J.B., *Gandhi: His Life and Thought*, New Delhi, Publications Division, Ministry of Information and Broadcasting, Government of India, 1968.

Kurt, Lewin, *Resolving Social Conflict*, New York: Harper Bros., 1948.

Laszol, E. *et al.*, *Goals for Mankind*, New York: Dutton, 1977.

Lawerence, T.J., *The Principles of International Law*, Boston: Boston

Lentz, Theodore, *Towards a Science of Peace*, Varanasi: Navachetna, 1970.

Mahadev Desai, *Righteous Struggle*, Ahmedabad, Navajivan Publishing House, 1951.

McDougall, *An Introduction to Social Psychology*, London: London Press, 1943

McNeil, Elton B. (ed.), *The Nature of Human Conflict*, Englewood Cliffs, NJ.: Prentice Hall, 1965.

Mead, Margaret and Frances Bagley Kaplan, *American Report*, The Report of the President's Commission on the Status of Women and Other Publications of the Commission, New York, Scribner's, 1965.

Merrills, J.G., *International Dispute Settlement*, London, Sweet and Maxwell, 1984.

Millet, Kate, *Sexual Politics*, New York: Doubleday, 1970.

Mitchell, C.R., *Peacekeeping and the Consultant's Role*, Gower, Farnborough, 1981.

Mitchell, C.R. and K. Webb, (eds.), *New Approaches to International Mediation*, London, Greenwood Press, 1998.

Mitchell, Christopher R., *Handbook of Conflict Resolution: An Analytical Problem Solving Approach*, London, 1996.

Moore, Wilbert E., *Social Change*, Englewood Cliffs, N.J.: Prentice Hall, 1963.

Morris, W.H. Jones, "Mahatma Gandhi—Political Philosopher?" *The Indian Journal of Political Science*, Vol. XXXI, No. 3, July-September 1960.

Murphy, G., *Human Nature and Enduring Peace*, New York, Reynal and Hitchcock, 1945.

Murthy, K. Satchidananda and A.C. Banquet, *Studies in Problems of Peace*, Bombay, Asia Publishing House, 1960.

Natesan, G.A., *Speeches and Writings of Mahatma Gandhi*, Madras, G.A. Natesan and Co., 1933.

Niebuhr, Reinhold, *Moral Man and Immoral Society*, New York, Charles Scribner's Sons, 1947.

Oberschall, Anthony, *Social Conflict and Social Movements*, Englewood Cliffs, NJ.: Prentice Hall, 1965.

Park, Robert D. and Ernest W. Burgese, *Introduction to the Science of Sociology*, Chicago, University of Chicago Press, 1921.

Park, R.E., "The Social Function of War", *American Journal of Sociology*, Vol. XLVI, 1941.

Pauling, Linus, *World Encyclopaedia of Peace*, Oxford: Pergamon Press, 1986.

Philip C. Jessup, (ed.), *Neutrality: Its History, Economics, and Law,* New York, 1935-36, 4 vols.

Pigou, A.C., *The Political Economy of War,* London: London Press, 1921.

Polak, H.S.C., H.N. Brailsford and Lord Pethick, Lawrence, *Mahatma Gandhi*, London, Odham Press Limited, 1949.

Popper, Karl, *The Open Society and Its Enemies*, London, Routledge and Kegan Paul, 1949, Vol. II.

Power, Paul, F., *Gandhi on World Affairs*, London, George Allen and Unwin, 1961.

Pradhan, Ram Chandra, "Peace Education and Human Rights" in Laszlo, Erwin and Yoo, Jong Youl (eds.), *World Encyclopaedia for Peace,* Oxford: Pergamon Press, 1986.

Prasad, Rajindra, *Satyagraha in Champaran*, Ahmedabad, Navajivan Publishing House, 1951.

Pribram, K., *Conflicting Patterns of Thought,* Washinghton: Public Affairs Press, 1949.

Pyarelal, *Mahatma Gandhi, The Last Phase*, Ahmedabad, Navajivan Publishing House, 1958.

Raj Krishna, "Non-Violence, War and Peace", *Quest* 42, July September 1964

Rapaport, Anatal, *Fights Games and Debates*, Ann Arbor, University of Michigan Press, 1960.

Rapopart, Anatal and Orwant Carol, *Experimental Games: A Review*, Behavioural Science, 1962.

Rastogi, G.D., *Psychological Approach to Gandhi's Leadership*, Gorakhpur, Gorakhpur University, 1969.

Raymond, Aron, *Peace and War: A Theory of International Relations,* London: London Press, 1966.

Reno, William, *Warlord Politics and African Studies*, Boulder, Co. Lynne Rienner, 1998.

Romain Rolland, *Mahatma Gandhi: The Man Who Became One With the Universal Being*, New Delhi, Publications Division, Ministry of Information and Broadcasting, Government of India, 1990.

Ronald, H. Baiston, *Christian Attitude Toward War and Peace*, London, Hodder and Stoughton, 1961.

Sanders, P., *International Arbitration*, The Hague, Martinus Nijhoff, 1967.

Sapirstein, M.R., *Emotional Security*, London, Rider and Co., 1948.

Sarup, Bishan Sharma, *Gandhi As A Political Thinker*, Allahabad, Indian Press Pvt. Ltd., 1956.

Schelling, Thomas C., *The Strategy of Conflict,* New York: Galaxy Books, 1963.

Schulder, Diane, B., "Does the Law Oppress Women?" in Robin Morgan (ed.) *Sisterhood is Powerful*, New York, Vintage, 1970.

Shakhnazarov, G., *The Coming World Order,* Moscow: Progress, 1984.

Shand, A.T., *The Foundation of Character*, London, Macmillan, 1914.

Shridharni, K.L., *War Without Violence*, Bombay, Bharatiya Vidya Bhawan, 1962.

Sharma, Rashmi, *Gandhian Economics: A Humane Approach*, New Delhi, Deep and Deep, 1997.

Sharma, Jai Narain, *Gandhi's View of Political Power*, New Delhi, Deep and Deep, 1987.

Sharp, Gene, *The Politics of Non-Violent Action: The Dynamics of Non-violent Action Part III*, Boston, Porter Sarget Publishers, 1973.

Sherif, M. and C. Sherif, *Groups in Harmony and Tensions*, New York: Harper, 1953.

Shukla, Chandrashanker, *Reminiscences of Gandhiji*, Bombay, Vora and Company, 1951.

Siegel, Sidney and Fouraker, Lawrence E., *Bargaining and Group Decision Making: Experiments in Bilateral Monopoly*, New York, McGraw-Hill, 1960.

Small, Albion, W., "Socialism in the Light of Sociology", *American Journal of Sociology*, Volume XVII, 1972.

Simmel, George, *Conflict*, (translated by Kurt H. Wolff), New York: Free Press to Glance, Inc., 1956.

Simmel, George, "The Sociology of Conflict", *American Journal of Sociology*, Volume IX, 1904.

Simpson, J.L., Fox H., *International Arbitration*, London, Stevens,1959.

Sohn, L.B., *The Function of International Arbitration Today*, Hague Receuil, 1963.

Spainer, John W. and Nogee Joseph, *Two Politics of Disarmament: A Study in Soviet-American Gamesmanship*, New York, Praeger, 1962.

Speier, Hans and Alfred, Kahler, *War in Our Time*, New York: New York Press, 1939.

Spratt, P., *Gandhism: An Analysis*, Madras, The Huxley Press, 1939.

Star, S.A., *An Index of Social Tensions*, Glencoe: Free Press, 1954.

Strodtbeck, Fred, Rita M. James and Charles Hawkins, "Social Status in Jury Deliberation", *American Sociological Review*, 22 (December) 1957.

Sturzo, D.L., *Nationalism and Internationalism*, New York, Roy Publishers, 1946

Tendulkar, D.G., *Mahatma*, New Delhi, Publications Division, Ministry of Information and Broadcasting, Government of India, 1952.

The Collected Works of Mahatma Gandhi, New Delhi, Publications Division, Ministry of Information and Broadcasting, Government of India, 1965, (Vols. 1-100).

Thomas, N. Carver, "The Basis of Social Conflict," *American Journal of Sociology*, Vol. XIII, 1908.

Thomas, R.W., *Racial Unity: An Imperative for Social Progress*, Ottawa: Association for Bhai Studies, 1993.

Touval, S. and I.W. Zartman, (eds.), *International Mediation in Theory and Practice*, Boulder, Colorado, Westview Press, 1985, p. 255.

Turner, Ralph, "Collective Behaviour and Conflict", *Sociological Quarterly*, V, 122-32, 1964.

UNESCO, *Tensions That Cause Wars*, Chicago, University of Illinois Press, 1948.

Universal House of Justice, *The Promise of the World Peace*, National Spiritual Assembly of the Bahais of United States, 1985, p. 14.

Vasquez, John "Why Do Neighbours Fight? Proximity, Interaction and Territoriality," *Journal of Peace Research*, 32.

Vollenhoven, Van C., *The Law of Peace*, London: London Press, 1936.

Volkogonov, D.A. (ed.) *Problems of War and Peace*, Progress Moscow, 1972.

Weber, Max, *The Methodology of the Social Sciences*, translated by Edward A. Shills and Henry A. Finch, 1968.

Weisstan, Naomi, "Kinder, Kuche, Kirche' as Scientific Law: Psychology Constructs the Female," in Robin Morgan (ed.), *Sisterhood is Powerful*, New York, Vintage, 1970.

Westerfield II Bradford, *Foreign Policy and Party Politics: Pearl Harbor to Korea*, New Haven, Yale University Press, 1955.

Wetter, J.G., *The International Arbitral Process: Public and Private*, New York, Oceana, 1979.

Wilkins, E.H., (ed.), *Report of the Commission on the Coordination of Efforts for Peace*, Oberlin: Oberlin Press, 1933.

William, Jr. Robin, M., "Social Order and Social Conflict", *Proceedings of the American Philosophical Society*, Volume 114, June 1970.

Wilson, G.G., and G.F. Tucker, *International Law*, Boston: Boston Press, 1935.

Wright, Quincy, *A Study of War*, Chicago: University of Chicago Press, 1942.

Wright, Quincy, "Changes in the Conception of War", *American Journal of International Law*, Vol. XVIII, (October), 1926.

Wright, Quincy (ed.), *Public Opinion and World Politics*, Chicago: Chicago Press, 1933.

Wright, Quincy, "The Outlawry of War", *American Journal of International Law*, Vol. XIX, (January), 1925.

Young, Oran R., *The Intermediaries. Third Parties in International Crises*, Princeton, Princeton University Press, 1967.

Zaidi, A.M. and S.G. Zaidi (ed.) *The Encyclopaedia of Indian National Congress*, Vol. 9, 1925-1929, New Delhi, S. Chand and Co. Ltd., 1980.

Zartman, I. William (ed.) *Elusive Peace. Negotiating an End to Civil Wars*, Washington, D.C., Brookings, 1995.

Index